Francis Edward Paget

The Spirit of Discipline

Sermons Preached by Francis Paget

Francis Edward Paget

The Spirit of Discipline
Sermons Preached by Francis Paget

ISBN/EAN: 9783744744058

Printed in Europe, USA, Canada, Australia, Japan

Cover: Foto ©Thomas Meinert / pixelio.de

More available books at **www.hansebooks.com**

THE SPIRIT OF DISCIPLINE

The Spirit

OF

Discipline

SERMONS PREACHED BY

FRANCIS PAGET, D.D.

CANON OF CHRIST CHURCH, OXFORD; SOMETIME VICAR OF BROMSGROVE

TOGETHER WITH AN

INTRODUCTORY ESSAY CONCERNING ACCIDIE

LONDON

LONGMANS, GREEN, & CO.

AND NEW YORK: 15 EAST 16th STREET

1891

✠

QUEM · DEDIT · DOMINUS ·

QUEM · RECEPIT ·

RICARDUM · WILLELMUM · CHURCH ·

LUCEM · FIRMAMENTUM · DESIDERIUM ·

DILECTISSIMUM ·

AMORE · PROSEQUOR ·

✠

Preface

THE title of this book is meant to point towards a thought which under various aspects enters into most of the sermons here printed: the thought of the power which the grace of God confers on men to extend or strengthen, by dutiful self-discipline, the empire of the will. The reality of some such power is plainly suggested by the contrast between those lives in which more things seem possible year by year, and those in which more things continually seem impossible or intolerable; while, if there be such power within reach, clearly a man's happiness and usefulness depend to a great extent on his seeking and exercising it. An especial task in which it may be exercised is described in the introductory essay which precedes the sermons.

Contents

INTRODUCTORY ESSAY.

INTRODUCTORY ESSAY.

CONCERNING ACCIDIE.

" Yea, they thought scorn of that pleasant land, and gave
no credence unto His word; but murmured in their tents,
and hearkened not unto the voice of the Lord."

MOST men may know that strange effect of vividness
and reality with which at times a disclosure of
character and experience in some old book seems to
traverse the intervening centuries, and to touch the
reader with a sense of sudden nearness to the man
who so was tried, so felt and thought, so failed or
conquered, very long ago. We are prepared, of
course, for likeness, and even for monotony, in the
broad aspect of that ceaseless conflict through which
men come to be and to show what they are; for the
main conditions of a man's probation stand like birth
and death, like childhood, and youth, and age, awaiting
every human soul, behind the immense diversity of
outward circumstance. We expect that the inner
history of man will go on repeating itself in these
general traits; but when, out of an age whose ways

B

Ỳ ꝺ

imagination hardly represents to us with any clearness, there comes the exact likeness of some feature or deformity which we had thought peculiar to ourselves or our contemporaries, we may be almost startled by the claim thus made to moral kinship and recognition. We knew that it never had been easy to refuse the evil and choose the good; we guessed that at all times, if a man's will faltered, there were forces ready to help him quietly and quickly on the downward road; but that centuries ago men felt, in minute detail, the very same temptations, subtle, complex, and resourceful, which we to-day find hiding and busy in the darker passages of our hearts, is often somewhat unreasonably surprising to us. For we are apt, perhaps, to overrate the intensive force of those changes which have extended over all the surface of civilized life. We forget how little difference they may have brought to that which is deepest in us all. It is, indeed, true that the vast increase of the means of self-expression and self-distraction increases for many men the temptation to empoverish life at its centre for the sake of its ever-widening circumference; it may be harder to be simple and thoughtful, easier to be multifariously worldly now than once it was; but the inmost quality, the secret history, of a selfish choice or a sullen mood, and the ingredients of a bad temper, are, probably, nearly what they were in quieter days; and there seems sometimes a curious sameness in the tricks that men play with conscience, and in the main elements of a soul's tragedy.

The Bible is the supreme, decisive witness to this profound identity in the experience, the discipline, the needs of man through all generations. It is, indeed, greatly to be wished that people would realize rather more adequately the prerogative distinction which the Bible has in this (besides all other traits by which it stands alone), that it does thus speak to every age; that, through the utmost change of circumstances, it is found to penetrate with unchanged precision the hidden folds and depths of human character; that it can be at once universal and intimate in its sympathy. It is a sign of true greatness in a man if he can more freely than most men transcend even the pettier external differences of this world; but to be unchecked by the revolutions of centuries, and the severing barriers of continents and races, unchecked in piercing to the deepest elements of each man's being, unchecked in knowing him, with all his grandeur and his meanness, his duplicity and folly, his restlessness and fear and faint-heartedness and aspiration,—it is hard to think

to whom this freedom could belong, save to the King
of the ages, the Creator and the Judge of all men.
Surely any one who realizes how the life of Jesus
Christ, told in the four Gospels, has found and
formed the saints of every generation, and what the
Psalms have been to them, may feel fairly confident
of this to start with — that in human life the
recurrent rhythms of spiritual experience are profound and subtle, and that the Bible comes to us
from One Who, with unerring and universal insight,
knows what is in man.[1]

This constancy and freshness of the Bible's power
for the discipline of character is the central and
decisive witness to the substantial constancy of our
needs and dangers, our difficulties and capacities;
for in every age he who bends over the Bible and
peers into its depths,[2] may feel at times almost as
though his own life must have been in some strange
way lived before, when the words that speak to him
so intimately were written down. But elsewhere
also, as one would expect, one comes on hints and
fragments in which the same deep constancy is
betrayed, and that which seemed most closely

[1] Cf. W. Bright, "Lessons from the Lives of Three Great Fathers,"
Appendix iii., and the Bishop of Derry's "Bampton Lectures," Lectures
iv. and viii.
[2] Cf. St. James i. 25.

characteristic of one's self is found to have been no less vivid and intimate in the experience of men severed from those of the present day by the uttermost unlikeness in all the conditions of their life. We may be somewhat surprised when we discover how precisely Pascal, or Shakespeare, or Montaigne can put his finger on our weak point, or tell us the truth about some moral lameness or disorder of which we, perhaps, were beginning to accept a more lenient and comfortable diagnosis. But when a poet, controversialist and preacher of the Eastern Church, under the dominion of the Saracens, or an anchoret of Egypt, an Abbot of Gaul, in the sixth century, tells us, in the midst of our letters, and railway journeys, and magazines, and movements, exactly what it is that on some days makes us so singularly unpleasant to ourselves and to others—tells us in effect that it is not simply the east wind, or dyspepsia, or overwork, or the contrariness of things in general, but that it is a certain subtle and complex trouble of our own hearts, which we perhaps have never had the patience or the frankness to see as it really is; that he knew it quite well, only too well for his own happiness and peace, and that he can put us in a good way of dealing with it—the very strangeness of the intrusion from such a quarter into our most private affairs may secure for him a certain degree of our interest and attention.

There may be those who will be drawn by some such interest to weigh what has been said at various times about the temptation and the sin with which the first sermon in this volume is concerned—the temptation and the sin of accidie. The present writer was some years ago brought to think a little about the subject by a striking and suggestive passage in the fifth chapter of Maria Francesca Rossetti's "Shadow of Dante," and by the vivid words quoted from Chaucer in Mr. Carlyle's note on the hundred and twenty-third line of the seventh canto of the "Inferno." The reference to St. Thomas Aquinas in the "Shadow of Dante" led on to Cassian; and the Benedictine Commentary on Cassian pointed to some others who had added more or less to the recognition of this "enemie to every estate of man," this deep and complex peril of men's strength and happiness. It may be shown that there are not wanting, in the life and literature of the present day, signs of the persistence and reality of that peril; and it will perhaps be worth while to gather together in this essay some of those passages in which, under widely diverse circumstances, and in generations many centuries apart, men have spoken what may always seem home-

truths about the sin of accidie. No pretence can
be made to a thorough treatment of the subject, nor
to the learning which such a treatment would
require; but a few representative witnesses may be
gathered out of four distinct groups of writers, and
these may be enough to show how steadily the
plague has hung and hangs about the lives of men,
while they may perhaps help some of us to see it as
it is, and to deal with it as we ought.

I. Cassian, whose long life nearly covers the latter
half of the fourth century and the former half of the
fifth, may be placed first in the first group of those
who have written concerning ἀκηδία, acedia, or accidie.[1] Trained during his early years in a monastery
at Bethlehem, he had spent a long time among the
hermits of the Thebaid, before he turned to his great
work of planting in the far West the monasticism
of the East, founding his two communities at Mar-
seilles, and writing his twelve books, "De Cœnobiorum Institutis,"[2] and his "Collationes Patrum in

[1] Concerning the orthography of the Greek word there can be no
doubt. The Latin form here given is that employed, *e.g.*, by Cassian
and by St. Thomas Aquinas, and justly defended by the Benedictine
Commentator on Cassian. The English form, while, in common with
the Italian, it conceals the derivation of the word, has the decisive
sanction of Dr. Murray's Dictionary, *q.v.*; cf. also Ducange, *s.v.*

[2] Entitled by some, " De Institutis Renuntiantium." On the life
of Cassian, cf. P. Freeman, " Principles of Divine Service," vol. i. pp.

Scythica Eremo Commorantium." The tenth book of
the former work is entitled "De Spiritu Acediæ;"
and in the first chapter of that book he gives a pro-
visional and somewhat scanty indication of its subject. "Acedia" may be called a weariness or distress
of heart; it is akin to sadness; the homeless and
solitary hermits, those who live in the desert, are
especially assailed by it, and monks find it most
troublesome about twelve o'clock: so that some of
the aged have held it to be "the sickness that de-
stroyeth in the noonday," the "dæmonium meridia-
num" of the ninety-first psalm. But the most striking
part of all that Cassian has to say about accidie is the
description in the second chapter of a monk who is
suffering from a bad attack of the malady. When
the poor fellow is beset by it, he says, it makes him
detest the place where he is, and loathe his cell; and
he has a poor and scornful opinion of his brethren,
near and far, and thinks that they are neglectful and
unspiritual. It makes him sluggish and inert for
every task; he cannot sit still, nor give his mind to
reading; he thinks despondently how little progress
he has made where he is, how little good he gains or

249-253, and I. Gregory Smith's article in the "Dictionary of Christian Biography." There is a very elaborate account of his work, published at Lyons in 1652, by J. B. Quesnay, S.J.

does,—he, who might so well direct and help others
and who, where he is, has nobody to teach and
nobody to edify. He dwells much on the excellence
of other and distant monasteries; he thinks how pro-
fitable and healthy life is there; how delightful the
brethren are, and how spiritually they talk. On
the contrary, where he is, all seems harsh and
untoward; there is no refreshment for his soul to
be got from his brethren, and none for his body from
the thankless land. At last he thinks he really
cannot be saved if he stops where he is; and then,
about eleven or twelve o'clock, he feels as tired as if
he had walked miles, and as hungry as if he had
fasted for two or three days. He goes out and looks
this way and that, and sighs to think that there is no
one coming to visit him; he saunters to and fro, and
wonders why the sun is setting so slowly; and so,
with his mind full of stupid bewilderment and
shameful gloom, he grows slack and void of all
spiritual energy, and thinks that nothing will do
him any good save to go and call on somebody, or
else to betake himself to the solace of sleep. Where-
upon his malady suggests to him that there are
certain persons whom he clearly ought to visit,
certain kind inquiries that he ought to make, a religious lady upon whom he ought to call, and to

whom he may be able to render some service; and
that it will be far better to do this than to sit profit-
less in his cell.

In two later chapters Cassian traces some of the
results which follow from the lax and desultory dis-
sipation of the inner life that is thus allowed. But
the main part of the book is taken up with the
praises of hard work, as the true safeguard against
accidie; especial stress being laid on the counsel and
example of St. Paul in this regard ; and mention
being made of a certain abbot who, to keep himself
busy and steady his thoughts and drive off this
temptation, toiled all through the year, and every
year burnt all the produce of his labour; the excuse
for this economic enormity lying in the fact that he
lived so far from a town, that the carriage of the
produce would have cost more than its market price.

Much, however, which other writers link with
accidie is assigned by Cassian to sadness, of which
he speaks in the preceding book, "De Spiritu
Tristitiæ." The severance of sadness from accidie
is deliberately censured by St. Thomas Aquinas; and
certainly the sullen gloom which Cassian describes
in this ninth book forms a congenial and integral
part in the complex trouble which accidie generally
denotes, while it is clearly present in that picture

of the "accidious" monk which has just been cited from Cassian himself. Thus we may fairly perhaps complete, from the delineation of "Tristitia," the conception of "Acedia." For the sadness of which Cassian speaks is the gloom of those who ought not to be sad, who wilfully allow a morbid sombreness to settle down on them; it is a mood which severs a man from thoughts of God, "and suffers him not to be calm and kindly to his brethren." "Sometimes, without any provoking cause,[1] we are suddenly depressed by so great sorrowfulness, that we cannot greet with wonted courtesy the coming even of those who are dear and near to us, and all they say in conversation, however appropriate it may be, we think annoying and unnecessary,[2] and have no pleasant answer for it, because the gall of bitterness fills all the recesses of our soul." Those who are sad after this fashion have, as St. Gregory says, anger already close to them; for from sadness such as this come forth (as he says in another place) malice, grudging, faint-heartedness, despair, torpor as to that which is commanded, and the straying of the mind after that which is forbidden.[3]

---

[1] Cf. "Collationes Patrum," Collatio V., cap. ix.
[2] Cf. F. W. Faber, "Growth in Holiness," p. 244.
[3] S. Gregorii, "Reg. Past.," III. iii.; "Moralium," liber xxxi.

The Κλῖμαξ, or *Scala Paradisi*, from which St. John of the Ladder takes his distinctive title, rests on the experience of some sixty years spent in the ascetic life. It was composed after the writer had been called from his solitude as an anchoret, to become Abbot of the Monastery of Mount Sinai, at the age of seventy-five. He speaks of ἀκηδία with striking force and vividness; it is one of the offshoots of talkativeness—a slackness of the soul and remissness of the mind, a contempt of holy exercise, a hatred of one's profession; it extols the blessedness of a worldly life, and speaks against God as merciless and unloving; it makes singing languid, prayer feeble, service stubborn. So peculiarly does it tell upon the voice, that when there is no psalmody, it may remain unnoticed; but when the psalms are being sung, it causes its victim to interrupt the verse with an untimely yawn.—Then ἀκηδία is personified. She sees the cell of the anchoret and laughs to herself, and goes and settles down close by him. She suggests all sorts of good reasons why he well may leave his prayers and gad about. She recalls to him the words of Scripture as to the Christian duty of visiting the sick; and in the middle of his

§§ 87–89.   Cf. S. Isidorus Hispalensis, "Quæstiones in V. T.," in Deuteronomium, xvi.

devotions she reminds him of urgent business to be done elsewhere. Lastly, in a fine and instructive passage, the voice of accidie is heard, acknowledging what forces are her allies and her enemies. "They who summon me are many; sometimes it is dulness and senselessness of soul that bids me come, sometimes it is forgetfulness of things above; ay, and there are times when it is the excess of toil. My adversaries are the singing of psalms and the labour of the hands; the thought of death is my enemy, but that which kills me outright is prayer, with the sure hope of glory." [1]

It seems strange at first, but true to facts when one begins to think, that accidie should be thus linked both with talkativeness and with that deadness and dulness of the voice which seems to be indicated by ἀτονία ψαλμωδίας. Similarly St. Isidore of Seville [2] puts gossiping and curiosity together with listlessness and somnolence among the troubles born of accidie; and St. John of Damascus defines ἄχος (which the commentators seem to identify with accidie) as a grief which engenders voicelessness. [3] The comment

---

[1] S. Joannes Climacus, "Scala Paradisi," xiii.; cf. xxvii. 2.

[2] S. Isidorus Hispalensis, "Quæstiones in V. T.," in Deut. cap. xvi.

[3] S. Joannes Damasc., "De Orth. Fid.," ii. 14, λύπη ἀφωνίαν ἐμποιοῦσα, v. ed. Basil, 1518.

appended to these words directly applies the defini-
tion to the sin of accidie, which is "a sorrowfulness so weighing down the mind that there is no
good it likes to do. It has attached to it as its
inseparable comrade a distress and weariness of soul,
and a sluggishness in all good works, which plunges
the whole man into lazy languor, and works in him
a constant bitterness. And out of this vehement woe
springs silence and a flagging of the voice, because
the soul is so absorbed and taken up with its own
indolent dejection, that it has no energy for utterance, but is cramped and hampered and imprisoned
in its own confused bewilderment, and has not a
word to say."

II. Concerning the witness of two mediæval
teachers, St. Thomas Aquinas and Dante, something
has been said in the course of the first sermon in this
volume; and the writer has no hope of speaking at
all worthily about those profound, majestic ways of
thought in which they, with their great companions
and disciples, move. He would only try to suggest
for inquiry or consideration three points which seem
especially needed to supplement what he was trying to
convey in the sermon.

(*a*) The first is the affinity which St. Thomas marks
between accidie and envy. Both alike are forms

of sinful gloom, antagonists to that joy which stands second in the bright list of the effects of *Caritas*. But the joy that comes of *Caritas* is twofold : there is the joy that is found in God, the quiet exultation of the soul that knows His goodness and His love, the joy of loving Him ; and there is also the joy which concerns one's neighbour's good, the gladness of the soul that feels a brother's welfare or happiness exactly as its own, and freely, simply yields to the delight of seeing others rightly glad. Neither, it may be, can perfectly be realized in this life ; but neither is unknown—that is begun in " the way," which is to be made perfect in " the country." [1] And over against these two fair gifts of pure and self-forgetful joy there stand, in hard and awful contrast, the two unlovely sorts of sinful gloom : [2] the gloom of accidie, which is " tristitia de bono divino "—a sorrowful despondency, or listlessness concerning the good things which God hath prepared for them that love Him ; and the gloom of envy, which is " tristitia de bono proximi "—the gloom of him

" Who so much fears the loss of power,
Fame, favour, glory (should his fellow mount

---

[1] Cf. S. Th. 2da 2^{dae}, xxviii. 3.
[2] Cf. S. Th. 2da 2^{dae}, xxviii., xxxv. (*ad init.*), xxxvi.

> Above him). and so sickens at the thought,
> He loves their opposite : " [1]

the gloom of the soul that sullenly broods over the
prosperity of others till . their success seems, to its
sick fancy, like a positive wrong against itself. Thus
envy may stand side by side with accidie ; and in
both we see that sorrow of the world, that heavy,
wilful, wasteful sadness, which is as alien from the
divinely quickened sorrow of repentance as it is from
the divinely quickened joy of love.

(b) In the second place, there seems to be reality and
justice, as well as comfort, in the distinction which
St. Thomas draws in answering the question whether
accidie is a deadly sin :—the distinction between its
complete and incomplete development. Fully formed,
discerned and recognized by the reason, and deepened
by its assent, it is a deadly sin, driving from the
heart the characteristic joy of the spiritual life, and
setting itself in irreconcilable antagonism to that
love which is inseparably linked with the Divine indwelling. "The fruit of the Spirit is love, joy,
peace ; " and these cannot live in the heart that
deliberately yields itself up to a despondent renunciation of all care and hope and effort concerning its

---

[1] Dante, " Purgatorio," xvii. 118-120 (Cary's translation). Cf. Ar.
Rhet., ii. x. 1, with Mr. Cope's note.

true calling and its highest good. But there is also a venial sort of accidie: a reluctance that is not deliberate, nor confirmed and hardened by a wilful choice; a sloth engendered by the persistent hanging back of a man's lower nature, which only a continuous exertion will keep up to the level or ambition of the higher life.[1]—It is with a curious answer that St. Thomas meets the contention that accidie can never be a deadly sin because it violates no precept of the Law of God. It violates, he replies, the commandment concerning the hallowing of the seventh day: for the moral import of that commandment is to bid us rest in the Lord; and gloominess concerning the good which is of God is contrary to that rest.[2]

(c) The different aspect of the sin of accidie in the "Inferno," where it has plunged on into the very depths of sullenness and gloom and wrath, and in the "Purgatorio," where only thoughts of sloth and of lukewarmness are prominent, is remarkable ; and the contrast seems to find its explanation in that view of the various stages towards the finishing[3] of the

[1] Cf. A. Lehmkuhl, "Theologia Moralis," vol. i. § 740.

[2] S. Th. 2da 2^{dae}, xxxv. 3, ad primum. Cf. also, as bearing on St. Thomas' conception of acedia, S. Th. 1ma, lxiii. 2, ad secundum; 2da 2^{dae}, clviii. 5; and "Quæstiones de Malo," Qu. xi.

[3] St. James i. 15.

C

sin which is presented by St. Thomas. Dante's teaching as to its beginning is given towards the close of the seventeenth canto; and it is very clearly brought out by Mr. Vernon in his "Readings in the Purgatorio." "Virgil begins to discourse at considerable length on the origin and cause from which the seven principal sins are derived, and he says that love is the cause of all." "He apparently means that pride, envy, and anger arise from the love of evil against one's neighbour; *accidia*, or sloth, from a tardy desire of discerning and acquiring the true good. The three remaining sins, avarice, gluttony, and self-indulgence, spring from an excessive love or desire of what is not the true good." Similarly Mr. Vernon quotes Benvenuto as saying that "*accidia* is a defective love of the highest good, which we ought to seek for ardently. It is, therefore, a kind of negligence, a tepid lukewarm condition, and as it were a contempt for acquiring the desirable amount of goodness."[1] And so the last two instances of accidie, which arc brought before us in the eighteenth canto, are instances in which a great vocation was dismally forfeited through faint-heartedness, through lack of faith and courage. For accidie was a part,

[1] W. W. Vernon, "Readings in the Purgatorio of Dante," i. 455. Cf. M. F. Rossetti, "A Shadow of Dante," pp. 114, 117.

at least, of their sin who "would not go up" to win "that pleasant land," but "murmured in their tents;" to whom God sware "that they should not enter into His rest," "because of unbelief;" and of their sin, too, who forewent the glory of "a share in founding the great Roman Empire," the degenerate, slothful band, who stayed behind in Sicily—

"Who dared not hazard life for future fame." [1]

The various phases of restlessness and discontent, of sullenness, and hardening, and resentment, and rebellion, through which the defective love of good passes into the horrid, dismal mood, which is shown in the seventh canto of the "Inferno," are described by St. Thomas when he is answering the question whether accidie ought to be set down as a capital sin.[2] But they are shown, somewhat less systematically, it may be, yet with the finest power and vividness, by Chaucer, whose account of accidie, in "The Persones Tale," may fitly stand with those which have been cited in this second group. It seems as though nothing could be more forcible and arresting than the picture he has drawn of it; in which this especially is noteworthy, that from the first he fastens on the traits of irritation and ill

[1] Verg., Æn., v. 751.
[2] S. Th. 2da 2^{dae}, xxxv. 4, "Quæstiones de Malo," Qu. xi. 4.

temper as essentially characteristic of it. "Bitter-
nesse is mother of accidie;" and "accidie is the anguish
of a trouble[1] herte," and "maketh a man hevy,
thoughtful, and wrawe."[2] Then, in four stages, the
great misery and harmfulness of the sin is shown. " It
doth wrong to Jesu Crist, inasmoche as it benimeth[3]
the service that men shulde do to Crist with alle
diligence;" to the three estates, of innocence, of
sinfulness, of grace alike, "is accidie enemie and
contrary, for he loveth no besinesse at all;" it is "eke
a ful gret enemie to the livelode of the body, for it
ne hath no purveaunce ayenst temporal necessitee;"
and fourthly, it "is like hem that ben in the peine
of helle, because of hir slouthe and of hir hevinesse."
That listless, joyless, fruitless, hopeless, restless
indolence, more tiring and exacting than the hardest
work, more sensitive in its dull fretfulness than any
state of bodily suffering,—how apt and terrible a
forecast it presents of their fierce sullenness who
can come to hate love itself for being what it is!
The rest of Chaucer's stern portrayal of " this roten
sinne" consists of a long list of all the vices that
follow in its train; and a dismal crew they are.
"Slouthe, that wol not suffre no hardnesse ne no
penance;" and "wanhope, that is, despeir of the

---

[1] *i.e.* dark, gloomy.   [2] *i.e.* peevish, angry.   [3] *i.e.* taketh away.

mercy of God." (And "sothly, he that despeireth
him is like to the coward champion recreant, that
flieth withouten nede. Alas! alas! nedeles is he
recreant, and nedeles despeired. Certes, the mercy
of God is ever redy to the penitent person, and is
above all His werkes.") "Than cometh sompnolence,
that is, sluggy slumbring, which maketh a man hevy
and dull in body and in soule;" "negligence or
rechelessness that recketh of nothing," "whether
he do it well or badly;" "idelnesse, that is the yate
of all harmes," "the thurrok[1] of all wicked
thoughtes;" "*tarditas,* as whan a man is latered,
or taryed, or he wol tourne to God (and certes, that
is a gret folie);" "lachesse,[2] that is, he that whan
he beginneth any good werk, anon he wol forlete
it and stint;" "a maner coldnesse, that freseth all
the herte of man;" "undevotion, thurgh which a
man is so blont that he may neyther rede ne sing in
holy Chirche, ne travaile with his hondes in no good
werk;" "than wexeth he sluggish and slombry, and
sone wol he be wroth, and sone is enclined to hate
and to envie;" "than cometh the sinne of worldly
sorwe swiche as is cleped *tristitia,* that sleth a man,
as sayth Seint Poule."

Such are the main points in Chaucer's wonderful

---

[1] *i.q.* the hold of a ship.　　　　[2] Slackness.

delineation of the subtle, complex sin of accidie.
In strength of drawing, in grasp of purpose, in
moral earnestness, in vivid and disquieting penetration, it seems to the present writer more remarkable and suggestive than any other treatment of the
subject which he has found; or equalled only by
the endless significance of that brief passage, where
the everlasting misery of those who wilfully and to
the end have yielded themselves to the mastery of
this sin is told by Dante in the "Inferno."

III. Two voluminous writers concerning accidie at
a later date (one in the seventeenth, the other in the
eighteenth century) bring into prominence certain
points of interest; while, with a great elaboration
of detail, they show some loss of power and reality
and impressiveness in the general conception: the
element of sloth being developed and emphasized
somewhat to the overshadowing of all other traits
and tendencies.

The curious work entitled "Tuba Sacerdotalis,"
and published by Marchantius (a pupil of Cornelius
à Lapide, and a priest of the Congregation of St.
Charles) about the middle of the seventeenth century, sets a high example of consistency in the use
of metaphors; for its closely printed folio pages, to
the number of 109, are steadily ruled by the one idea

of representing the seven deadly sins as the seven
walls of Jericho, and showing how they are to be
thrown down by the trumpet of the preacher's voice.
In the case of each wall, its metaphorical dimensions
are carefully described, its height of structure and
depth of foundations, its breadth (with the bricks of
which it is composed) and its length, or circumference.[1] Then appear the seven trumpets at whose
blast it is to fall; seven utterances from the Law,
the Sapiential Books, the Prophets, the Gospels, the
Epistles, the conscience of man, the judgment of God ;
and then, with a bold extension of the unbroken
metaphor, seven battering-rams are brought forward,
in the form of seven effective considerations for the
demolition of that particular wall. Lastly, there is
in regard to each wall a spiritual application of the
curse pronounced in the Book of Joshua upon him
who should rebuild Jericho ;[2] and a description of the
corresponding wall in the sevenfold circuit round
Jerusalem. It seems a quaint, cramped plan for
saying what one wants to say ; though possibly some
of our literary methods may have graver faults. But
if one finds it hard to understand the mind to which

---

[1] Each wall is also regarded as being especially under the care of
one evil spirit; the wall of accidie being, for some reason, entrusted to
Behemoth.

[2] Josh. vi. 26; 1 Kings xvi. 34.

this seemed the best scheme for an ethical treatise, the signs of power and penetration and insight, and the modern-looking passages on which one comes, are surely thereby made the more remarkable. And as, in the nine chapters of his seventh Tractate, Marchantius describes in every detail and dimension the great wall of accidie, so high that it shuts out the light of God, and hides from those whom it encloses all His love and mercy; so deeply founded that it reaches right down to despair;[1] built broad and strong, with diverse kinds of stones and bricks, such as lukewarmness, love of comfort, sleepiness, leisureliness, delay, inconstancy; and drawn out to an immense length by the multitude of hands that toil in building it:—as he expounds all this with a good deal of care, learning, and shrewdness, he says so many things worth thinking of that one may almost forget the pedantic form in which his work is cast. Perhaps the finest passage is that "De Septemplici Ariete Murum Acediæ Evertente," where he dwells on seven thoughts which ought to dislodge this sin from its place in a man's heart: the thought of our Saviour's ceaseless, generous toil for us; of the labours of all His servants, saints, and martyrs; of the unwearied

---

[1] Cf. the very striking passage on hardness of heart, in the fourth paragraph of the third chapter.

activity of all creation, from the height where, about the throne, the living creatures rest not day and night, down to herbs and plants continually pressing on by an instinctive effort to their proper growth ; the thought that came home so vividly to St. Francis Xavier, of the immense energy and enterprise of those who seek the wealth of this world, "in their generation wiser than the children of light ; " the thought of the shortness of this life and the urgency of its tasks, because " there is no work, nor device, nor knowledge, nor wisdom in the grave ; " the thought of one's own past sins, with the need that they entail ; and lastly, the thought of heaven and of hell.

There are some suggestive words in another and a less ambitious work by the same author, his " Resolutiones Quæstionum Pastoralium," where, in dealing with the question, "Of what sort is the sin of accidie ? " he indicates a distinction analogous to that drawn by St. Thomas, between its incomplete and complete forms, and says, " His sin is deadly who is gloomy and downcast by the deliberate consent of his will, because he was created for grace, for good deserts, for glory." [1] The words may point, perhaps, to a reason why the conception of " accidie " seems to belong

---

[1] Marchantii Hortus Pastorum, etc., p. 996 (ed. 1661). Cf. also the " Praxis Catechistica," pp. 1026, 1027.

especially to Christian ethics; why one finds (so far as the present writer is aware) nothing like so full and serious a recognition of the temper it denotes in Theophrastus,[1] for instance, or in Aristotle. The true perversity and wrong-heartedness of gloom and sullen brooding could not be realized until the true joy for which the love of God had made man was disclosed : and the wickedness of a listless, cowardly, despondent indolence might seem less before men fully knew to what they were called by God, and to what height He bade their ventures, efforts, aspirations, rise; before they knew by what means and at what a cost the full power of attainment had been brought within the reach of those who truly seek it. It was the revelation of these things in the faith of Jesus Christ that gave distinctness to the great duty of hopefulness and joy, and corresponding clearness and seriousness to the sin of accidie.

"Exterminium Acediæ" is the title of a volume of addresses for a retreat of three days' duration, published by Francis Neumayr, a Jesuit, in 1755.[2] One

---

[1] The μεμψίμοιρος, or grumbler, who "represents the passive form of discontent," comes nearest to the idea among the Characters of Theophrastus ; but the interval of difference is wide and manifold and significant.

[2] The writer is indebted to the Rev. R. W. Randall for the knowledge of this book. Cf. "Retreat Addresses and Meditations," by R. W. Randall, p. xix.

finds here the appearance, at least, of another sort of
artificiality ; and it is not easy to be reconciled to
the elaborate preparation of effects of sudden impulse,
somewhat like those

> " In the off-hand discourse
> Which (all nature, no art)
> The Dominican brother, these three weeks,
> Was getting by heart." [1]

But, in spite of touches which may thus jar upon
one here and there, the book is certainly impressive
and remarkable; and there is teaching in the very
fact that the author could choose this one sin to be
the central subject of meditation and self-examination throughout the exercises of the three days. His
one text, as it were, for all his addresses is that bidding of our Lord's which most directly challenges
the desultory, listless, nerveless languor of the "accidious:" "Strive (*contendite*) to enter in at the
strait gate:" [2] and he shows how accidie is "the foe
of those three adverbs" which should characterize our
serving God—*speedily, seriously, steadily* ; and how
sorrow, love, and fear should help to drive it from
our hearts ; while he marks how vast a multitude of
lives are ruined by the sin, and how few people ever
speak of it, or seem conscious of its gravity. But the

[1] R. Browning, "The Englishman in Italy," v. 64.
[2] St. Luke xiii. 24.

freshest and most interesting part of his book is that in which he deals with the excuses of those clergy who "enjoyed bad health," and made some bodily weakness or indisposition the excuse for a great deal of accidie. This excuse is attacked with that sort of downright and inconsiderate good sense which directed the discipline of many English homes half a century ago, and which, while it may often have involved some harshness and suffering, yet surely fought off from very many lives the intractable misery of imagined ailments. Let us listen to the relentlessly healthy Neumayr. "I hear some one complaining, 'I don't mind work. But what am I to do? Again and again, when I should like to work, I can't. I am indisposed.'[1] Now, this objection I must answer with care, because there is scarcely any corner into which accidie as it flees betakes itself with greater security against its pursuers. I ask, therefore, what is the meaning of this pretext, 'I am indisposed'? Do you mean, 'I am not able,' or 'I do not like' to work? If you mean the former, then this abnormal inability must be due to a change that has taken place, either in the solid or in the liquid parts of the body." These two sorts of changes are

---

[1] "Non sum dispositus." The phrase is, perhaps, intentionally ambiguous. *Vide* Ducange, *s.v. Indispositus.*

discussed according to the pathology with which Neumayr was acquainted; any damage to the solid parts must be seriously and thoroughly treated, "morboque vacandum esse sana Ratio postulet;"—a disorder of the liquid parts (specified as "humores, sanguis, phlegma, bilis") may be due to any one of many diverse causes; and if it does not yield to change of diet and a good night's sleep, then, says Neumayr, try patience : let the love of the Cross come in ; and when the lower nature says, "I'm indisposed," let the generous soul make answer, "Then you must not be." [1] "Truly," he continues in a later passage, "truly the desire of a long life hinders very many from a happy life: for only by toiling can we win a happy life, and they who love life dread toil, lest they may hurt their health. So do we love to be deceived. I, too, myself have hugged like maxims : 'Spare thyself. Take care of thy health.' 'My strength is not the strength of stones, nor is my flesh like brass.' 'A living dog is better than a dead lion.' Bah! who so beguiled me that I did not hear the hissing of the serpent in such words ? Who talks like that save accidie itself ? " "My Saviour, let my days be few, if only they may be well filled.[2] But

---

[1] "Exterminium Acediæ," pp. 142, 143 (ed. 1758).
[2] "Pauci sint dies mei, modo pleni sint" (ibid., p. 168).

art not Thou the Lord of life? I pray Thee, then,
grant me a long life; but for no other end than this, that
I may redeem the time which I have lost by accidie."

Yet one more passage must be quoted from this
writer before the witness of the present day is heard
—a passage which may be at least suggestive of some
disquieting thoughts for many of us. He has been
speaking of that call to strenuous co-operation with
Divine grace which comes to us because we are human
beings; and then of that especial challenge to a
vigorous life, a brave self-mastery, which comes to men
in the prerogative dignity of their sex. And yet, are
men really more brave, more strenuous than women
in self-discipline and self-sacrifice? "Certainly the
greater part of our teachers favour the opinion that
there are more women than men in the way of salvation; and that not so much because many of them
show more love than men for a secluded life, nor
because they have more time for prayer, and are
kept apart from the perilous duties which men have
to bear, but because they do violence to their own
wishes more than men do; and that is seen in the
manly chastity of virgins, in the patience of wives, in
the constancy of widows."[1]

---

[1] "Id quod satis docet *virilis tot virginum continentia, tot uxorum
patientia*, tot viduarum constantia" (ibid., p. 210).

Without presuming to follow the speculation that there is in these words as to the hidden things of God, we surely may find something to think about in the reason that is suggested for the writer's venturesome opinion; there is some truth in that thought concerning human life, and the division of its real burdens, which the Jesuit put before his brethren in their retreat a century and a half ago.

IV. Professor Henry Sidgwick, in his " Outlines of the History of Ethics," after saying that the list of the deadly sins " especially represents the moral experience of the monastic life," adds that " in particular the state of moral lassitude and collapse, of discontent with self and the world, which is denoted by ' Acedia,' is easily recognizable as a spiritual disease peculiarly incident to the cloister."[1] The brief description of the predominant elements in the sinful temper of accidie is excellent; but the apparent implication that the noxious growth is indigenous among monks, and rarely found elsewhere, seems disputable, and, for lack of due qualification, likely to be misleading.[2]

---

[1] H. Sidgwick, " Outlines of the History of Ethics," iii. § 5, *ad fin.*

[2] It is interesting to contrast Mr. Ruskin's emphasis on Dante's juxtaposition of *Anger* and *Sorrow* in the seventh canto of the "Inferno." "There is, perhaps, nothing more notable in this most interesting system" (*i.e.* the system of the seven circles into which the nether world is divided) " than the profound truth couched under the attach-

Doubtless it is true that a special and very virulent form of accidie was often to be found in monasteries, among "such as gave themselves to a one-sidedly contemplative life, without having the power or the calling for it, and who were filled with a disgust of all things, even of existence, while even the highest religious thoughts became empty and meaningless to them."[1] Cassian and St. John Climacus show full consciousness of this; and one may well believe that in the Spanish cloister, into which Mr. Browning got so vivid and terrible a glimpse, a long indulgence of this sin in its worst forms preceded that rancorous

ment of so terrible a penalty to sadness or sorrow. It is true that idleness does not elsewhere appear in the scheme, and is evidently intended to be included in the guilt of sadness by the word 'accidioso;' but the main meaning of the poet is to mark the duty of rejoicing in God, according both to St. Paul's command and Isaiah's promise, 'Thou meetest him that rejoiceth and worketh righteousness.' I do not know words that might with more benefit be borne with us, and set in our hearts momentarily against the minor regrets and rebelliousnesses of life, than these simple ones—

'Tristi fummo
Nell' aer dolce, che del sol s' allegra,
Or ci attristiam, nella belletta negra.'

' We once were sad,
In the sweet air, made gladsome by the sun ;
Now in these murky settlings are we sad.' " *

[1] H. Martensen, "Christian Ethics (Individual)," Eng. trans., p. 378. Cf. the following page for a careful qualification of that which might seem to be here implied.

_____

* J. Ruskin, "The Stones of Venice," ii. 325 (ed. 1886).

hate which fastened on poor Brother Lawrence, in his intolerable harmlessness and love of gardening.[1] But it would be incautious and, the present writer believes, profoundly and perilously untrue, if any one were to think that the temptation and the sin belong to a bygone age, or need not to be thought about and fought against in the present day, even under such circumstances as may seem to have least of the cloister or of asceticism in them. It may have changed its habit, covered its tonsure, and picked up a new language; but it is the same old sin which centuries ago was wrecking lives that had been dedicated to solitude and to austerity, to prayer and praise; the same that Cassian saw in Egypt, and St. Gregory in Rome—that St. Thomas analysed in one way, and Chaucer in another; the same as that of which Dante marks the sequel in those who have and in those who have not entered on the way of penitence.

Clearly the grounds for such an assertion as this can be but very partially adduced : in large part they must be furnished to each man by his own experience of life and his own conscience.[2] But there are some

---

[1] R. Browning's "Poetical Works," vi. 26.

[2] There is much that is very clever and suggestive in the chapter upon "Spiritual Idleness," in F. W. Faber's "Growth in Holiness." But, to the present writer's mind, it is a book marred by many blemishes.

fragments of more general and external witness which may be here alleged.

Poetry may not to the legal mind be evidence ; and there may not always be a valid inference from the self-disclosure of poets to the character of their age ; there may, perhaps, be some who would say that even monks are not more abnormal in their experience than poets.[1] But, nevertheless, it surely is a significant fact that so very many of the chief and most characteristic poets of our age have seemed to speak of a temper very like accidie, as having been at times a besetting peril of their work and life. It is seen in Wordsworth, in the conflict and crisis of his soul, after the shock of the French Revolution, when, he says—

> "I lost
> All feeling of conviction, and, in fine,
> Sick, wearied out with contrarieties,
> Yielded up moral questions in despair.
>   This was the crisis of that strong disease,
> This the soul's last and lowest ebb ; I drooped,
> Deeming our blessèd reason of least use
> When wanted most."[2]

There are passages in the "Christian Year"[3] and in

---

[1] Κοῦφον γὰρ χρῆμα ποιητής ἐστι καὶ πτηνὸν καὶ ἱερόν, καὶ οὐ πρότερον οἷός τε ποιεῖν, πρὶν ἂν ἔνθεός τε γένηται καὶ ἔκφρων καὶ ὁ νοῦς μηκέτι 'ν αὐτῷ ἐνῇ (Plat. Ion., 534, B).

[2] "The Prelude," bk. xi. Cf. Mr. John Morley's Introduction, pp. li, lii.

[3] Third Sunday after Easter.

the "Lyra Innocentium"[1] which could hardly have
been written save by one who himself had felt the
power, at once penetrating and oppressive, of the
moods which are described; but, in two letters to Sir
John Coleridge, Keble takes away all doubt upon the
subject, and tells very frankly and very touchingly
the severity of his struggle against " a certain humour
calling itself melancholy; but, I am afraid, more truly
entitled proud and fantastic, which I find very often
at hand, forbidding me to enjoy the good things, and
pursue the generous studies which a kind Providence
throws so richly in my way; . . . a certain perverse
pleasure, in which, perhaps, you may not conceive
how any man should indulge himself, of turning over
in my thoughts a huge heap of blessings, to find one
or two real or fancied evils (which, after all, are sure
to turn out goods) buried among them."[2]—In all the
strangely manifold wealth of Archbishop Trench's
work, certain of his poems seem to stand apart with
a distinctive power for the help of many troubled
souls; and some of us, it may be, have to thank him
most of all for this—that he had the courage and the
charity to let men see not only the songs he wrote
when he had won his victory over the besetting

[1] iv. 10, " Ill Temper."
[2] Sir J. D. Coleridge, " Memoir of the Rev. J. Keble," pp. 66, 68.

gloom, but also those which came out of a time when
he hardly knew which way the fight might go—a time

> "Of long and weary days,
> Full of rebellious askings, for what end,
> And by what power, without our own consent,
> Caught in this snare of life we know not how,
> We were placed here, to suffer and to sin,
> To be in misery, and know not why;"

a time in which he knew

> "The dreary sickness of the soul,
> The fear of all bright visions leaving us,
> The sense of emptiness, without the sense
> Of an abiding fulness anywhere;
> When all the generations of mankind,
> With all their purposes, their hopes and fears,
> Seem nothing truer than those wandering shapes
> Cast by a trick of light upon a wall,
> And nothing different from these, except
> In their capacity for suffering."
>
> "Our own life seemed then
> But as an arrow flying in the dark,
> Without an aim, a most unwelcome gift,
> Which we might not put by." [1]

Mr. Matthew Arnold, in the " Scholar-Gipsy," shows
with rare, pathetic beauty how such miseries as these
are fastened into the " strange disease of modern
life;" [2] and Lord Tennyson, in his fine and thoughtful

[1] R. C. Trench, Poems: "On leaving Rome." Cf. also "Ode to
Sleep," and "Despondency;" and "Letters and Memorials," chapters
iii. and vi.

[2] Cf. also "Growing Old;" a poem which it is interesting to com-
pare with one on "Latter Years," in "Iona and other Verses," by
W. Bright.

poem, " The Two Voices," tells the course of that great battle which so many hearts have known, and the strength of that victory which all might win, fighting against " crazy sorrow," against sullen thoughts, until

"The dull and bitter voice was gone."

But surely no poet of the present day, and none perhaps since Dante, has so truly told the inner character of accidie, or touched more skilfully the secret of its sinfulness than Mr. Robert Louis Stevenson, in the graceful, noble lines which he has entitled " The Celestial Surgeon "—

> " If I have faltered more or less
>   In my great task of happiness;
> If I have moved among my race
> And shown no glorious morning face;
> If beams from happy human eyes
> Have moved me not; if morning skies,
> Books, and my food, and summer rain
> Knocked on my sullen heart in vain;—
> Lord, thy most pointed pleasure take
> And stab my spirit broad awake;
> Or, Lord, if too obdurate I,
> Choose Thou, before that spirit die,
> A piercing pain, a killing sin,
> And to my dead heart run them in." [1]

" *Sullen were we in the sweet air, that is gladdened by the sun, carrying lazy smoke within our hearts; now lie we sullen here in the black mire.*" [2] Surely the

[1] R. L. Stevenson, " Underwoods, " No. xxii.
[2] Dante, " Inferno," vii. 121–124.

fourteenth and the nineteenth centuries are not very far apart in their understanding of the nature and the misery of accidie. It may have found its way very easily to the cells of anchorets and monks; but it is not very far from many of us, in the stress and luxury and doubt of our day.

One, indeed, there is, and he the one whom many hold to be the greatest poet of our day, who seems to show in all his work no personal knowledge of such cloudy moods as gather round a man in accidie. In reading what Mr. Browning has left us, there is a sense of security somewhat like that with which those who had the happiness of knowing him always looked forward to meeting him, to being greeted by him; a confident expectation of being cheered by the generous and hopeful "geniality of strength."[1] It has been well said that "in this close of our troubled century, the robust health of Robert Browning's mind and body has presented a singular and a most encouraging phenomenon."[2] Whatever may be denied to him or criticized in him, this surely may be claimed without misgiving by those who have learnt from him and loved him—that he never failed to make effort seem worth while. To many of our poets

[1] E. Gosse, "Robert Browning : Personalia," p. 82.
[2] Id. ibid., p. 91.

we may owe this debt, that they have rebuked despondency and helped us to dispel it: Mr. Browning's
beneficence lies in this—that he shows us how a
thoughtful man may keep his work untouched by it.
It is, indeed, a high standard of courage that he sets
before us on the last page he gave us, in the epilogue
to his verses, and to his life;—but it is a standard
by which we need not fear to try his work; for he
teaches us in truth as

> " One who never turned his back but marched breast forward,
>   Never doubted clouds would break;
>   Never dreamed, though right were worsted, wrong would triumph;
>   Held we fall to rise, are baffled to fight better,
>   Sleep to wake." [1]

V. No words could seem more apt than these to
carry us forward to thoughts of that high grace
which stands out foremost among the antagonists of
accidie; and such thoughts may point towards a
further ground for doubting whether some forms
of accidie may not even be among the peculiar
dangers of the present day.

"Ayenst this horrible sinne of accidie, and the
braunches of the same, ther is a vertue that is called
fortitudo or strength, that is, an affection thurgh
which a man despiseth noyous thinges. This vertue

[1] R. Browning, "Asolando," p. 157. Cf. "Prospice:" Poetical
Works,' vii. 168.

enhaunseth and enforceth the soule, right as accidie abateth and maketh it feble : for this *fortitudo* may endure with long sufferance the travailles that ben covenable." "Certes this vertue" (in its first kind, which "is cleped magnanimitee, that is to say gret corage") "maketh folk to undertake hard and grevous thinges by hir owen will, wisely and resonably."[1]

"A virtue that is called strength"—the wise and reasonable undertaking of hard things. One sees directly how the excellence of which Chaucer so speaks is indeed the very contrary of that despondent and complaining listlessness, that self-indulgent, unaspiring resignation to one's moral poverty, which is at the heart of accidie. In accidie a man exaggerates the interval and the difficulties which lie between himself and high attainment; he measures the weight of all tasks by his own disinclination for them; his way "is as an hedge of thorns," and with increasing readiness he says, "There is a lion without; I shall be slain in the streets." He teaches his circumstances to answer him according to his reluctance; the real hardness of that which is noble seems in his imagination nearer and nearer to impossibility; with

---

[1] Chaucer, "The Persones Tale: Remedium Accidiæ." Cf. St. Thomas Aquinas, S. Th., 2da 2^{dae}, Qu. cxxiii., cxxviii., cxxxix., cxl.

increasing shamelessness he declines the venture which is an element in most things that are worth doing, and a condition of all spiritual progress; and so he settles down into a deepening despondency concerning that good to which God calls him, a refusal to aspire, or to venture, or to toil towards a higher life. And from such despondency the more positive traits of accidie are seldom very far removed; resentment, fretfulness, irritation, anger, easily find access to a heart that is refusing to believe in the reasonableness of lofty aims, and lazily contenting itself with a low estimate of its hopes, its powers, and its calling. Plainly that which men are losing, that of which they are falling out of sight, when they sink back into this dangerous and dismal plight, is the grace, the virtue, the sense of duty and of shame, which should lead them to the wise and reasonable undertaking of hard things. They ought to be steadily repelling the temptation to think any fresh thing impossible or indispensable to them. For it is a temptation which comes on apace when once a man has begun to yield it ground; it is a temptation which does more than many which may look uglier to make life fruitless and expensive and unhappy; and it is a temptation which finds useful allies among the characteristic troubles of the present day. Surely

it is a time of risk that comes to many men, in the
ways of modern life and modern medicine, when
the pressure of their work or the unsteadiness of
their nervous system has begun to make them watch
their own sensations, and look out too attentively for
signals of fatigue. It may even be as harmful to
make too much as it is to make too little of such
signals; they may, indeed, be well marked and heeded,
as warning us that the undertaking of hard things
should be wisely and reasonably limited; but there
is apt to be a pitiful loss of liberty and worth and
joy out of any life in which they come to command
an ever-increasing deference, encroaching more and
more upon the realm of will, discouraging a man from
ventures he might safely make, and filching from
him bit by bit that grace of fortitude which is the
prophylactic as well as the antidote for accidie.[1]

But there is another way, more serious and more
direct, in which the sin of accidie gathers power and
opportunity out of the conditions of the present day.

[1] " Comparez la vie d'un homme asservi à telles imaginations, à
celle d'un laboureur se laissant aller aprez son appetit naturel,
mesurant les choses au seul sentiment present, sans science et sans
prognostique, qui n'a du mal que lorsqu'il l'a; où l'aultre a souvent
la pierre en l'ame avant qu'il l'ayt aux reins; comme s'il n'estoit
point assez à temps pour souffrir le mal lorsqu'il y sera, il l'anticipe
par fantasie, et luy court au devant" (" Essais de Montaigne," ii. 12;
vol. iii. p. 128, ed. 1820).

The moral influence of any form of unbelief which is largely talked about, reaches far beyond the range of its intellectual appeal; it is felt more widely than it is understood; in many cases it gets at the springs of action without passing through the mind. And this is likely to come about with especial readiness when the prevalent type of unbelief makes little demand for precise knowledge or positive statement, and easily enters into alliance with a general inclination of human nature. The practical effect of agnosticism is favoured by these advantages, and it mixes readily with that pervading atmosphere of life which tells for so much more in the whole course of things than any definite assertion or any formal argument. Hooker noticed long ago that trait of human faultiness which is always ready to befriend suggestions such as those of agnosticism. "The search of knowledge is a thing painful, and the painfulness of knowledge is that which maketh the will so hardly inclinable thereunto. The root hereof, Divine malediction; whereby the instruments being weakened wherewithal the soul (especially in reasoning) doth work, it preferreth rest in ignorance before wearisome labour to know."[1] It is very easy to translate into the sphere of action that renunciation of sustained

---

[1] R. Hooker, "Of the Laws of Ecclesiastical Polity," I. vii. 7.

and venturesome and exacting effort which in the
sphere of thought is sometimes called agnosticism;
and so translated it finds·many tendencies prepared
to help its wide diffusion. If "the search of knowledge is a thing painful," the attainment of holiness
does not come quickly or naturally to men as they
now are; and it is not strange that while many are
denying that it is possible to know God, many more
are renouncing the attempt to grow like Him. Two
brilliant and thoughtful writers,[1] with equal though
diverse opportunities of studying some of the most
stirring life of our day, in Boston and in Birmingham,
have marked, with impressive coincidence of judgment,
how widely spread among us is the doubt whether
high moral effort is worth while, or reasonable. " We
are so occupied with watching the developments of
fatalistic philosophy in its higher and more scientific
phases, that I think we often fail to see to what an
extent and in what unexpected forms it has found
its way into the life of men, and is governing
their thoughts about ordinary things. The notion of
fixed helplessness, of the impossibility of any strong
power of a man over his own life, and, along with
this, the mitigation of the thought of responsibility
which, beginning with the sublime notion of a man's

---

[1] Mr. Phillips Brooks and Dr. R. W. Dale.

being answerable to God, comes down to think of him only as bound to do his duty to society, then descends to consider him as only liable for the harm which he does to himself, and so finally reaches the absolute abandonment of any idea of judgment or accountability whatever,—all this is very much more common than we dream."[1] There is something very terrible and humiliating in the swiftness with which a great deal of energy and aspiration is unstrung the moment even a light wreath of mist passes over the aspect of the truths that held it up. So much less time and reasoning and probability may suffice for the relaxation of a high demand than were required to enforce its recognition. And thus the thinnest rumour of negative teaching seems enough in some cases to take the heart out of a man's struggle against sloth or worldliness. If a considerable number of articles in magazines imply that it is impossible to know God, it does not seem worth while to get up

---

[1] Phillips Brooks, "Lectures on Preaching," p. 222. Cf. R. W. Dale, "Nine Lectures on Preaching," p. 195: "The issue of the controversy largely depends, for the moment, upon the vigour and authority of conscience, and upon the ardour and vehemence of those moral affections which are the allies of conscience and the strong defenders of her throne. . . . Teach men that it is the prerogative of human nature to force and compel the most adverse circumstances to give new firmness to integrity and new fire to enthusiasm." Cf. also p. 241, for a striking passage on the duty of joy.

half an hour earlier in the morning to seek Him before the long day's work begins; if, in various quarters and on various grounds, the claims of Christ are being set aside or disregarded, then, though the arguments against those claims may never have been carefully examined, the standard of the Sermon on the Mount begins to seem more than can be expected of a man; and if it is often hinted that sins which Christianity absolutely and unhesitatingly condemns may be condoned in an ethical system which takes man as it finds him, and recognizes all the facts of human nature, the resolute intention of the will is shaken, and the clear, cherished purpose of a pure and noble life recedes further and further, till it almost seems beyond the possibility of attainment, beyond the range of reasonable ambition. And so there settles down upon the soul a dire form of accidie; the dull refusal of the highest aspiration in the moral life; the acceptance of a view of one's self and of one's powers which once would have appeared intolerably poor, unworthy, and faint-hearted; an acquiescence in discouragement, which reaches the utmost depth of sadness when it ceases to be regretful; a despondency concerning that goodness to which the love of God has called men, and for which His grace can make them strong.

Surely it is true that, amidst all the stir and changefulness which makes our life so vastly different from that of which Cassian, for instance, wrote, there are many whose alacrity, endurance, courage hopefulness in pressing on towards goodness, in "laying hold on the eternal life," is, insensibly perhaps, relaxed and dulled by causes such as these; whether by the encroachment of imaginary needs upon the rightful territory of a resolute will, or by the suspicion, hardly formulated or recognized, it may be, yet none the less enfeebling, that Christianity has set the aim of moral effort unreasonably high, that men have been struggling towards a goal which they were never meant to think of, and that it is not worth while to try for such a state of heart and mind as the Bible and the saints propose to us. And wherever any such renunciation is being made, there is the beginning of accidie; for that listlessness or despondency concerning the highest life has always been a distinctive note of it. It would be cruelly and obviously unjust to link the sin too closely with such tendencies as have here been indicated. There are very many who go on (not knowing, it may be, by Whose strength they persevere), bravely lifting up the aim and effort of their life high above the reach of doubts which yet they cannot dissipate; there are very many who, professing full belief of all that can give worth and hope and seriousness to a man's life, yet yield their joyless hearts to sloth or sullenness, as though the love of God had brought no call to strive, no strength for victory, no hope of glory among the trials of this world. All that is here asserted is that there are characteristic troubles of our age which easily fall in with the assailing force of accidie; that the evidence of its persistence does not lie wholly in individual experience; and that it would be unwise to think that we may abate in any way our watchfulness against it.

And now, as ever, over against Accidie rises the great grace of Fortitude; the grace that makes men undertake hard things by their own will wisely and reasonably. There is something in the very name of Fortitude which speaks to the almost indelible love of heroism in men's hearts; but perhaps the truest Fortitude may often be a less heroic, a more tame and business-like affair than we are apt to think. It may be exercised chiefly in doing very little things, whose whole value lies in this, that, if one did not hope in God, one would not do them; in secretly dispelling moods which one would like to show; in saying nothing about one's lesser troubles and vexations; in seeing whether it may not be best to bear a burden before one tries to see whither one can shift it; in refusing for one's self excuses which one would not refuse for others. These, anyhow, are ways in which a man may every day be strengthening himself in the discipline of Fortitude; and then, if greater things are asked of him, he is not very likely to draw back from them. And while he waits the asking of these greater things, he may be gaining from the love of God a hidden strength and glory such as he himself would least of all suspect; he may be growing in the patience and perseverance of the saints. For most of us the chief temptation to lose heart, the chief demand upon our strength, comes in the monotony of our failures, and in the tedious persistence of prosaic difficulties; it is the distance, not the pace, that tries us. To go on choosing what has but a look of being the more excellent way, pushing on towards a faintly glimmering light, and never doubting the supreme worth of goodness even in its least brilliant fragments,—this is the normal task of many lives; in this men show what they are like. And for this we need a quiet and sober Fortitude, somewhat like that which Botticelli painted, and Mr. Ruskin has described. Let us hear, by way of ending for this essay, his description of her.[1]

[1] J. Ruskin, "Mornings in Florence," iii. 57, 58.

E

"What is chiefly notable in her is—that you would not, if you had to guess who she was, take her for Fortitude at all. Everybody else's Fortitudes announce themselves clearly and proudly. They have tower-like shields and lion-like helmets, and stand firm astride on their legs, and are confidently ready for all comers.

"But Botticelli's Fortitude is no match, it may be, for any that are coming. Worn, somewhat; and not a little weary, instead of standing ready for all comers, she is sitting, apparently in reverie, her fingers playing restlessly and idly—nay, I think, even nervously—about the hilt of her sword.

"For her battle is not to begin to-day; nor did it begin yesterday. Many a morn and eve have passed since it began—and now—is this to be the ending day of it? And if this—by what manner of end?

"That is what Sandro's Fortitude is thinking, and the playing fingers about the sword-hilt would fain let it fall, if it might be; and yet, how swiftly and gladly will they close on it, when the far-off trumpet blows, which she will hear through all her reverie!"

CHRIST CHURCH,
Christmas, 1890.

I.

THE SORROW OF THE WORLD.[1]

"The sorrow of the world worketh death."

2 COR. vii. 10.

WHEN Dante descends to the Fifth Circle of the Inferno, he finds there a black and loathsome marsh, made by the swarthy waters of the Stygian stream pouring down into it, dreary and turbid, through the cleft which they have worn out for themselves. And there, in the putrid fen, he sees the souls of those whom anger has ruined; and they are smiting and tearing and maiming one another in ceaseless, senseless rage.[2] But there are others there, his master tells him, whom he cannot see, whose sobs make those bubbles that he may mark ever rising to the surface of the pool—others, plunged further into the filthy

---

[1] It is hoped that this sermon differs widely enough from the preceding essay, both in substance and in treatment, to warrant its insertion here, in spite of the recurrence in it of some thoughts already touched.

[2] "Inferno," vii. 100–116.

swamp. And what is the sin that has thrust them
down into that uttermost wretchedness? " Fixed in
the slime, they say, ' *Gloomy* were we in the sweet
air, that is gladdened by the sun, carrying sullen,
lazy smoke within our hearts; now lie we *gloomy*
here in the black mire.' This hymn they gurgle
in their throats, for they cannot speak it in full
words." [1]

Surely it is a tremendous and relentless picture of
unbroken sullenness—of wilful gloom that has for
ever shut out light and love; of that death which
the sorrow of the world worketh.

" The sorrow of the world." No discipline or
chastening of the soul; no grief that looks towards
God, or gropes after His Presence in the mystery of
pain ; no anguish that even through the darkness—
aye, even, it may be, through the passing storms of
bitterness and impatience—He can use and sanctify,
for the deepening of character, the softening of
strength, the growth of light and peace. No, none
of these ; but a sorrow that is only of this world,
that hangs in the low and misty air—a wilful sorrow
that men make or cherish for themselves, being, as
Shakespeare says, " as sad as night only for wanton-

---

[1] " Inferno," vii. 121–126; *vide* Mr. Carlyle's translation, almost
exactly followed here.

ness."[1] This is, surely, the inner character of "the sorrow of the world." This makes its essential contrast with the sorrow that could be Divine; the sorrow that Christ shared and knows and blesses; the grief with which He was acquainted. This is the sorrow that worketh death; the sorrow that the great poet of the things unseen sets close by anger. Let us try to think about it for a little while.

The sin whose final issue, in those who wholly yield their souls to it, with utter hardness and impenitence, Dante depicts in the passage which I have quoted—the sin whose expiation, in those who can be cleansed from it, he describes in the eighteenth canto of the "Purgatorio"[2]—was known in his day, and had been known through many centuries of human experience, by a name in frequent use and well understood. It was ranged, by writers on Christian ethics, on the same level with such sins as hatred, envy, discord; with pride, anger, and vainglory; it would be recalled in self-examination by any one who was taking pains to amend his life and cleanse his heart; it was known as prominent and cruel among a man's assailants in the spiritual combat. Through all the changeful course of history, nothing, I suppose, has changed so little as the

---

[1] "King John," IV. i. 15.   [2] "Purgatorio," xviii. 91–138.

conditions and issues of that combat. And yet now the mention of this sin may sound strange, if not unintelligible, to many of us; so that it seems at first as though it might belong essentially to those bygone days when men watched and fought and prayed so earnestly against it; and there is no one word, I think, which will perfectly express its name in modern English. But we know that the devil has no shrewder trick than to' sham dead; and so I venture to believe that it may be worth while to look somewhat more closely at a temptation which seems to be now so much less feared than once it was.

I. The sin of "acedia," or, according to the somewhat misleading form which the word assumed in English, "accidie," had, before Dante's time, received many definitions; and while they agree in the main, their differences in detail show that the evil was felt to be subtle and complex. As one compares the various estimates of the sin, one can mark three main elements which help to make it what it is —elements which can be distinguished, though in experience, I think, they almost always tend to meet and mingle; they are *gloom* and *sloth* and *irritation*. The first and third of the three seem foremost in Dante's thoughts about the doom of accidie; the second comes to the front when he is thinking how

the penitent may be cleansed from it in the intermediate state. Gloom and sloth—a sullen, heavy,
dreary mist about the heart, chilling and darkening
it, till the least thing may make it fretful and angry ;
—such was the misery of the " accidiosus." So
one Father is quoted as defining the sin to be
" fastidium interni boni "—" a distaste for the soul's
good ; " another calls it " a languid dejection of
body and soul about the praiseworthy exercise of
virtues ; " and another, " a sluggishness of the mind
that cares not to set about good works, nor to keep
them up." [1] And so, too, in later times, it was said
to be " a certain sadness which weighs down the
spirit of man in such wise that there is nothing
that he likes to do ; " or " a sadness of the mind
which weighs upon the spirit, so that the person
conceives no will towards well-doing, but rather feels
it irksome." [2] So Chaucer also, " Accidie or slouth
maketh a man hevy, thoughtful, and wrawe. Envie
and ire make bitterness in heart, which bitterness is
mother of accidie, and benimeth [or taketh away]
the love of all goodness : than is accidie the anguish
of a trouble heart. . . . Of accidie cometh first that a

[1] Cf. Commentator on Cassian, " De Cœnobiorum Institutis,"
Lib. x.

[2] Quoted by M. F. Rossetti, " A Shadow of Dante," p. 51.

man is annoyed and encumbered for to do any goodness. . . . For accidie loveth no besinesse at all." [1]
Lastly, let me cite two writers who speak more
fully of the character and signs and outcome of the
sin.

The first is Cassian, who naturally has a great
deal to say about it. For all the conditions of a
hermit's life, the solitude, the sameness, the austerity,
the brooding introspection, in which he lived, made
it likely and common that this should be his besetting sin; and Cassian had marked it as such during
the years he spent among the solitaries of the
Egyptian deserts. In that book of his "Institutes"
which he devotes to it,[2] he defines it as a weariness
or anxiety of heart, a fierce and frequent foe to those
who dwell in solitude; and elsewhere he speaks of
it as a sin that comes with no external occasion, and
often and most bitterly harasses those who live apart
from their fellow-men. There is something of humour
and something of pathos in the vivid picture which
he draws of the hermit who is yielding to accidie:
how utterly all charm and reality fade for him out
of the life that he has chosen—the life of ceaseless
prayer and contemplation of the Divine Beauty; how

---

[1] Quoted by Mr. Carlyle on "Inferno," vii. 121-126.
[2] Lib. x., "De Spiritu Acediæ."

he hates his lonely cell, and all that he has to do there; how hard, disparaging thoughts of others, who live near him, crowd into his mind; how he idles and grumbles till the dull gloom settles down over heart and mind, and all spiritual energy dies away in him.[1]

It is a curious and truthful-seeming sketch, presenting certain traits which, across all the vast diversity of circumstance, may perhaps claim kindred with temptations such as some of us even now may know.

But of far deeper interest, of surer and wider value, is the treatment of acedia by St. Thomas Aquinas. The very place which it holds in the scheme of his great work reveals at once its true character, the secret of its harmfulness, its essential antagonism to the Christian life, and the means of resisting and conquering it.—"The fruit of the Spirit," wrote St. Paul to the Galatians, "is love, joy, peace." And so Aquinas has been speaking of love, joy, peace, and pity, as the first effects upon the inner life of that *caritas* which is the form, the root, the mother, of all virtues.[2] *Caritas*, that true friendship of man

---

[1] The description is cited at greater length in the "Introductory Essay."

[2] S. Th. 2da 2dae, xxvii.-xxx.

with God; that all-embracing gift which is the fulfil-
ling of the Law; that "one inward principle of life,"
as it has been called, " adequate in its fulness to meet
and embrace the range of duties which externally
confront it;"—*caritas*, which is in fact nothing else
but " the energy and the representative of the Spirit
in our hearts,"[1] expands and asserts itself, and makes
its power to be known by its fruits of love, joy, peace,
and pity in the character of man.   Mark, then, how
joy springs out at once as the unfailing token of the
Holy Spirit's presence, the first sign that He is having
His Own way with a man's heart.   The joy of the
Lord, the joy that is strength, the joy that no man
taketh from us, the joy wherewith we joy before God,
the abundant joy of faith and hope and love and
praise,—this it is that gathers like a radiant, foster-
ing, cheering air around the soul that yields itself
to the grace of God, to do His holy, loving Will.—But,
over against that joy,[2] different as winter from summer, as night from day, ay, even as death from life,
looms the dreary, joyless, thankless, fruitless gloom
of sullenness, the sour sorrow of the world, the sin of
accidie; the wanton, wilful self-distressing that numbs
all love and zeal for good; that sickly, morbid weari-

[1] J. H. Newman, "Lectures on Justification," p. 53.
[2] S. Th. 2ᵈᵃ 2ᵈᵃᶜ, xxxv.

ness in which the soul abhors all manner of meat, and
is even hard at death's door ; that woful lovelessness
in which all upward longing fails out of the heart
and will—the sin that is opposed to the joy of love.
So St. Thomas speaks of accidie, and so he brings
it near, surely, to the conscience of many men in
every age.

II. Yes, let us put together in thought the traits
which meet in the picture of accidie; let us think of
it in its contrast with that brightness of spiritual joy
which plays around some lives, and makes the name-
less, winning beauty of some souls—ay, and even
of some faces—and we may recognize it, perhaps, as
a cloud that has sometimes lowered near our own
lives; as a storm that we have seen sweeping across
the sky and hiding the horizon, even though, it may
be, by God's grace only the edge of it reached to
us—only a few drops fell where we were. Heaviness,
gloom, coldness, sullenness, distaste and desultory
sloth in work and prayer, joylessness and thankless-
ness,—do we not know something of the threatenings,
at least, of a mood in which these meet ? The mood
of days on which it seems as though we cannot
genuinely laugh, as though we cannot get rid of a
dull or acrid tone in our voice ; when it seems impossible frankly to " rejoice with them that do rejoice,"

and equally impossible to go freely out in any true, unselfish sympathy with sorrow; days when, as one has said, "everything that everybody does seem inopportune and out of good taste;"[1] days when the things that are true and honest, just and pure, lovely and of good report, seem to have lost all loveliness and glow and charm of hue, and look as dismal as a flat country in the drizzling mist of an east wind; days when we might be cynical if we had a little more energy in us; when all enthusiasm and con- fidence of hope, all sense of a Divine impulse, flags out of our work; when the schemes which we have begun look stale and poor and unattractive as the scenery of an empty stage by daylight; days when there is nothing that we *like* to do—when, without anything to complain of, nothing stirs so readily in us as complaint. Oh, if we know anything at all of such a mood as this, let us be careful how we think of it, how we deal with it; for perhaps it may not be far from that "sorrow of the world" which, in those who willingly indulge and welcome and invite its presence, "worketh death."

III. It occurs to one at once that this misery of accidie lies on the border-line between the physical and the spiritual life; that if there is something to be

---

[1] F. W. Faber, "Growth in Holiness," p. 244.

said of it as a sin, there is also something to be said
of it as an ailment. It is a truth that was recognized long ago both by Cassian and by St. Thomas
Aquinas, who expressly discusses and dismisses this
objection against regarding accidie as a sin at all.[1]
Undoubtedly physical conditions of temperament and
constitution, of weakness, illness, harassing, weariness,
overwork, may give at times to such a mood of mind
and heart a strange power against us; at times the
forces for resistance may seem frail and few. It is
a truth which should make us endlessly charitable,
endlessly forbearing and considerate and uncritical
towards others; but surely it is a truth that we
had better be shy of using for ourselves. It will do
us no harm to over-estimate the degree in which
our own gloom and sullenness are voluntary; it
will do us very great harm to get into the way of
exaggerating whatever there may be in them that
is physical and involuntary. For the border-line
over which accidie hovers is, practically, a shifting
and uncertain line, and "possunt quia posse videntur"
may be true of the powers upon either side of it. We
need not bring speculative questions out of their
proper place to confuse the distinctness of the practical issue. We have ample warrant, by manifold

[1] S. Th. 2da 2^{dae}, xxxv. 1, ad 2^{dum}.

evidence, by clear experience, for being sure for ourselves that the worth and happiness of life depend
just on this—that in the strength which God gives,
and in the eagerness of His service, the will should
ever be extending the range of its dominion, ever
refusing to be shut out or overborne, ever restless in
defeat, ever pushing on its frontier. Surely it has
been the secret of some of the highest, noblest lives
that have helped the world, that men have refused
to make allowances for themselves; refused to limit
their aspiration and effort by the disadvantages with
which they started; refused to take the easy tasks
which their hindrances might seem to justify, or to
draw premature boundaries for the power of their
will. As there are some men to whom the things
that should have been for their wealth are, indeed, an
occasion of falling, so are there others to whom the
things that might have been for their hindrance are
an occasion of rising; "who going through the vale
of misery use it for a well, and the pools are filled
with water."—And "they shall go from strength to
strength"—in all things more than conquerors through
Him Who loveth them; wresting out of the very
difficulties of life a more acceptable and glorious
sacrifice to lift to Him; welcoming and sanctifying
the very hindrances that beset them as the conditions

of that part which they, perhaps, alone can bear in the perfecting of His saints, in the edifying of the body of Christ. And in that day when every man's work shall be made manifest, it may be found, perhaps, that none have done Him better service than some of those who, all through this life, have been His ambassadors in bonds.

IV. Lastly, then, brethren, let me speak very simply of three ways in which we may, God helping us, extend and reinforce the power of our will to shut out and drive away this wasteful gloom, if ever it begins to gather round us; three ways of doing battle against this sin of accidie.

(1) In the first place, it will surely be a help, a help we all may gain, to see more, to think more, to remember and to understand more, of the real, plain, stubborn sufferings that others have to bear ; to acquaint ourselves afresh with the real hardships of life, the trials, and anxieties, and privations, and patience of the poor—the unfanciful facts of pain. For "blessed is he that considereth the poor and needy; the Lord shall deliver him in the time of trouble." It is one part of the manifold privilege of a parish priest's life that day by day he has to go among scenes which almost perforce may startle him out of any selfish, wilful sadness :—

"When sorrow all our heart would ask,
We need not shun our daily task,
And hide ourselves for calm;
The herbs we seek to heal our woe
Familiar by our pathway grow,
Our common air is balm."[1]

Of old it was thought to be the work of tragedy
that the spectator should be lifted to a higher level,
where action and passion are freer and larger, so that
he might be ashamed to go home from the contemplation of such sorrows to pity or alarm himself about
little troubles of his own.[2]   But if the disasters of the
stage could teach men to be brave and quiet under
trials that were less indeed, but still were real, how
much more should that great ceaseless tragedy of
actual anguish and distress that day and night goes
on around us, rouse and shame us all out of the idle,
causeless gloom that sometimes hangs about men's
hearts?

Those are very noble words of one who in our day
has frankly and faithfully shared with the world
his own profound experience both of despondency
and of deliverance.   "Suffer me not, O Lord, suffer
me not to forget how at the very moment when, it
may be, I am thus playing with a fantastic grief, it

[1] "Christian Year," First Sunday after Easter.
[2] Cf. Timocles in Meincke's "Poetarum Comicorum Græcorum
Fragmenta," p. 613; and Arist. Poetica: vi, ad init.

is actually faring with multitudes of my fellows, many times better and truer and holier than myself. Think, O my soul, of all those—the mourners who have survived everything, even hope itself, the incurables who pace the long halls of pain in the vast hospital of this world; its deposed, discrowned, and disinherited, for whom all the ornament of life has for ever departed, perhaps by their own fault, perhaps by that of others, but in either case gone, and so gone that it never can come back again; long pain the road by which, and death the goal to which, they must travel."[1] Surely the sin of accidie seems most hateful and unmanly in the presence of such thoughts as these.

(2) There is another very safe and simple way of escape when the dull mood begins to gather round one, and that is to turn as promptly and as strenuously as one can to whatever work one can at the moment do. If the energy, the clearness, the power of intention, is flagging in us, if we cannot do our best work, still let us do what we can—for we can always do something; if not high work, then low; if not vivid and spiritual work, then the plain, needful drudgery. Virgil's precept has its place in every way of life, and certainly in the inner life of all men—

[1] R. C. Trench, "Brief Thoughts and Meditations," p. 113.

F

" Frigidus agricolam si quando continet imber,
Multa, forent quæ mox cœlo properanda sereno,
Maturare datur." [1]

When it is dull and cold and weary weather with
us, when the light is hidden, and the mists are thick,
and the sleet begins to fall, still we may get on with
the work which can be done as well in the dark days
as in the bright; work which otherwise will have
to be hurried through in the sunshine, taking up its
happiest and most fruitful hours. When we seem
poorest and least spiritual, when the glow of thankfulness seems to have died quite away, at least we
can go on with the comparatively featureless bits of
work, the business letters, the mechanism of life, the
tasks which may be almost as well done then as ever.
And not only, as men have found and said in every
age, is the activity itself a safeguard for the time,
but also very often, I think, the plainer work is the
best way of getting back into the light and warmth
that are needed for the higher. Through humbly and
simply doing what we can, we retrieve the power
of doing what we would. It was excellent advice of
Mr. Keble's, " When you find yourself overpowered as
it were by melancholy, the best way is to go out, and
do something kind to somebody or other." [2]

---

[1] Virg. Georg. I. 259–261.
[2] " Letters of Spiritual Counsel," p. 6.

(3) But there is yet one way, above all other ways, I think, in which we ought to be ever gaining fresh strength and freedom of soul to rise above such moods of gloom and discontent; one means by which we should be ever growing in the steadiness and quiet intensity of the joy of love. It is the serious and resolute consideration of that astounding work of our redemption which the Love of God has wrought at so immense a cost. It is strange indeed—it would be inconceivable if it were not so very common—that a man can look back to Calvary and still be sullen; that he can believe that all that agony was the agony of God the Son, willingly chosen for the Love of sinful men, and still be thankless and despondent. Strange that he should be sullen still, when he believes that that eternal and unwearied Love is waiting, even during the hours of his gloom and hardness—waiting, watching at his dull, silent heart, longing for the change to come; longing just for that turn of the will which may let in again the glad tide of light and joy and health. Strange that any one should be able to think what a little while we have in which to do what little good we may on earth, before the work is all sealed up and put aside for judgment, and yet take God's great trust of life, and wilfully bid the heaven be dark at noon, and wrap himself in an untimely night wherein

no man can work. Strange, most strange, that any one should believe that this world is indeed the place where he may begin to train his soul by grace for an everlasting life of love and praise and joy, prepared for him in sheer mercy by Almighty God, and still be sullen. Ah! surely, it can only be that we forget these things; that they are not settled deep enough in our hearts; that in the haste of life we do not think of them, or let them tell upon us. For otherwise we could hardly let our hearts sink down in any wilful, wanton gloom, or lower our eyes from that glory of the western sky which should ever brighten our faces as we press towards God; that glory which our Blessed Lord was crucified to win for us; that glory whither the high grace of God the Holy Ghost has been sent forth to lead us.

II.

LEISURE THOUGHTS.

" Whatsoever things are true, whatsoever things are honest, whatsoever things are just, whatsoever things are pure, whatsoever things are lovely, whatsoever things are of good report; if there be any virtue, and if there be any praise, think on these things."

PHIL. iv. 8.

"THINK on these things"—consider these things, and keep the current of your thoughts set towards them: let your minds be busy with them; and let them tell on all your view of life. Such seems to be the force of the word which St. Paul rather strangely uses here.[1] He is giving a rule, I believe, in regard to a part of our life and a field of self-discipline which deserves far more care than it often gets. He does not seem to be speaking of thought with an immediate regard to action, for his advice as to outward conduct is given in the next verse; nor is he speaking here of meditation as a religious exercise, for the lines of thought to which he points would

---

[1] $\tau a\hat{v}\tau a\ \lambda o\gamma i\zeta\epsilon\sigma\theta\epsilon.$

seem too wide and general for that. Rather, he is
telling us, I think, how we ought to set and train and
discipline our minds to use their leisure; how they
ought to behave, so to speak, when they are not on
special duty, when there is no present task to occupy
them. There are spaces day by day in almost every
life when the attention is not demanded for any
definite object; when we are or may be free to think
of what we will. They are the times in which some
people are simply listless, and hardly conscious of
thinking at all; some build castles in the air; some
think of their ambition, or of the scraps of praise
that they have heard; some of their anxieties; some
of their grievances; some of their dislikes; some,
happily, of their hobbies; some, very unhappily, of
their health; and some, one must fear, of thoughts
that are wholly ruinous and shameful.—It is this
"no man's land," this unclaimed, fallow ground that
St. Paul would have rescued from its uselessness or
misuse; and he points us to the right and wholesome
use for it : " Whatsoever things are true, whatsoever
things are honest, whatsoever things are just, whatsoever things are pure, whatsoever things are lovely,
whatsoever things are of good report; if there be
any virtue, and if there be any praise, think on these
things."

I. Surely it is a matter of greatest moment, a matter well worth some real pains and firmness with ourselves, if we can indeed so set the ordinary drift and habit of our minds; so form or transform by God's grace their ordinary inclination. Not only because to Him all hearts are open, and from Him no secrets are hid—that would be reason enough—but there is yet more. There is the tremendous power of habit; the constant, silent growth with which it creeps and twines about the soul, until its branches clutch and grip like iron that which seemed so securely stronger than their little tentative beginning. So the mind spoils its servants, till they become its masters; and the leisure time of life may be either a man's garden or his prison.—Thus there is, perhaps, nothing on which the health and happiness and worth of life more largely turn than on this—that the habitual drift, the natural tendency of our unclaimed thought, should be towards high and pure and gladdening things.

And then, yet again, we may learn the importance of our leisure thoughts, if we remember the certainty of our unconscious self-revealing. That inner world of wilful imaginations and of cherished desires is not so wholly hidden from others as we may sometimes fancy. We may believe that we can keep it quite

apart from our outward life—that we can huddle it
all out of sight when we meet and deal with our
fellow-men; but the habits of the mind will quite
surely tell, sooner or later, more or less clearly, on
those subtle shades of voice and bearing and expression by which, perhaps, men most often and most
nearly know one another. "Out of the abundance
of the heart the mouth speaketh;" and not only out
of that which at the time a man may choose for
utterance:—"his heart gathereth iniquity to itself;
and when he goeth abroad, he telleth it." It is a
grave and anxious thought, surely, that there is this
law of unconscious self-revealing in human life; that,
whether we wish it or no, what we are, or what we
fain would be and are striving to become, within, will
come out somehow, even in this world, forestalling
in part that bare and utter disclosure when this world
is done with. We have all known, I trust, something
of that gracious and unstudied radiance which issues
forth from a pure and true and loving character;
that air of joy and health which some men seem to
bring with them wherever they are; the inevitable
self-betrayal of moral beauty, of fair thoughts and
hopes within. Must it not be true that (however it
may be checked and counteracted by the grace of
God, or by the ministry of angels) there is also some

unconscious effluence of gloom, distrust, unkindness,
or impurity from the mind that is habitually allowed
to drift in its solitude or leisure towards uncomely, or
greedy, or suspicious thoughts ? The inner habit is
always tending to work its way out. " Do not think,"
wrote a great Bishop of our day, " that what your
thoughts dwell upon is of no matter. *Your thoughts
are making you.* We are two men, each of us—what
is seen, and what is not seen. *But the unseen is the
maker of the other.*" [1]

Perhaps I have said more than was needed about
the obvious importance of the leisure habits of our
minds, their drift and tendency in unclaimed times.
But somehow, I think, many do forget how much
it matters what they mostly think of when they may
be thinking of whatever they choose. And then
there are many things that tend to make us listless
and careless in the matter. It needs, for some of us
at least, a good deal of watchfulness and effort. And
the demands that must be met in daily life are many ;
and we are tired or lazy, and it seems hard if we
may not sometimes think of nothing particular. And
then, just as many people repeat unkind or foolish

[1] Bishop Steere, ", Notes of Sermons," 1st series, p. 273. The writer
desires to acknowledge an especial debt to these fresh and thoughtful
Notes.

things because they have nothing particular to say,
so in many minds the vacant spaces are invaded
by thoughts which had better never come, which
would not have come if the room had not been
empty.

II. So, then, let us go on to see what kind of
thoughts St. Paul, taught by the Holy Ghost, Who
knows us wholly, through and through, would have
us make at home in our minds and hearts.

He gives us a wide choice. The list is by no means
limited to what is ordinarily called sacred or religious ;
it includes all bright and pure and generous thoughts
—all that makes up the best grace and helpfulness
of life. " Whatsoever things are true: " all that is
frank and straightforward and sincere—that has no
cowardice, no fear of coming to the light. " Whatsoever things are grave : " not with that sham gravity
which so often discredits the word; not with the
gravity of self-importance, or narrowness, or gloom ;
but with a free and noble reverence for ourselves
(since God has made us and dwells in us), and for all
that is great and reverend around us—the grace of
thought that guards us from mere stupid flippancy.[1]
" Whatsoever things are righteous : " so that in all
our thoughts we may be exactly doing justice to

---

[1] Cf. Phillips Brooks, " Lectures on Preaching," pp. 54–59.

others; giving them credit for all the good we know
or well may hope of them; making allowance for
the difficulties we cannot measure; casting out all
scornfulness and all suspicion; and using, in all our
thoughts of our fellow-men, that generosity which is
simple justice. "Whatsoever things are pure:" all that
is innocent and safe and guileless; all the simple and
spiritual beauty that we can find in nature or in art; all
that can stay fearless and unchecked in the presence
of the perfect and eternal purity of Christ our Lord:
for so may we be growing in that only steadfast
strength, the strength of a stainless mind. And then
St. Paul yet further widens out the kind of thoughts
we are to welcome and habituate in our hearts. "All
that is lovable, and all that is attractive:" all that
adds to the courtesy and kindliness of life; all that
will make good men glad to be with us, and bring a
bit of cheering and encouragement, of gentleness and
sympathy to anxious or wounded souls; all that
rightly wins for us the love of men, and opens out
their hearts to us, and makes them trust us with the
knowledge of their highest life.

But yet, again, St. Paul has something more to add.
He will leave out nothing which can keep our minds
astir with harmless, gladdening thoughts;[1] he would

---

[1] Cf. Bishop Lightfoot, *in loco.*

not slight the virtues or excellences of which men
talked even in the heathen society of his day; nay,
the mind may well be busy in its leisure about any
honourable strength or skill that can win men's
praise; the doing well in any worthy and unselfish
rivalry—it may be intellectual, or it may be athletic
(I think he would have said,)—"If there be any
excellence, or if there be any praise, think on these
things."

III. Such is the fair and ample list that St. Paul
commends to us; such are the things with which he
would have us train and occupy our minds. It is,
I think, a sphere of self-discipline in which many
of us have much to learn; much need of stronger,
steadier self-mastery than we have yet attained.

For plainly there is nothing in this world much
more worth gaining than the happiness of a mind
that tends to dwell on pure and generous thoughts.
All through our hours of waking, thoughts of one kind
or another must be thronging through our minds; and
by God's grace we may do much to determine of what
kind they shall be. And all experience would teach us
to expect that every year, if we are not careful, it
will grow harder to change the habitual bearing, the
ingrained likes and dislikes which give tone and
direction to our leisure thoughts; we might win

now, perhaps, with a little firmness of self-discipline, that which some few years hence we may have to fight for inch by inch, and may hold only with constant effort and distress. And certainly these mental ways and habits of which the Apostle speaks to us will make the gladness of whatever leisure and loneliness and silence may come in the years of life that may be still before us.—Ah! but there is something more than this—a deeper, higher reason for striving after such self-mastery, for watching over all the habits of our minds. It is a wonderful happiness if we tend instinctively to bright and clear and whole-some thoughts; but yet, I think, St. Paul is here marking out for us only the beginning of that which may be; he is only showing us how to get our minds ready, as it were, for that which God may have in store for us. For it is in pure and bright and kindly lives that the grace of God most surely takes root downward, and bears fruit upward; that the presence of our Lord unfolds the fulness of its power, and achieves its miracles of transforming love. He works unstayed, untroubled, in the soul that has been trained to think in all its leisure times of true and high and gentle thoughts. He enters in and stays there, not as a wayfaring man, but as a willing, welcome Guest in a house that has been prepared and

---

decked and furnished as He loves to see it. There the surpassing brightness of His presence issues forth unchecked, and there the will of His great love is freely wrought.—Yes, and there too the Voice of God is clearly heard. There is no knowing whither God might call us, if only we would keep our minds, by His help, free and true to hear His bidding when it comes. He may have for any one of us a task, a trust, higher far than we can ask or think; some work for His love's sake amidst the sufferings of this world; some special opportunity of witnessing for Him, or of ministering to others, of winning to Him those who know Him not. And on the drift and tone which our minds are now acquiring it may depend whether, when the time comes, we recognize our work or not; whether we press forward with the host of God, or dully fall away, it may be, into the misery of a listless, aimless life.

Oh, then, brethren, for your own sakes, for the sake of your own chief happiness, for the sake of a world that needs your help, for the sake of God, Who seeks your love that He may crown your joy, be trying day by day, with watchfulness and prayer, to gain continually more of this high self-mastery in thought; to set the current of your thinking as St. Paul would have it flow; to turn it right away from

all impurity, suspicion, sullenness, jealousy, self-
deception, or ambition, and to guide it wholly towards
those pure and bright and thankful ways where it
may pass on surely into the peace of God, into the
light of His countenance and the welcome of His
love.

III.

THE HOPE OF THE BODY.[1]

"Glorify God in your body."

1 Cor. vi. 20.

In this brief command St. Paul sums up the practical
outcome of the argument with which he has been
occupied. These few words will stick in men's
memories; they may tell on thought and action at
innumerable points; they fix the true aim in a task
that has got miserably tangled and perplexed. And
so St. Paul ends with them this division of his letter;
for it seems evident that the words which follow
them in our version did not form part of the original
text.

I. "Glorify God in your body." The demand is
closely linked with the thoughts of the foregoing
verses; and though it clearly reaches far beyond the
subject with which they are especially concerned, it

[1] The writer has repeated and amplified some of the thoughts of
this sermon in an essay in *Lux Mundi*, on Sacraments.

is in them that we must learn the depth and intensity of its meaning. For it is the positive rule involved in those great truths with which St. Paul has been meeting the sophistry used by some to palliate a most degrading sin.

It is not necessary for us to examine in detail their arguments, or their bold misuse of St. Paul's own language. It is enough at present to follow him as he drags to light the fundamental and fatal error of their position. That error was a shamefully inadequate idea of the human body; of its meaning and purpose and capacity. Men who talked as they did must, plainly and avowedly, be thinking of the body as incapable of anything above the level or beyond the limits of this world; as adapted to find its full occupation and satisfaction among the things of sense; as having neither use, nor hope, nor fellowship in any higher life; as sensitive to no transforming power from above. In their estimate the body itself had no greater importance than such as was indicated by its transient desires and processes of nourishment during this short stage in its development. They thought that its career lay wholly between birth and death, and that the only forces to which it could answer were the ordinary conditions of animal existence; and, with the ruinous confidence of moral

G

short-sightedness, they made up a corresponding theory as to its proper treatment and occupation. The beginning and the end of the body, they said, all its life and use and receptivity, is here, is sensuous. And so they saw nothing terrible in taking it and imprisoning it here; in surrendering it wholly to earthliness; in shutting out all voices and all light that might have reached it from above, and deeming that in silence and in darkness it might find the fulfilment of its purpose; since it was only meant to grovel and enjoy itself after the fashion of its kindred, with the beasts that perish. So they seemed to think who, in the congenial air of Corinth, were constructing a system of Christian ethics in which sins of impurity should be treated as matters of indifference. And it is against the fatal tyranny of such insolent ignorance that St. Paul displays the truth, in all its liberating strength; the truth which determines the bearing of Christianity on the life of the body. There are, indeed, more things in heaven and earth than are dreamt of in that philosophy of complacent self-degrading.

"The body is not for fornication, but for the Lord ; and the Lord for the body." Decisively, abruptly, universally, all is changed when that is seen. No contrast could be more absolute or more transforming.

At once the full light of Easter flashes out upon the
gross darkness of the guilty conscience, blinded and
stupefied by the lie that it has begun to love. "The
body is . . . for the Lord; and the Lord for the body."
In the risen humanity of the Incarnate Son, complete and spiritual, is revealed its ultimate purpose.
Through whatever processes of preparation and
development it has reached its present condition, yet
greater changes lie before it; the meaning of its union
with a living spirit, a spirit that can know God, is
not yet disclosed. For Christ will change the body
of our humiliation so that it shall be conformable to
the Body of His glory.

Not, then, for a mere transient purpose of discipline
or probation, and far less for a ministry of sensual
gratification, do we find ourselves in this world so
mysteriously, so inextricably, united with a material
frame. There is a deep and wonderful prophecy in
that inscrutable interaction of soul and body which
may sometimes startle, or bewilder, or distress us;
it hints at the hope of the body, the opportunity of
the soul; it means that the body also is accessible
to the Divine life; that there are avenues by
which the power of the Resurrection can invade it;
that it is capable of a transfiguration; that for
it too the Lord from heaven is a quickening Spirit.

And on that belief rests first of all an astounding
hope.   For, as St. Paul continues, " God hath both
raised up the Lord, and will also raise up us by His
own power ; " or, as he elsewhere expresses the same
truth, " He that raised up Christ from the dead shall
also quicken your mortal bodies by His Spirit that
dwelleth in you." The Holy Sepulchre was empty
upon Easter Day ; the Body which the Word of God
had taken in the Virgin's womb had passed on into
a new sphere and manner of being ; through suffering
and death it had been brought to perfection ; by a
change which could not but be inscrutable to us,
it had become a spiritual Body, wholly penetrated
and transformed by the unhindered glory of God.
And thus in the Resurrection of Jesus Christ had
been made known the transforming power that can
bring a human body to the state for which the love
of God has fashioned and prepared it.—And surely,
even if this were all, if men only knew that a frame
like their own had been so dealt with, and that the
hope of such a change was set before them also, the
knowledge might make them reverent and expectant
and watchful in the ordering of the bodily life ; they
could not dare to dishonour or enslave that in whose
likeness so great a glory had been once revealed, that
for which so transcendent a destiny might be in store.

II. But this is very far from being all; there is
something else to be remembered in this matter which
is yet more quickening and controlling than the most
splendid hope could be. For St. Paul goes on to
appeal to two well-known axioms of the Church's
teaching, as amplifying and bringing right into the
heart of daily life the truth which must dispel the
sophistry of his Corinthian antagonist. He need not
dwell upon these axioms, he need only just recall
them; for they are the primary and characteristic
notes of Christian faith and life; they are absolutely
essential to the reasonableness of its initial ceremony,
and of all its highest acts; so that, if they are forgotten or denied, Christianity loses at once its hold on
life, and recedes into the distance, attenuated and
impoverished, and dwindling into a mere matter for
speculative or poetic treatment. They are the closely
united truths of the present fellowship of Christians
with the risen humanity of Christ, and of the indwelling of the Holy Ghost. "Know ye not that your
bodies are members of Christ?" "Know ye not that
your body is the temple of the Holy Ghost Which is
in you?" These are the present facts in which the
higher possibility, the spiritual calling of the body, is
made known. Even now Christ leaves not Himself
without witness in its life; even here it may receive

the presence, it may yield to the power, of the Spirit by Whom it shall be raised, incorruptible and wholly spiritual, at the last day. There is a continuity, howsoever it may be hindered or threatened, in the perfecting of a human nature; it is wrought by the same Agent and the same Instrument from the beginning to the endless end; from the first stirring of the Holy Spirit's influence to the day when spirit, soul, and body are presented blameless before the throne of God. The change begins on earth: already the body is for the Lord, to be uplifted by His power, informed by His Spirit, possessed and realized in · His service; and already the Lord is for the body. In His glory He abideth not alone. He rose again for us. His risen and ascended Manhood, taken wholly into the conditions of spiritual existence, is now the unfettered organ of His eternal life, the free and all-sufficing means whereby He visiteth the earth and blesseth it; whereby, remaining in Himself, He maketh all things new, and in all ages, entering into holy souls, maketh them friends, ay, and children of God. "He rose again for our justification." He has, as one has said, "elevated His material nature to be for evermore the instrument of spiritual action." His risen Body, free and unhindered now at the disposal of the Spirit, is "a

real centre of energy for the transformation of our
lives." [1]   And it is an energy which, issuing from His
complete and perfect Manhood, is borne by the indwelling Spirit to every part of our human nature ;
here and now beginning that which may hereafter
be fulfilled and known ; here and now making strange
things possible even in the body of our humiliation ;
hinting at changes which can but be begun on earth ;
achieving in some the earnest of the future victory ;
interrupting all that we call natural with fragments
of the true nature that as yet we know but dimly
and in part ; disturbing any narrow and premature
completeness with unaccountable traits of " somewhat
above capacity of reason, somewhat divine and
heavenly, which" reason " with hidden exultation
rather surmiseth than conceiveth ; " [2] and sending

> " Through all this fleshly dress
> Bright shoots of everlastingness." [3]

Not only is the body for the Lord hereafter—hereafter to be raised to that perfection whither He through
suffering has passed before—but here also and already

---

[1] Cf. R. M. Benson, " The Life beyond the Grave," p. 23 ; and W.
Milligan, " The Resurrection of our Lord," p. 130.   To these two
books the writer is indebted for much help in regard to the subject of
this sermon.

[2] Hooker, I. xi. 4.

[3] H. Vaughan, " Silex Scintillans," p. 31 : " The Retreate."

it may be reached, and touched, and cleansed, and
quickened by the mysterious energy of His Manhood;
it may own the brightness and the dominion of His
Presence, as the Holy Spirit dwelling in it reveals its
unsuspected capacity of life and freedom, and raises
it into closer union with its risen Lord.

III. Such is in part the import of those truths with
which St. Paul rebukes the Corinthian apologist for
sensuality. He could appeal to them as certain to
be in the front of every Christian's mind; as secure
of an immediate recognition by any one who bore
Christ's Name. Must we not own that, quite apart
from anything which is ordinarily called loss of faith,
they do not now hold the place which he demands
and presumes for them in Christian thought? That
our very bodies may be affected by a real energy
from the indwelling of the Spirit of Christ, and
the communication of His risen Manhood; that
the power of His Resurrection may extend even
to the physical conditions of our life; that, very
slowly and partially, it may be, with limits that
are soon reached, and hindrances that will not yield,
yet, for all that, very truly and practically, the
redemption of our body may be begun on earth:
—surely these thoughts are stranger to many of us
than they clearly were to St. Paul and to his converts;

stranger than they should be; stranger than they
have been to many who were far removed from
mysticism and incapable of unreality. For instance,
few of us, I venture to think, are quite ready for such
words as these of Hooker's, "Doth any man doubt
but that from the flesh of Christ our very bodies do
receive that life which shall make them glorious at
the latter day, and for which they are already accounted parts of His blessed Body? Our corruptible
bodies could never live the life they shall live were
it not that here they are joined with His Body which
is incorruptible, and that His is in ours as a cause of
immortality—a cause by removing, through the death
and merit of His own flesh, that which hindered
the life of ours."[1] I would not try to speak, for I
have neither time nor insight, of the hopes which
seem to be astir in words and thoughts like these.
But I would suggest, brethren, that we should, in
careful reverence and humility, be trying to know
more and more of this power of the Resurrection in
the life of the body. And there are many ways in
which we may be watching for its tokens and learning its reality. In the lives of the saints; in their
clearness and freedom; their successful resolution not
to be brought under the power of the things which

[1] V. lvi. 9.

domineer over most men; their calmness in tumult;
their steadiness of judgment through fatigue and
suffering; their thankfulness in all things; their self-
possession in the face of death. Or, again, in some
few careers which have in our own day arrested and
controlled men's thoughts by their strange impressiveness; careers in which the intensity of spiritual force
appeared in a power of endurance or of command
which common opinion instinctively called supernatural; careers such as those of Hannington or
Gordon—men born and nurtured in conditions like
our own, and yet so splendidly unhindered by the
things which keep us back. Or we may turn to the
history of ethics; and we are told that " it is a simple
historical fact that, among all nations and in all
ages, belief in Christ alone has fought and mastered
the sins of the flesh." [1]—We must own, indeed, with
bitter shame the hideous disfigurement that has pre-
vailed, that still prevails, in nations nominally His;
but still there has been a change clear and steady
enough to demand attention and explanation. The
power of the Resurrection has conquered, and is conquering day by day, passions which made havoc
almost unchecked until Christ came.—And then,
surely, in the history of art, we find a remarkable

[1] Mr. Wilson, cited by R. L. Ottley, " The Discipline of Self," p. 22.

acknowledgment, conscious or unconscious, that a transforming power has told upon the visible world so as to change men's estimate of art's highest theme. Was it not the intense, surpassing interest of those traits and lines and looks in which the work of the Spirit was seen in human faces—faces wasted, it may be, and harassed by the very greatness of the life that was astir, yet wrought even by their pain to a beauty which made all mere physical perfection seem thenceforward cold and poor and dead,—was it not this that drew the artist's gaze away from that which had seemed highest upon earth, to watch for the disclosure of that which was least in the kingdom of heaven, that he might "bring the invisible full into play"; that he might so paint that men should have fresh knowledge of the hidden work of God ? [1]

And so, brethren, in connexion with this witness from the history of art, I would venture very tentatively to speak of one more way in which, I think, we might be learning something of the real power of the Holy Spirit in the life of the body. Surely we might trace it sometimes in the faces and in the voices of those who, in penitence and prayer and love, with suffering or long self-discipline, have yielded up their

---

[1] R. Browning, "Old Pictures at Florence," Poetical Works, vol. vi. pp. 81–85 (ed. 1889).

wills, their lives, to Him—have truly longed that He should have His way with them. The thought is beautifully told in a well-known book on the Resurrection of our Lord.[1] But I cannot help citing a curious and merely incidental expression of it from a very different source. One of the cleverest of modern novels has for its central character a young American artist —Roderick Hudson—brilliant, unprincipled, conceited. He has been living a wholly selfish life in Rome for some time, when his mother and her adopted daughter, Mary Garland, come from America to visit him. And the first time he sees them,—simple, pious, loving folk, who have been living in constant anxiety for his sake,—he turns suddenly to his mother, in the middle of a sentence, and asks abruptly, " What makes you look so odd ? What has happened to your face these two years ? It has changed its expression." "Your mother has prayed a great deal," said Mary, simply. " Well, it makes a very good face," answers Roderick ; " very interesting, very solemn. It has very fine lines in it." [2]—Yes, brethren, there are many faces about this world, I think, in which prayer and patience and humility have, by God's grace, wrought a beauty which may be the

---

[1] W. Milligan, " The Resurrection of our Lord," Lecture V. p. 190.
[2] Henry James, " Roderick Hudson," vol. ii. pp. 43, 44.

nearest approach that can be seen in this life to the glory of the Resurrection—the glory that is to be revealed in those who shall then be wholly penetrated and transfigured by the Spirit of the Lord.

IV. Such may seem to be some of the ways in which we may mark the real power of the Resurrection in the life of the body. But, after all, by far the best, the surest, the happiest, verification of St. Paul's great claim must be made by each man for himself in the effort of obedience to the bidding of the text; in the hidden discipline of life; through pain and toil and fear, it may be, yet, by the grace of God, not without some earnest of a victory whose faintest, briefest forecast is better than all the pleasures of compromise—the victory of self-possession for the glory of God. It is pitiful to imagine how much of strength and liberty and joy is being missed or marred day after day by the mistakes men make in dealing with their bodies. I am not thinking now of the misery and havoc wrought by sheer misuse—by gluttony and drunkenness and lust. Quite apart, and utterly different from sins like these, there are misunderstandings of the body's meaning, and one-sided ways of treating it, which, with little or no blame perhaps, still hinder grievously the worth and happiness that life might have, and that the love of God

intended for it. There are the two mistakes that
Plato has for ever characterized in the third book of
the "Republic;" there is the mistake of a narrow and
exclusive athleticism, in which excellent means are
just spoilt by the lack of an adequate end; and there
is the far more serious, expensive, and persistent
blunder of the valetudinarian—the exacting worship
of a thankless idol, which would probably fare much
better if the rich man, like the artisan, had no
time to be ill, and thought it not worth while to
live νοσήματι τὸν νοῦν προσέχοντα, τῆς δὲ προκειμένης
ἐργασίας ἀμελοῦντα."[1] But must we not own that
there is also, in much of our Christian thought and
teaching, I would not say a mistake, but an omission
which has involved some serious loss? On every
ground it is right that the lesson of the Cross
should come first, and stand ever foremost in the
discipline of the Christian life; but is there not
room, and need also, for the lesson of the Resurrection? Probably we all of us know well enough
why the note of Lent should be ever clear and strong
in our lives; but should not the note of Easter
too be constant—the note of thankful welcome for
that stream of life and light and health which issues

[1] Plato, "Republic," 406 D. Cf. Dorner's "System of Christian
Ethics," p. 458, English translation.

from a fount that our sins can never sully, that our prayers and penitence may always reach ? We need not be one whit less firm and watchful in self-discipline, less mindful of the war we wage, because we lift our hearts in wondering joy to greet the strength that is made perfect in our weakness—the Presence that can preserve both body and soul unto everlasting life. Suffer me to put into another form what I am trying to express.

On Thursday last I was standing on the hill between Cumnor and North Hinksey, and delighting in one of those effects of contrast which seem the peculiar glory of an April sky. Over all the west and north there loomed an angry storm: black and wild and ominous, with here and there a lurid tinge, it spread from Faringdon almost to Godstow. But constantly, against that sullen mass, the larks were rising into the fresh air, as though they were resolute that no threats or fears should stay their song of praise for spring; and when one turned towards the east, the clouds were light and few, and the distant hills were clear, and the white Cross near Bledlow was gleaming in the sun. May there not be something like that contrast in the inner life—something like that voice of joy even in the face of all that is so dark and threatening; ever some steadiness of light about

the east; ever some radiance of the Resurrection
falling on the Cross—the Cross of shame and suffering and conquest? Certainly, when men were most
of all in earnest about self-discipline, the joy of the
risen life was not weak or uncertain in them. Let
us recall some words which may have a peculiar
force for us to-day, since he who wrote them has
so recently been taken from among us: "Mediæval
Christianity is reproached with its gloom and austeri-
ties; it assigns the material world, says Heine, to the
devil. But yet what a fulness of delight does St.
Francis manage to draw from this material world itself,
and from its commonest and most universally enjoyed
elements—sun, air, earth, water, plants! His hymn
expresses a far more candid sense of happiness, even
in the material world, than the hymn of Theocritus.
It is this which made the fortune of Christianity—
its gladness, not its sorrow; not its assigning the
spiritual world to Christ and the material world to
the devil, but its drawing from the spiritual world a
source of joy so abundant that it ran over upon the
material world and transfigured it."[1]

V. Many, perhaps, will recognize whose words
those are. In Oxford to-day,[2] even one who had not

[1] "Essays in Criticism," p. 207.

[2] Mr. Matthew Arnold died in the week preceding the Sunday on
which this sermon was preached.

the distinction and delight of Mr. Matthew Arnold's friendship may be allowed to speak of him, and may be pardoned, I trust, if he speaks unworthily; since it was difficult to be silent. Mr. Arnold has, beyond dispute, enriched the life of our day with such true help as always comes from perfect workmanship. To him we owe a high standard and example of excellence in the critic's work—and this alone were no indifferent gift; for there would be far more reverence and simplicity and charity among men if criticism always were as he would have it be, "a disinterested endeavour to learn and propagate the best that is known and thought in the world." To him we owe the disclosure of a beauty in our language such as only two or three perhaps at most beside him in this age have attained. And this, again, is far more than a mere adornment of human life. A deeper debt is due to those who so advance the ideal of expression; for many hard and foolish and untrue things might be left unsaid if men would only wait till they could say them in good English. Thankfully, too, let us recall how much his delicate and eager sense of beauty, and his faultless happiness of utterance, have added to the pure gladness and refreshment men may find in nature. Surely it is a triumph of poetic power and beneficence to have

H

linked for ever with our Oxford scenery thoughts
almost as exquisite and high as those which Wordsworth found among his nobler hills and vales. But
yet we owe to Mr. Arnold even greater debts than
these. I should fail, brethren, in the sincerity due
alike to his memory and to the trust I hold, if I
were to shrink from saying of parts of his work that
I believe they make (however utterly against his
earnest wish) for the impoverishment of life and for
the darkening of light. But there are great truths
which it was granted him to bear into the mind
of his day with a power and purity perhaps unique.
The meanness and vulgarity of self-satisfaction; the
absurdity of self-centredness and self-advertisement;
the ludicrous littleness of unreality;—it is worth while
to have had these things made quite clear and vivid to
us by a master's hand. But, as a poet, he has done
far more for us than this. With a power of buoyancy
which would have made it easy to disguise, or even
to forget at times, all grief, he never has kept back
from us the sorrow that had come to stay where
faith had been—the sorrow which is perhaps the
noblest witness that a doubting mind and a pure
heart can bear to truth. And he has told (as none, I
think, has ever told save he) the depth and solitude
and greatness of the buried life—" the mystery of

this heart which beats so wild, so deep in us." And, above all, with his loyal abhorrence of acquiescence in poor and stunted thoughts of life, he has never failed to bid us, one and all, to live with undivided care, with absolute allegiance, by the very highest hope that our hearts descry.—There is light and help for all in teaching such as this; and he whose pure and gracious skill has borne it into many souls has earned, indeed, our reverent and prayerful gratitude.

IV.

FREEDOM OF THOUGHT.

"Where the Spirit of the Lord is, there is liberty."
2 COR. iii. 17.

WE may almost seem to hear a change in the tone
of St. Paul's voice, and to see a new light glisten in
his eyes, as, in the course of his letter to the Church
at Corinth, he dictates these words to his amanuensis.
For they are words of transition into a region and
atmosphere of thought very different from that in
which he has before been moving. He has been
working out, with some complexity and elaboration
of detail, the contrast in substance, in circumstance,
and in method between the ministry of the old
covenant and the ministry of the new; between the
transient and fragmentary disclosure of an external
Law, and the inner gift of a quickening Spirit, steadfast in the glory of holiness, and endless in its power
to renew, to ennoble, to illuminate. With close and
tenacious persistence the deep, pervading difference

between the two systems has been traced; and then
St. Paul seems to lift up his eyes, and to speak as one
for whom the sheer wonder of the sight he sees finds
at once the words he needs. He has finished his
argumentative comparison; and now the vision of
the Christian life, the triumph of God's love and pity
in the work of grace, the astonishing goodness that
has made such things possible for sinful men, holds
his gaze. As the traveller who, in the Alps or the
Pyrenees, has climbed the northern side of a pass
halts when he reaches the summit, and feasts his
sight with the wealth and brightness of the southern
landscape, so St. Paul seems here to pause in his discussion, and to forget all else as he looks at the
beauty and fruitfulness which God the Holy Ghost
achieves in human lives. And as that sight fills his
heart, one word rises to his lips (a word that he has
not used before in this Epistle): with an insight like
that of the poet or the artist who sees into the life of
nature and brings out immediately the inner quality
of a scene, he seizes on the one distinctive note of
the work at which he is looking; one word tells the
peculiar glory of the characters that are surrendered
to the influence of the indwelling Spirit; one remarkable and penetrating word: " Where the Spirit of the
Lord is, there is *liberty*."

Liberty, then, according to St. Paul, is the characteristic token of the Holy Spirit's work in a man's
life : he who is really led and strengthened by the
Spirit will differ from other men in this especially,
that he will have more liberty, that he will move
more freely and (in the highest sense of the word)
more naturally than they. Let us think this morning
of the great claim that is thus made on behalf of
that Power which, in its fulness, came to mankind
on Whitsunday.—There are two spheres in which
we commonly speak of the enjoyment and exercise
of liberty—the spheres of thought and of conduct :
we speak of free thinkers and of free agents. Let us
this morning take St. Paul's claim into the former
of these two spheres, and try to see its meaning
in regard to our intellectual life.

I. Freedom of thought. We know what are the
associated ideas which the expression is apt to raise
in most men's minds. It would not be, I suppose,
unjust to say that there are some who hold that
only by setting aside all that St. Paul meant
when he spoke of the Spirit of the Lord, only
by getting rid of all the ideas with which he was
occupied, can men really attain to liberty of thought;
and that the belief in any teaching as divinely
revealed is the great, prevailing hindrance to intel-

lectual freedom. It seems sometimes to be quite sincerely taken for granted that, whatever may be lost, freedom, at all events, is gained when a man has renounced the Christian creed. Men speak of having shaken off the fetters of orthodoxy; and some, it may be, who still hold to the historic faith cannot quite resist a secret hankering after the liberty which is thus supposed to belong to those who have ceased to call themselves Christians. There is a wide and often a sincere opinion, not merely that authority in matters of belief has been and is sometimes misused and mis-understood—it would be strange if that were not so, —but that Christianity and thinking freely cannot go together. And yet St. Paul seizes upon liberty as the essential characteristic of the life of faith.

Can so direct a contradiction be in any way accounted for? How is it that different men can look honestly at facts virtually the same and come to conclusions so plainly opposite?

II. Surely, a large part of the answer to that question lies in this—that men have widely different ideas as to what the liberty of the intellect really is. For real freedom of thought is something much more than thinking what one likes; it is something much more difficult and less common. It is easy to say that one has no definite belief, and that

so one is going to speculate freely and to think for
one's self. But how hard, how rare, that freedom in
thinking for one's self really is! There is, indeed, a
certain sense in which none of us might find it
difficult to think freely; but it is a sense like that
in which we might say that a little child plays
freely when its untrained hands fall indiscriminately
and with equal satisfaction on any number of dis-
cordant notes. There is a certain sense in which
it is easy to judge for one's self; but it is a sense
like that in which we might say that a man is
judging for himself when he saunters in utter indifference past all the noblest pictures in a gallery,
and finds nothing to enjoy save some trivial and
shallow thing that takes his fancy by appealing to a
prejudice or an association of ideas in his own mind.
Let the child know something of what music means,
let the man begin but to suspect the joy that a true
artist finds where the pure and great spirits of past
ages live and speak their thoughts, and then the
vision of another freedom comes in sight.—And so in
the yet graver exercises of the intellect. The mere
liberty of thinking what one likes is not that liberty
of which St. Paul speaks—the liberty by which a
man is indeed ennobled and realizes himself and
serves his generation. There is much to be done,

and much to be undone, in every one of us before he can be free indeed in the sphere of thought.

(*a*) To be free from prejudice and conventionality; free from wilfulness and pride; free from despondency and sloth; free from self-interest and the desire of praise; free from our moods and tempers; free from the taint of our old sins, and the shame and misery of those that still beset us; free from all delight in saying clever things; free from the perverting love of originality, or paradox, or theory, or completeness; free from the yet wilder perversions of jealousy, or party strife, or personal dislike; free from the secret influence of timidity or impatience;—are these conditions of the intellect's true liberty easily to be secured? How many of us can say that we are even near to obtaining this freedom?

(*b*) And yet all these conditions, great as they are, are but the beginning of that liberation which sets a man really free to think. For besides all these there must be the watchful discipline of mind and heart; they must be trained to take the true measure of things; to see things as they are; to be sensitive to the faintest glance of light that may betray the hidden truth and mark the place of its emergence; they must be growing in that fineness of spiritual sense which will discern and disengage the living

germ of reality in the complex mass that is thrown
before it. The intellect that is to be free indeed
must not be cramped, bewildered, hindered, and misdirected by its own deformity; and perfect health
and symmetry of mind are not easily to be gained or
kept.

(*c*) And yet, again, there is wanted something
more than all this. For if intellectual liberty is to
be what in some it has been, what it may conceivably
hereafter be in us, there is need of something beyond
all that can be won even by the most watchful discipline of heart and mind, something more than self-
control and justice of insight. For liberty, in the
highest sense, cannot be found with the listless, or
indifferent, or desultory. The powers that are to
grow in freedom must be keen and vivid; their liberty
must be realized and deepened and assured in ordered
use; they must be ever winning for themselves fresh
strength and light as they press along their line of
healthful growth towards the highest aim they can
surmise. And so there can be no liberty of thought
without the love of truth—that quickening and
ennobling love which longs for truth, not as the
gratification of curiosity, not as the pledge of fame,
not as the monument of victory, but rather as that
without which the mind can never be at rest, or find

the meaning and the fulness of its own life—a love more like the love of home; a love sustained by forecasts of that which may be fully known hereafter; by fragments which disclose already something of truth's perfect beauty, as its light streams out across the waves and through the night, to guide the intellect in the strength of love and hope to the haven where it would be.

III. It seems strange indeed that people should ever talk as though it were easy to think freely, as though a man could attain to intellectual liberty simply by renouncing his belief in revelation and adopting whatever view of life may seem to him most likely. For it can be but slowly and painfully that any of us may move towards perfect liberty of thought; and we shall never reach it, I suppose, in this world; even as we shall never here be wholly free from sin. But we may grow in freedom if we will; we may be learning how to think; we may be casting out or bringing under sharp control the tendencies that trouble and confuse us; we may be redeeming our intellect from all that enslaves, dishonours, and enfeebles it. And for all this we certainly need help and guidance; we need that some Presence, pure and wise and strong beyond all that is of this world, should bend over us, should come to us, should lead

us out into the light.   The truth must make us free.
We must learn "the law of liberty," even as, to go back
to a former illustration, the child must learn the rules
of music before it can begin to gain the true freedom
of the trained musician.   And it was to make known
to us the law of liberty, to write it in our hearts,
to make it paramount over the activities alike of
intellect and will, that the Holy Spirit came down
to dwell in men.   Yes; if we would know more
of intellectual liberty, let us see whether it is not
really to be gained by simply and humbly bringing
our lives into more constant and more thankful sub-
mission to His guidance, to His enlightening and
renewing Presence.   For is not this a part of His
work?   Through the ministry of grace and truth
He makes known to men the love of God, shown
forth in Jesus Christ our Lord; and as the astounding
tenderness and glory of that love begins to dawn
upon them, He stirs in them some sense of what might
be the joy and strength and peace of a human life
that was filled with such a love as that; and then He
bears into their hearts the hope that, for Christ's sake,
that life, if they will have it, may even yet be theirs.
And in proportion as that hope grows real and pure
and clear within them, they begin with single-mindedness to look towards God and to live as in His sight;

and so the things of this world—its praise, its prizes, its contentions, its prejudices—loose their hold upon the mind, and a new sense of strength and independence come to it, as it begins to see even afar off its rest for ever in the truth of God. And then the Holy Spirit shows the way of liberty and growth: for there has been one human life lived upon this earth in perfect freedom ; one life in which every faculty was at every moment wholly free; and in proportion as a man is growing in likeness to our Lord Jesus Christ and following the blessed steps of His most holy life he will not walk in darkness, but will have the light of life. For there is the royal law of liberty ; there is the way where mind and heart alike may be becoming free indeed. And then as men falter and grow weary in the way, or as sin besets and overclouds them, He brings pardon and renewal ; He makes possible those "fresh beginnings, which are the life of perseverance;" He refreshes soul and body with the communion of their Redeemer's Manhood. Yes, and even in this world men find it true that " where the Spirit of the Lord is, there is liberty "—there the intellect really does attain to a steadiness of insight, a quiet decision, a strength against perplexity and sophistry, a firmness of right choice, which sometimes stand in strange contrast with the vacillation and mistakes of natural ability ; and there are those in every rank of life, on every level of education, who have in this way reached a degree of intellectual liberty such as the cleverest of men might envy if he was wise enough to recognize it. The true *liberty* begins in this world ; but it is only when the Spirit of the Lord has perfected the work of grace that the full meaning of that great word can be disclosed ; and when men are sinless, when they see God, when they know Him as also they are known, and when they serve Him day and night, then at last they may understand what it is for the intellect to be free indeed.

V.

THE KNOWLEDGE OF GOD.

" Now I know in part; but then shall I know even as also
I am known."

1 Cor. xiii. 12.

THERE is in these words another contrast besides
that which we see at once, between partial knowledge and complete. It is not only that the field of
knowledge is to be extended; there is to be a change
also in the act itself—a change in what knowing
means, in the relation it expresses. For there is
between the verbs used in the two clauses a difference which our translators have wisely despaired of
reproducing. Yet the distinction was, I think, full
of significance to St. Paul; it rests on a clear conviction in his mind about the attainment of knowledge
concerning the things of faith; and it may have
some especial teaching for us, in times when many
are rejecting Christianity because it does not satisfy
expectations which it has expressly and steadily
discouraged.

I. The two verbs, then, are γιγνώσκειν and ἐπιγιγνώ-
σκειν: but it is in the corresponding substantives, γνῶσις
and ἐπίγνωσις, that the difference is most clearly and
suggestively marked both by St. Paul and by St. Peter.
And in regard to the latter word a careful and unen-
thusiastic critic has said, on the Second Epistle of St.
Peter, that " this ἐπίγνωσις is the central point of the
Christian life, both theoretically and practically considered." [1]

What, then, is the meaning of the word ? What
is the distinction by which it goes beyond the simpler
word γνῶσις ? It seems, in the use of it which we
are here considering, to mark a higher degree of
intensity, an energy of deeper penetration. It is not
a quiescent state, the resting in an acquirement, but
the advance of one to whom every attainment is but
the impulse of fresh effort; one who is not content
to know, but ever, in Hosea's words, " follows on to
know "—" knowing in order to follow, and following
in order to know; as light prepares the way for
love, and love opens the mind for new light." [2]   It

---

[1] " It is the vehicle of the Divine agency in us, and so of our
highest participation of God; it is the means of escape from the pol-
lutions of the world—the crowning point of Christian virtues; the
means of access into Christ's kingdom " (Alford's Commentary, vol. iv.
part i. " Prolegg.," p. 141).

[2] Cf. E. B. Pusey on Hos. vi. 3.

seems analogous to that which many of us may have experienced, the strong intention with which one looks into a great picture; at first, perhaps, with some surprise at the high language that has been used about it; but gradually, hour after hour, it may be, seeing in it depths beyond depths of thought and beauty; never turning away from it without a feeling that we were, perhaps, on the very verge of seeing something unsuspected hitherto; leaving it at last with a certainty that we have by no means exhausted all that it contains.

Analogous again, and more closely analogous, is that advancing knowledge which we may gain, if we are patient and reverent, of a really great and deep character. As we watch the ways and try to enter into the mind of one who, through the dutiful effort of a long life, has done justly, and loved mercy, and walked humbly with his God, there may seem no end to the depths of strength and beauty which are disclosed; we are always feeling how little we have really known, how much there is yet to be understood. It was a surprise to us, perhaps, when first we penetrated at all beyond the reserve which has guarded the inner wealth from the squandering of common talk; but beyond that first surprise we see by fragments, and by indications slowly recog-

I

nized, how far more complex and costly and mysterious a thing real moral greatness is than we had ever thought. Knowing, we follow on to know; and as we advance, fresh revelations are released where we had suspected nothing.

II. Such, in regard to the things of faith, is that "larger and more thorough knowledge," that more penetrating discernment, which ἐπίγνωσις seems to mean. And thus it is striking to mark at what point in his life St. Paul brings the word into frequent use in speaking of the knowledge of God. It is seldom so used in his earlier letters; but it comes into sudden prominence in those written while he was for the first time a prisoner at Rome. It is a frequent and emphatic word with him as he writes from his imprisonment; and surely we may make a fair conjecture as to the cause. A lull has come in the outward activity of his life; that restless energy is checked from its manifold and ceaseless tasks; there is no longer the same necessity to be continually entering into the minds of others and becoming all things to all men; to a certain extent he is bidden to come apart and rest awhile. And in that comparative quietude he sees with deeper, steadier insight how boundless is the space of ever-growing light through which the soul of man may move forward

in the knowledge of God ; he sees how in that knowledge, rightly understood, there is the highest exercise
for every faculty of the inner life—for mind and
heart and will, to learn, to love, to worship; how
through that knowledge a man may come to realize
himself, to know the end for which God called him
into being, and what it means so to lose one's life
that one may find it. He sees further into that all-
embracing truth—that this is life eternal, the true
life, the life for which the love of God created and
redeemed men, that they may know the only true
God, and Jesus Christ, Whom He has sent; knowing
Him with a knowledge that ever presses on, and that
can never be distinct from love. Surely it may be
with some such experience of progress in the knowledge of God that St. Paul, in every letter which he
writes from his imprisonment, makes it a part of his
entreaty for his converts that they too may be led
forward in that deepening knowledge ; that God may
give unto them the spirit of wisdom and revelation
in the knowledge of Him ; that their love may abound
yet more and more in knowledge; that they may
increase in the knowledge of God and of His will;
that their deeds of charity may become effective in
the knowledge of every good thing. "In all the
Epistles of the Roman captivity," says Bishop Light-

foot, "St. Paul's prayer for his correspondents culmi-
nates in this word."[1] Above all else he longs that
they may continually advance in that knowledge
which has been the especial blessing, the uplifting
gladness of his time of bondage.

III. Our knowledge of God, then, in this life, must
be a constant "moving forward in the twilight;"
fragmentary, and perhaps unequal; but by His grace
increasing, as we "follow on to know;" starting from
a venture, demanding an effort; and to the end of
this life a knowledge only in part. But after this
life, if we have endured and persevered unto the end,
there shall be a change. "Then shall I know even as
also I was known." When the things which keep
us back have loosed their hold on us; when sin and
indolence and doubt are done with; when all the
anxieties that we have suffered here to fret us and
divide our hearts are put away for ever; when,
through whatsoever discipline, in this world or beyond
it, God has wrought His perfect work on us; then
will the broken and faltering effort pass into an
unhindered energy, and we shall know Him even as
also we were known. Even as from the first He has
known us; as, when He made us His, when He called

---

[1] Bishop Lightfoot, on Philemon 6. Cf. also his notes on Phil. i. 9
and on Col. i. 9.

us to Himself, when He gave us our work to do, He knew us; as now, in all the discipline of life, in all His dealings with us, His gaze penetrates at once the inmost depths of our being; so shall we be ever moving forward, with intensity then undivided and unwearied, in the realization of His infinite truth and goodness.

Let us try to see our present duty in this regard. Some measure of the knowledge of God is within the reach of all who really desire it and will really strive for it.[1] Through many ways He is waiting to reveal Himself more clearly to every one of us— through conscience, through nature, through the Bible, through the lives of the poor and of those who suffer patiently, through all moral beauty, and above all, in the life and teaching of our Lord. Through all these ways, it may be, hints and glances of His glory have already come to us; through all these ways we may know in part, and follow on to know continually more. But, undoubtedly, there is need of venture—the venture of faith, to commit ourselves to Him; to trust the light we see, even though we see it faintly and unsteadily. Knowledge will never grow in that cold and sceptical mind which Dr. Newman has described so well; the mind

---

[1] Cf. Bishop Harvey Goodwin, " The Foundations of the Creed," p. 30.

" which has no desire to approach its God, but sits at
home waiting for the fearful clearness of His visible
coming, Whom it might seek and find in due measure
amid the twilight of the present world."[1]—And then,
with the venture of faith, there is need of self-discipline and of effort. We cannot expect to grow in
the knowledge of God while our sins are unrepented
of; while our temper is uncontrolled; while purposes
of self-indulgence, half recognized and connived at,
are suffered to hang about our cowardly and lazy
hearts—no, nor yet while our prayers are hurried
and heedless; while devotion is costing us no care
and no firmness of daily self-concentration. And then,
above all, there is need of loyal obedience to the
truth we have already grasped; a resolute determination, " by God's grace, not to flinch from any duty "
we have recognized;[2] to follow where the way is
clear, even though it be rough and steep, and though
at first we see but a few steps in front of us. These
are plain conditions of growing in the knowledge of
God; and they can never be easy to any of us; they
may at first be very hard. But when we are quiet,
when we are true to ourselves, we know, thank God,

[1] " University Sermons," p. 220.
[2] Cf. Wilfrid Ward, " William George Ward and the Oxford Movement," Appendix B.

one thing, at all events, quite certainly—that in that way of effort and self-discipline and prayer lies our only hope of peace; our one chance of living as every man would fain have lived when the time comes for him to die. Far ahead of us, it may be, on that way we see some who have had faith to venture and strength to persevere; we see what they, God helping them, have made of life and of themselves; we feel how they have grown in the knowledge and the love of God, and how that knowledge and that love have lifted them above the passions and the fears, the selfishness and insincerity, which make so many weak and miserable; and so we may gather courage to press on; while God, of His great mercy, seldom leaves men long without some earnest of that increase of light which ever waits upon the pathway of obedience; that they may understand more clearly, as they will to do His Will, what is the hope of His calling, and what the riches of His glory, and the exceeding greatness of His power.

VI.

DRUDGERY AND HEROISM.

"I came down from heaven, not to do Mine own will, but
the will of Him that sent Me."

ST. JOHN vi. 38.

I. In almost every calling of life we can trace two
very different elements or parts. There is, on the
one hand, the ordinary routine of daily work; there
is, on the other hand, the occasional demand for a
great act of courage or self-sacrifice. On the one
hand, the level course of common tasks; on the other,
the rare opportunity of heroism. On the one hand,
the plain business that must be done; on the other,
the chance of realizing, of acting up to the noble
idea which belongs to one's profession. So it is, for
instance, in a doctor's life. He may go on, through
week after week, of clear and obvious tasks, just
doing his best for the cases that he has to deal with;
and then, suddenly, it may be, he has a chance of
doing, or not doing, a splendid deed; of saving
another's life at the risk of his own; of showing how

far the highest thought of his calling has a hold
upon him. And so, again, in a priest's life. There
may be long spells of quiet and safe and almost
uneventful work; and then comes the call to a real
venture of self-sacrifice—the opportunity, it may be,
of bearing part in some perilous mission-work; the
outbreak of fever or cholera in the squalid alleys
of a crowded parish; the choice between worldly
prospects and loyalty to Divine truth: and he, too,
must show what he really means, of what sort he
really is, and how far the Gospel he preaches and the
example of his Lord have indeed been taken into
his own heart. And so it is, most evidently, I suppose, in a soldier's life:[1] there especially one may seem
to see these two elements—the ordinary routine and
the magnificent opportunities, the commonplace business and the heroic ventures. It must be so throughout all ranks. Every soldier, to whatever branch of
the service he belongs, and whatever trust he holds
in it, will have his share of plain and unexciting
work, of tasks that may look more or less like
drudgery; and then to every soldier there may come
the opportunity of realizing at some critical moment,

[1] This sermon was preached on the 18th of June, in St. Paul's
Cathedral, at the Annual Festival of the Army Guild of the Holy
Standard.

in some decisive act, the highest ideal of greatness;
the opportunity of laying down his life for his
friends; of lifting higher the standard of courage,
of endurance, of self-control, and of self-sacrifice, by
swift and generous daring—by a deed to be remembered and reverenced, perhaps, on earth through
many generations; a deed never to be forgotten,
surely, there, where the memory of a man's unselfishness matters most.—The riches of a nation are the
records of such acts—acts that long live on to shame
men out of listlessness and vanity, and to make them
discontent with easy, selfish lives and paltry aims;
acts which, by the grace of God, ennoble every way
of life, however humble and obscure; but which
nowhere glow with a more vivid radiance than in the
histories of military service. So absorbing is men's
interest in such exploits, that they often give hardly
any thought to the uneventful background out of
which they come; to the long tracts of quiet routine
which may be just as real and characteristic a part
of a true soldier's life as the brilliant ventures of
fearlessness and self-devotion.

Now, if there are these two parts in our lives,
surely what we want to learn is how we may
best be preparing ourselves, as we go on with our
regular and ordinary work, for the demand, the

opportunity, which may come to us; how we may
be getting ready to do the right thing, and to quit
ourselves like men, when the crisis, the time of trial,
is on us. For two things, I think, we may mark if
we study men's characters and ways a little. First,
that the ready and the unready man, the man who will
not fail and the man who may, look very much alike
sometimes. The difference is deep down in them, and
it does not show in fair weather; it is the sudden
demand, the need for something great, that brings it
out—just as it was not till the cry came at midnight,
when it was too late to mend matters, that the
foolish virgins found that they had no oil for their
flickering and failing lamps. And secondly, most men
are likely to be at a crisis more or less what they
have been beforehand. Where their treasure is, there
will their heart be found; they will make their choice
then—save for a miracle of God's grace—as they
have been choosing all along. It seems, indeed, one
of the gravest and deepest of moral laws, that under
the stress of trial men will strongly tend at least to be
whatever in quieter hours they have made themselves.

II. Is there, then, any one great principle, any universal law, which reaches over the whole course of a
man's life; which holds good alike in all its parts, and
under all conditions? Is there any one ruling motive

which we can so welcome and settle and enthrone
in our hearts by daily practice, that in the time of
fiercest strain it may, God helping us, hold us firm
and keep us straight? Can we make routine the
school of heroism?

Yes, indeed, my brothers; and in this, as in all
else, our Blessed Lord and Saviour teaches us quite
plainly and quite perfectly the way of peace and
strength. He Who died to set us free to live as men
should live; He Who ever lives to plead for us; He
Who deigns to come to us in the holy Mysteries
which He has ordained;—He shows us by His own
example how a life may be sure and steadfast through
all the changes of this world; how the plainest tasks
may be our training for the very noblest deeds. "Not
to do Mine own will, but the will of Him that sent
Me." In those words He tells us the central principle of His own life on earth; and in those words
He gives us the one sure rule for handling our own
lives rightly. Other aims may call out a high degree
of energy and ability in a man; the passion for glory,
the love of money, personal ambition, thirst for
power,—all these will nerve a man for great enter-
prises, great endurance; high things have been dared
and done for motives such as these; but none of
these is sufficient even for this present life; none will

guide a man with equal, steady light and help alike through the calm and through the storm, through the quiet and through the exciting times. Men spend their strength for these things; they gain it in allegiance to God. "Not to do Mine own will, but the will of Him that sent Me."' To ask myself each morning, not—How far can I to-day advance my own interest, increase my reputation, enjoy myself? but—How can I, in the duties and opportunities of this day, fulfil the will of God?—this is the way in which a man grows strong and fearless; this is the way in which the plainest round of daily tasks may be his training-ground for some splendid act of self-devotion that will thrill and gladden and uphold the hearts of all true men. "Not to do Mine own will, but the will of Him that sent Me." Only let a man—whatsoever his work may be—renew each day that purpose in his heart, and seek God's grace to keep it, and then, be sure of it, two things will come about. First, that for him even the most ordinary tasks, the mere routine of life, will be ennobled; the very drudgery will shine with some reflection of the obedience of heaven; it will seem like those most attractive of all faces, in which there may be no natural beauty, in the usual sense of the word, which may be even plain, but in which there certainly is a supernatural

charm of moral beauty that we may learn a little
to understand as life goes on. And secondly, in that
routine he will be bringing his inner life into a habit
of attention and allegiance to the voice of duty; by
constant drilling and discipline he will be training
his heart almost to take it for granted that at all
times duty is the one thing to be thought about,
and that whatever clashes with duty must give way;
and so, whenever the time comes, he will be ready.
If the voice of duty, clear, austere, yet not ungentle,
calls even for the sacrifice of life itself, he will not
be perplexed or staggered; he will not have to weigh
this and that, or to call in the straggling forces of his
will; that is certainly the voice that he has always
followed; he will rise and follow it now; it has kept
him straight so far, and he will not now begin to
distrust it; he will answer, in simplicity and thankfulness, "I come to do Thy will; I am content to
do it; yea, Thy Law is within my heart;" he will
keep the path of duty, and will leave the rest to
God. Yes, the love of duty is the strength of heroes;
and there is no way of life in which we may not set
ourselves to learn that love.

III. Let me point you, brethren, in conclusion, to
two splendid instances of the controlling greatness of
character which may be reached by that steadfast

and unselfish loyalty to duty of which I have been trying to speak. We cannot forget what night it is on which we are gathered here—the night of Waterloo. We are within a few minutes of the very time at which the battle was decided; the time at which, as the imperial guard passed up the ridge held by our troops, the Duke of Wellington gave orders for that simultaneous attack in front and in flank to which Napoleon himself ascribed the loss of the battle.[1] As we look back to that day—the most critical and the most fateful, I suppose, in modern history— perhaps the best lesson for us all to learn may be seen when the two great commanders who met upon that field are set in contrast; and the lesson of that contrast is, I think, nothing else than this—the unique strength and greatness of allegiance to duty. On both sides of the contrast we may see in rare magnificence the same commanding qualities of in- tellect, the same unwearied energy, the same personal courage, the same masterful intensity of will; but, writes the historian, "Napoleon was covetous of glory; Wellington was impressed with duty." "Single- ness of heart was the characteristic of Wellington, a sense of duty was his ruling principle; ambition pervaded Napoleon, a thirst for glory was his in-

[1] Alison, ch. xciv., § 30, and note.

variable incentive. . . . There is not a proclamation
of Napoleon to his soldiers in which glory is not
mentioned, nor one in which duty is alluded to ; there
is not an order of Wellington to his troops in which
duty is not inculcated, nor one in which glory is
mentioned." [1] It would be hard, I think, to measure
what Europe owed to the victory at Waterloo; but
surely this stands high, if not supreme, among its
abiding results—that the splendour of that day
arrays the form of duty, that it arrested and struck
down a policy of personal ambition.

Let us turn for our last lesson to a very different
scene, but yet a scene in which the majesty of
dutifulness held the gaze of Europe. As on this very
day last year, one whom I would venture to call one
of the greatest soldiers of our age was carried to his
grave. The Emperor Frederick had given up his
heart to the love of duty in his boyhood; through
his years of splendid action he had been steadfast
and true in that allegiance ; and through the long
weeks of yet more splendid patience God Almighty
kept him dutiful to the very end. Forty years ago,
before he was eighteen, he had entered upon active
service ; and his father introduced him to the officers
of the regiment to which he was attached, in these

[1] Alison, ch. xciv., § 64-66.

words: "I entrust my son to you in the hope that he will learn obedience, and so some day know how to command." Then, turning to his son, he simply said, "Now go and do your duty." The note that these words touched sounded again in the first public utterance of the youthful prince about six months later: "I am still very young," he said, "but I will prepare myself with love and devotion for my high calling, and endeavour some day to fulfil the anticipations of my people, which will then become a duty entrusted to me by God."[1] And so year after year, through times of peace and times of war, he laboured to prepare himself; in steadfast allegiance to duty he kept storing up the strength and wisdom and self-mastery that he would need when he should be called to his yet greater duties as the Emperor of Germany. But God had another—may we not, as we look towards the Cross of Christ, be bold to say an even greater?—use for all that strength and wisdom and self-mastery. Not to sway for a few years the course of that one nation's history, but for all times and through all lands to set a great example of unmurmuring patience; to teach and to encourage men to do their duty, simply and quietly, even through the weariest days of suffering and weakness;

[1] Rennell Rodd, "Frederick, Crown Prince and Emperor," pp. 35, 36.

K

to show how the love of home and duty may go unfaltering, not with a sudden venture but with slow and painful steps, through ever-growing anguish, on into the very face of death ;—this was the privilege of the most dutiful soldier whose greatness has ennobled our day. Thus did men see in "the short and speechless reign" of the Emperor Frederick how vast a strength is stored in those whose hearts are resolutely set not to do their own will, but the will of Him Who sent them.

VII.

THE PERILS OF THE VACANT HEART.

" When the unclean spirit is gone out of a man, he walketh
through dry places, seeking rest, and findeth none. Then
he saith, I will return into my house from whence I came
out; and when he is come, he findeth it empty, swept, and
garnished. Then goeth he, and taketh with himself seven
other spirits more wicked than himself, and they enter in
and dwell there : and the last state of that man is worse than
the first."

ST. MATT. xii. 43–45.

I. THESE strange, disquieting words seem to come into
the course of our Lord's teaching with the tone, the
feeling, the climate, as it were, of another world than
that with which, at the moment, He is engaged. As
He speaks, His disciples are round about Him; His
opponents are cavilling at His words and works, and
trying to lead Him to a false step; the man whom
He has just healed is sitting, it may be, at His feet
and looking up into His face, in the first rapture of
recovered health; and the multitude are pressing
in on the little group. But He Who is the Centre
of all this interest and hatred and affection, is not

looking at any of the people who surround Him ; His gaze does not meet with theirs; for His eyes are fastened upon a scene beyond the visible, and none of those who are about Him have any suspicion of the tragedy which He is watching. He is marking the course of a great disaster in that hidden and mysterious world which lies behind the things of sense, behind the ways of men; and suddenly, in words at once most vivid and most mysterious, He tells His hearers what it is that He is seeing. What is it that He speaks of ?   What is it that He is watching ?—It is the dreary, wasteful, ruinous disappointment that comes wherever a moral victory is left unused.   First, He sees the unclean spirit—some tyrannous power of darkness and defilement—driven out of a man's heart, driven from the throne it had usurped; He sees the heart relieved of that vile presence, of that cruel oppression. And then He marks how the evil spirit, hateful and hating—the spirit that has been driven out—goes restlessly straying to and fro, in the dreary impotence of baffled cruelty. At last He sees it turn again to the heart whence it had been dislodged; and, lo! that heart is empty. It is like a place that is decent indeed, and orderly enough ; no great harm has come as yet, no shameful sin defiled it; it looks neatly swept and garnished :

but it is empty. No ruling principle or passion has come to occupy it; no strong affection, no controlling love, no masterful enthusiasm, has been welcomed as sovereign over the man's life, and lord of his allegiance: the great opportunity, the critical moment of liberty, has been missed, and the throne is vacant. "Then goeth he, and taketh with himself seven other spirits more wicked than himself, and they enter in and dwell there: and," our Lord adds, in words which sound like the dreariest death-knell that ever rang over a wasted life, words so desperately sad that, however a man may be living, he could hardly bear to imagine them spoken of himself,[1] "the last state of that man is worse than the first."

II. Mysterious and astounding the scenery of this pitiful drama may seem to us; we may feel that it is like a fragment of a world which lies, save in so far as our Lord reveals it, quite beyond our ken. But however weird and dark the story of that wasted opportunity, that unused and therefore forfeited victory, may seem to us, we may feel that it tells of a disaster which we can clearly understand; that it points to a very plain law of human life and character. For we know that in the moral, as in the

---

[1] Cf. J. B. Mozley, "Parochial and Occasional Sermons:" *Growing Worse*, pp. 118–120.

physical order, nature abhors a vacancy. Consciously
or unconsciously, as the years go by, all men more
and more submit their lives to some allegiance; with
whatever uncertainty and changefulness, some one
motive, or group of motives, grows stronger and
stronger in them; they tend, at least, to bring every
thought into captivity to some one obedience. For
better or for worse, things which seemed difficult or
impossible a few years ago will come almost naturally
to a man a few years hence; he will have got ac-
customed to take a certain course, to obey certain
impulses or principles wherever they appear. We may
indeed distinguish three states in which a man may be.
He may be yielding his heart more and more to the
love of self, in whatsoever way of pride, or avarice,
or lust, or sloth. Or he may be yielding his heart
more and more to the love of God, falteringly, it may
be, with many struggles and failures, but still really
getting to love God more, to move more readily and
more loyally to do God's Will wherever he sees it.
Or, thirdly, he may be like the man of whom our
Lord spoke. He may, by God's grace, have cast out
an evil spirit from his heart; he may have broken
away from the mastery of some bad passion, some
tyrannous hunger or hatred; and he may be hesi-
tating, keeping his heart swept, clear and empty; his

will may be poised, as it were, between the one love and the other. Ah! but that can only be for a very little while. That balance never lasts; one way or the other the will must incline; one service or the other must be chosen, and that soon.[1]

For no man is ever safe against the love, the service of sin save by the power of the love of God. There is no sure way of keeping the evil out save by letting Him in—by the glad welcome, the trembling, thankful, adoring recognition of Him Who made us, that we might find our freedom in His service, and our rest in His engrossing love. Yes, for here is the deepest pathos of that empty throne of which our Saviour speaks — that heart so easily reoccupied by the unclean spirit that has been driven out of it:—that all the while Almighty God is waiting, pleading that He may enter in and dwell there; that he may bring into the wavering and aimless soul that growing peace and harmony and strength which no man knows save in the dedication of his life to God. God, and "the seven Spirits which are before His throne," would enter in and dwell there; and then the last state of that man might be in the beauty of holiness, in the joy of his Lord, in the peace that passeth

[1] Cf. Bishop Steere, "Notes of Sermons," second series, p. 95; and H. Drummond, "Natural Law in the Spiritual World," pp. 100, 101.

all understanding. Surely, brethren, it is pitiful to think how many lives are passed in perpetual peril and hesitation; how many hearts grow tired and feeble in the desultory service of they know not what; against how many names that woeful record is being written day by day, " The last state of that man is worse than the first;" while all the time it is only a little courage, a little rousing of one's self, a little venture in the strength of faith, that is needed to enthrone above the empty, listless soul the one love that can give joy and peace and clearness through all the changes of this world; the One Lord Who can control, absorb, ennoble, and fulfil all the energies of a spiritual being.—The love of God ; the growing realization of all that His love has done and borne for me ; the thrilling discovery, the steady recognition of the patience, the forbearance, the unwearied gentleness wherewith He has been waiting and working that, after all, I might not lose the bliss for which His love created me ;—here is the motive power which has made the saints; here is the force which still day after day comes rushing in to occupy some heart which "the Lord hath redeemed and delivered from the hand of the enemy." It is that love which alone gives meaning and harmony and strength to every life that is humbly and thankfully yielded to its service. It is that love, quickened and increased by the sacramental grace of God, which garrisons the soul against all who hate it, and keeps it in His perfect peace, so that no harm can happen unto it, so that no power of the evil one can enter in and dwell there.

III. The application of these thoughts to the great work upon which you will soon be entering[1] seems clear and direct; let me try to speak of it very briefly in three ways.

(a) First, then, we must never, in any work that we try to do in God's Name, set before ourselves or others a negative aim. The aim, the hope, the constant thought, must be not only to cast out sin, but to bring in love. It will never do, as Gordon wrote once, "to wish for the absence of evil, and yet not to desire the Presence of God."[2] It is, indeed, a great thing if we can help some one who is touched by the mission to escape from the mastery of some sin that has dragged down his life; to drive out the evil spirit of drunkenness, or gambling, or impurity, or avarice; to break away from associations which are ruining him, or to resolve that he will think no more of a

---

[1] This sermon was preached in the Church of St. Columba at Sunderland, to those who were to take part in the Sunderland Mission.

[2] C. G. Gordon's "Reflections in Palestine," p. 95.

grudge that has for years, perhaps, made it impossible for him ever really to say the Lord's Prayer;[1]—aye, it is a great thing, a thing worth living, toiling, praying for.   But it is not all; that victory is only the opportunity for another and a greater.   It will never do to "wish for the absence of evil, and yet not to desire the Presence of God."   Nothing is secured until He is there; until His love is shed abroad in the heart. Only when His Holy Spirit rules and guides and cheers a man, teaching him the love of God, bringing home to him the astounding message of the Cross, disclosing to him the power of renewal that Christ's infinite compassion won for us, making him feel how marvellously God has borne with all his ingratitude and rebellion, and waited that He might have mercy on him,—only then will the evil spirit, if he dares to return and tries to enter in, feel that a Stronger than he has occupied and garrisoned the heart.

(*b*) And then, secondly, that we may thus aim high, we must, thoughtfully and steadily, realize the spiritual capacities of the human heart; we must try, by frequent prayer, by humility and watchfulness, to understand and remember, so far as our hearts and minds can reach, what God is willing to do in those to whom He sends us.   I am sure that it is a very

---

[1] Cf. Francois Coppée, " Le Pater."

common mistake to underrate the spiritual capacity
of those with whom we have to do, especially among
the poor. Because their lives are hard and rough, and
their pleasures unlike ours; because they may have
little time for prayer; because they cannot express
themselves, or use religious language; because the sins
which beset them happen to be, in most men's eyes,
more disfiguring than those which beset educated and
prosperous people; therefore we seem almost to think
that the aim for them cannot be very high; that
they cannot receive the very highest truth. We forget
that God the Holy Ghost is ready to make them to be
numbered with Christ's saints. Never let us forget
that; for the earnest of that work of His in the lives
of the poor is the most glorious and beautiful thing,
perhaps, a man can ever see; and one will never see
it unless one is gentle and hopeful and reverent in
all one's thoughts of them. But then we may learn
how the grace of God, the light and life that flow
from His indwelling, can lift the very weariest and
hardest-driven soul into a dignity of endurance, a
radiance of faith, a simplicity of love, far above all
that this world can give or take away. Yes, right
through the constant stress of need; right through the
daily hardships, and in the midst of all the storms of
temptation round about them, there is indeed a beauty

and a joy that comes into men's homes and lives, aye, and into their very faces, when, through the revelation of His love and through the power of His sacraments, He enters in and dwells with them, to take the vacant throne of their hearts, to claim them for his own and be their God. And I think there is no beauty and no joy so well worth working for, so wonderful to see, as that; and none that seems so like an earnest of the life of heaven.

(*c*) And then, lastly, if we think of the greatness of the capacities that are to be realized, if we think of the high aim that is to be kept in view, we may be sure that there will be need of great patience in the work; of that true patience which has been called the queen of the virtues; the patience which includes both endurance and perseverance; the quiet, constant, undiscouraged maintenance of a noble purpose.[1] A high aim will always demand great patience; and to remember often what the aim is may help you patiently to persevere, however long the strain and effort may prove to be. For often, I think, the reason of impatience is a poor idea of what is to be attained. So, when children are watching any one at work, they will wonder why he does not get on faster, why he is taking such a time over it; because

[1] Cf. R. C. Trench, " New Testament Synonyms," pp. 197, 198.

they cannot see, as the workman does, how exact and
finished and perfect the result is to be. So, again,
when people have to bear great suffering, some may be
offended and inclined to rebel; because they cannot
see the everlasting glory, the unspeakably high calling,
for which that suffering is helping to prepare the
soul. They put the outcome of it all too low. And
so, too, in this case. Remember the height of the
aim, the splendour of the hope; not simply to produce here and there some amendment in the outward
look of things; but to bear, by the grace of the Holy
Ghost, the love of God into the hearts of men; to
help them to yield themselves to Him; to teach them
to be glad with the true happiness which He designs
for them; to bring the calm, pure light of heaven
among the troubles and sorrows and difficulties of this
earth. Remember that, and surely it will not seem
strange if for such a hope there may be need, after
the mission has passed, of even years of watchfulness
and prayer and loving service. For so may God
achieve the full work of His compassion; that those
who, by His grace, have driven out the evil from their
hearts, may go on to bring their lives more and more
perfectly under the glad mastery of His love, abiding
ever in that increasing strength and brightness which
issue from the indwelling presence of His Holy Spirit.

VIII.

THE DISASTERS OF SHALLOWNESS.

"Some fell upon a rock; and as soon as it was sprung up,
it withered away, because it lacked moisture."

St. Luke viii. 6.

"When the sun was up, they were scorched; and because
they had no root, they withered away."

St Matt. xiii. 6.

It is easy to bring before our minds the sight of
which our Lord here speaks. It may well be that as
He speaks His eyes are resting on it, and His hand
perhaps, is pointing to it.[1] In one part of a cornfield
sloping down towards the Sea of Galilee, He may
have marked how thin a coating of soil covered the
rock of the hillside. The seed sown in that shallow
ground has had a rapid and a feeble growth; the
rock has checked its roots from striking downwards
to reach the nourishment it needs; and so checked,
and forced, perhaps, into unnaturally quick development by the hot surface of the stone, the plant has, as

[1] Cf. R. C. Trench, "The Parables of our Lord," p. 66.

we say, run to stalk; the energy which should have
been spent in secretly penetrating to the sources of
sustenance and renewal has been all thrown into a
showy and ill-nourished growth. There may have
been a fair look of promise at the first; but there is
no reserve or reality of strength; there is no communication with the hidden springs of refreshment
when the need comes; and as soon as the fierce rays
of the Eastern sun beat down upon it, the thin
and frail and rootless and resourceless plant withers
away. The heat which might have advanced and
ripened and perfected it, had its growth been
gradual and well sustained, is too much for it now.
There is in it no robustness to bear the strain, no
substance to be matured by it; and because it has
no moisture and no root, when the sun is up it
withers away.

As we pass from the parable to its interpretation
let us fasten on this one point—that as, in the order
of nature, the agency, the influence, which ripens one
plant, may scorch and ruin another; so, in the analogous sphere of moral growth, what tells on one man
for the increase of strength and maturity and fruitfulness may be full of peril and misery, if not of
sheer disaster, in the life of another.[1] Our Lord Him-

[1] Cf. R. C. Trench, *ubi supra*, p. 73.

self seems to bring out for us this lesson in the parable. It is, He says, in time of trial, it is when affliction or persecution arises because of the Word, that those whose spiritual life is thus rootless and precarious fall away. " Blessed," He had said, " are they which are persecuted for righteousness' sake : for theirs is the kingdom of heaven." " Blessed are ye, when men shall revile you, and persecute you, . . . for My sake." But here it is just that persecution which reveals the weakness and works the ruin. The trouble, the discipline, which should have braced and ennobled the character, only demoralizes and overbears it; that which should have been, in the highest sense, for the man's wealth is unto him an occasion of falling. In a different figure the Prophet Jeremiah brings vividly before us the same terrible disappointment, the utter dreariness of fruitless discipline, when he speaks of the refiner's furnace heated to the uttermost, till all the lead that should act as a solvent is used up, and the bellows are burnt by the blaze, and still no silver is yielded; " the founder melteth in vain." [1] And it is, surely, the saddest failure we can ever see, when the stress of pain, or sorrow, or trouble comes upon a man, and leaves him no better than he was; no humbler, no gentler,

[1] Jer. vi. 29.

no more thoughtful for the cares and sufferings of others, no less worldly and selfish, no more nearly ready to die. It is a failure so dismal and barren that we can hardly bear to think of it; it seems at first the one part of the great mystery of pain into which no light penetrates. Mysterious indeed it is; though no one who has learnt the manifoldness of the uses of adversity, the diverse, hidden, complex ways through which it works on characters, and tells in lives that are even incidentally brought near to it, will venture to speak of any suffering as really fruitless, or to limit the silent energy with which even that which seems most hopelessly to fail as discipline may yet be working round to some great and far-off outcome of beneficence. Still, mysterious certainly it is that the opportunity of learning through suffering should be given, and neglected or abused; but the mystery, as has been truly said, belongs really to the problem of evil, not to the problem of pain.[1] That moral evil should perplex and thwart the work of suffering is not stranger than that it should be allowed in other ways to mar God's work and to disfigure human life; that men should spurn the teaching of pain and sorrow is not stranger than that they should abuse the gift

[1] J. R. Illingworth, in "Lux Mundi," p. 118.

L

of a great intellect or a splendid education; that suffering should make a man hard or sullen is not stranger than that culture should make him conceited or insolent. In both cases that which should have been for his wealth is unto him an occasion of falling; in both cases the gift of God is spoilt by the blindness and wilfulness of man; in both cases we find ourselves confronted with that stubborn and arresting fact of moral evil; that which has been called "the one irrational, lawless, meaningless thing in the whole universe;" that which reason will not enable us to explain, nor conscience, thank God, suffer us to explain away.[1]

We must, then, bear patiently the sense of strangeness and perplexity with which we think of those who suffer pain, and seem to learn no lesson and to gain no strength or beauty from it:—the secret of that defeat of love is hidden in the obscurity hanging round the certain fact of moral evil. It is for us to mark, for our own sake and for the sake of all on whom our life or influence may tell, what is the especial fault with which our Lord connects, in the Parable of the Sower, this pitiful misuse of discipline : what is the form of self-indulgence of which He

[1] A. L. Moore, "Oxford House Papers," p. 151; J. R. Illingworth, in "Lux Mundi," p. 116.

warns us here that it imperils or destroys the
capacity of understanding pain and sorrow when
they come to us.

Surely it is the self-indulgence of shallowness in
religion.—We know the disastrous perils of shallowness in the intellectual life; the weakness and fruit-
lessness of the mind that never really takes a truth
home to itself, never lets it put forth all its meaning,
never has the patience or the honesty thoroughly to
appropriate it; the mind that is content hastily to
receive and reproduce a phrase instead of toiling to
realize and interpret a fact. We know, perhaps by
some sad and humiliating experience of our own, the
poverty, the tentativeness, the insecurity under any
real strain, which that form of self-indulgence, the
self-indulgence of seeking high interest on scanty
capital, entails in the life of the intellect. It should
be, I think, the chief gain of a man's time here,[1] so
far as merely mental discipline is concerned, that he
should realize the unworthiness and discredit of all
such hasty forwardness. And closely analogous to
this is that great peril to which our Lord is pointing
when He speaks of the shallow soil, and the showy,
rootless growth that withered when the heat beat
down upon it. "He that heareth the word, and

[1] This sermon was preached at a College Service in Oxford.

straightway with joy receiveth it."—"*Straightway
with joy.*" The message that began, " Repent ye, for
the kingdom of heaven is at hand;" the message
that centres in the Cross, with its tremendous disclosure of the horror and awfulness of sin; the
message which speaks to us of the Son of God, made
subject for our sakes to hunger and weariness, to
scorn and hatred, to agony and death; the message
which declares again and again how we too must
take up our cross and follow Him if we would be
His disciples; the message which forces on our sight
the unspeakable gravity of human life, and of its
issues when this world is done with; the message
that speaks to us of the day of judgment, and
of the outer darkness, and of weeping and gnashing
of teeth; the message in which, as one has marked,
from the lips 'of Him Who loves us with the
love that passeth knowledge, there come, for His very
love's sake, "words which shake the heart with
fear;" [1]—surely this is not a message which a man
can really take in its entirety into his soul with
nothing but immediate, unhindered joy ; nothing but
a light-hearted gladness in the moral beauty it presents, the hopes of which it speaks, its promises of forgiveness, and its note of victory. Joy there is, indeed,

---

[1] Cf. R. W. Dale, " The Old Evangelicalism and the New," p. 40.

for all who truly take the message to themselves,
and humbly dare, God helping them, to seek to know
all that it has to say to them ; joy which has some
semblance, some forecast of that for which He endured
the Cross ; joy such as St. Paul and St. John write
about ; joy such as we may have seen sometimes in
the unearthly radiance of its victory over pain, and
death, and sorrow, and crying. Yes ; but there is
something else first ; something else, which seldom
"for the present seemeth to be joyous, but grievous ; "
something else, without which that inexpensive
brightness, that easy hopefulness that somehow
things will all come right with us, is apt to be a
frail, resourceless growth, withering away when the
sun is up, and the hot winds of trial are sweeping .
over it. For if Christianity is to be to us what we
know it has been, what we sometimes see it is to
Christ's true servants, in the time of trouble, when the
heat is beating down upon us, we must have opened
out our hearts to it, we must have broken up the soil
for it, that freely and deeply its roots may penetrate
our inner being ; we must have laid bare our life to
its demands ; we must have taken to ourselves, in
silence and sincerity, its words of judgment with its
words of hope ; its sternness with its encouragement ;
its denunciations with its promises ; its requirements

with its offer; its absolute intolerance of sin with its inconceivable and Divine long-suffering towards sinners.

Surely, surely we need to think more than many of us do think of these things; we need to realize that no religious life is strong which does not rest on penitence—penitence, thorough and sincere and living; penitence such as brings the soul, with all its secret sins, all its half-conscious self-deception, all its cherished forms of self-indulgence, right into contact with the demand, the sternness, the perfect holiness of Him Who died for it.

Often, I think, there are trials of doubt and onsets of unbelief, in which the endurance of a man's faith may depend on nothing else so much as on this— whether he has really known, not the evidences of Christianity, not its coherence as a theological system, not its appeal to our higher emotions in great acts of worship, not even the beauty of its moral ideal, but its power to penetrate the heart and to convince of sin; its power to break down our pride with the disclosure of God's love and patience with us, with our blindness and ingratitude, our obstinate rejection of His goodness to us; its power, then, to bear into a broken and a contrite heart the first glimmer and the growing radiance of that joy that cannot be till penitence has gone before—the joy that no man taketh from us; the joy that all the discipline of life may only deepen and confirm; and that, through the heat of sorrow and suffering and persecution, when and as God wills, may be ripened unto life eternal.

IX.

HALF-HEARTEDNESS.

" A double-minded man is unstable in all his ways."
St. James i. 8.

It does not seem necessary to enter into the
question as to the fitness with which this Epistle is
appointed for the Feast of St. Philip and St. James,[1]
—the question, that is to say, whether the writer
of the Epistle, generally identified with James, called
the Lord's brother, the first Bishop of the Church of
Jerusalem, is or is not to be further identified with
James, the son of Alphæus, who is the companion of
St. Philip in our calendar. A question which has been
undecided for fifteen centuries, and which has been the
subject of numberless treatises, seems probably out of
the reach of decision unless some fresh evidence should
emerge to settle it; while little practical teaching
could be gained from any hasty account of it. It
seems better to learn from the Epistle, as it is this
day brought before us, the clear, incisive lessons

[1] Upon which day this sermon was preached.

which it has to teach us. And so I would ask you to look with me at one of the clearest and the most incisive of these—a lesson which may seem, perhaps, to have some special force in our day.

I. "A double-minded [or half-hearted] man," St. James tells us, "is unstable in all his ways."—*A double-minded man.* The designation is wide in range and deep in penetration. Perhaps there may not be one of us to whom in some way, in some degree, it does not apply; not one of us who is not in some part of his life hindered and enfeebled and imperilled by the vacillation of half-heartedness. But in its outcome, if it be not checked, if a man does not, gradually at least, with advancing efforts of faith and courage, get free from it, it is a terrible misunderstanding and misuse of life. The word which St. James uses was taken forty years ago as the title of one of the most subtle, penetrating, pathetic poems of modern times—a poem such as only Oxford, one might think, and the Oxford of the last half-century, could have produced. In *Dipsychus* Mr. Clough has drawn with great power, with searching keenness, the irresolute waverings, the fore-doomed compromises, the inconsistent self-excusings, of the double-minded man; the man to whom even his tempter says at last, or nearly at last—

> "Heartily you will not take to anything;
> Whatever happen, don't I see you still
> Living no life at all? . . .
>   Will you go on thus
> Until death end you? If indeed it does.
> For what it does, none knows. Yet as for you,
> You hardly have the courage to die outright:
> You'll somehow halve even it." [1]

In Dipsychus the uttermost disaster of the double-minded man, with his "ineffective, indeterminate swaying," is set forth; but we are reminded that the inconsistency through which and in which he has moved towards that disaster is nothing uncommon; when, in the epilogue, an average, unimaginative, self-complacent critic, looking back to all the arguments of the evil spirit, Dipsychus' tempter, thinks that "if only it hadn't been for the way he said it, and that it was he who said it, much that he said would have been sensible enough." [2]

II. Yes, double-mindedness, half-heartedness. In widely varying degrees and ways it is indeed a most frequent secret of weakness and unrest, of failure and peril; it keeps men back from the task that was marked with their name; it takes the spring and brightness out of life; it is the foe of inner freedom, and of all health, and strength, and growth, and peace.—Let us look at three forms which the

[1] A. H. Clough, "Poems," p. 125.   [2] Id. *ibid.*, p. 133.

trouble takes—three parts of our life which it invades and mars.

(*a*) First let us think of that form of half-heartedness of which especially St. James is here speaking—the half-heartedness of a divided trust; half-heartedness in prayer. He is saying how wisdom, the wisdom that is from above, the wisdom by which people see their way through all the tangles of this world, is to be sought from God; and how surely God will give it. But, then, it must be asked in faith, with true, whole-hearted committal of one's self to God, with no doubting, no faltering irresolutely to and fro; for he who so doubts and falters is like a wave of the sea, driven with the wind and tossed about—and "let not that man think that he shall obtain anything from the Lord;" he is a half-hearted man, unsteady in all his ways.—What is the temper, the bearing of mind and heart, of which St. James is speaking? Not surely that imperfection of faith, that liability to days of dimness and of weakness, which very many may know whom God is truly leading on, nearer and nearer to Himself; not that hindered but true-hearted venture which spoke and was accepted in the prayer, "Lord, I believe: help Thou my unbelief." No, not that; but the temper which really has in it no clear element of venture or of self-committal at all; the temper which thinks of prayer as little more than something which may do some good and can do no harm; the temper of one who turns to pray by way of being on the safe side; the temper that is prepared, if the prayer be not granted, simply to look out for some other way in which the result may be attained; the temper that has never realized the deep and utter incongruity between the simplest act of prayer, and all cold-hearted scheming for one's own advantage— between prayer and selfishness. Half-heartedness in prayer it is when one half or some smaller fragment of the heart has some expectation from prayer, while the rest more solidly relies on shrewdness, or money, or influence, or self-will; when natural instruments of success are regarded not as means which may be (if they are humbly, faithfully, unselfishly employed) directed and hallowed by the blessing of the Almighty, but as alternative ways, resources in the background, second strings, if the prayer should not have the result which selfishness desired from it. It was a saying of General Gordon's, "Do not try planning and praying and then planning again; it is not honouring to God." [1] And it would be hard to measure how much of the extraordinary power of

[1] C. G. Gordon's Letters to his Sister, p. 5.

his life was due to this—that there was no reserve in his committal of himself to God; that he lived with an undivided trust; that he had marked and judged and dealt with the temptation to half-heartedness in prayer.

(*b*) Again, how many of us are hindered and confused by the half-heartedness of our love towards God; the divided and inconstant desire with which we seek the blessings of goodness, the joy of our Lord, the gladness of His service. We may have seen more or less clearly that there is indeed no steady happiness in life save the happiness of serving Him, the happiness of unselfishness, of self-forgetfulness for the sake of others. This may have been borne in on us through some of· the many ways in which God lets us see the truth; and we may be quite sure of it in our quieter times, when we have the opportunity and the courage to think.—But to let go of other things; to set our whole heart upon the kingdom of God and His righteousness; not to plan any other pleasures for ourselves, but to be willing that they should come to us when and as He wills, to be enjoyed as His gifts, with thankfulness to Him, with a heart that all along is quite free and ready for His work; to leave the ordinary well-known ways in which we have seemed fairly sure, at all events, of being comfortable, if not happy, of having occasional pleasures, even though we may be getting to care for them less and less; to do without excitement, or praise, or luxury, or a margin of leisure, and to make up our minds that we will plan for no happiness outside God's service, and that all that we enjoy shall be what freely comes, unplanned, from Him, as we go about the work that He has given us to do;— this is the real venture of faith; this needs some wholeheartedness of desire; this is what we find so hard. We want some gloss upon that stern saying of St. James, "The friendship of the world is enmity with God." Though we know it is no good, we cannot give up trying to get on well with both.

(*c*) And then, thirdly, lying very near to this, there is the half-heartedness of a divided intention. We do intend to do God's Will; but, then, it must not go too far from our way; it must not ask too much of us. Or, we intend to do God's will; but so that incidentally our own will may be gratified at the same time. We will press forward in His work, we will be strenuous and constant in the discharge of duty; but, then, there must be credit reflected, if not on ourselves, at least on the party to which we belong; we look that in some way or another it may prove

to have been a good thing for us that we were so
dutiful. If we do not pursue honesty as being the
best policy, at least we expect that it will appear to
be so in the end. And so the poor, unworthy motive
is always coming across us—the unowned purpose
must be kept in view; the secret intention claims
half our heart; and, almost without knowing it, the
strength and reality of our choice and will to do
God's work grows less and less.

III. Half-heartedness in faith and love and purpose
—most of us, I fear, know something of such things;
and most of us, I think, will own how exactly
St. James fastens upon the practical outcome of it all.
" The double-minded [the half-hearted] man is unstable
in all his ways." Unsettledness, disorder, inequality,
unsteadiness, restlessness, confusion, hesitation, bewilderment,—are not these, indeed, the characteristics
that prevail more and more in the half-hearted life;
these, with all the vacillation, the weakness, the dim-
sightedness, that they entail? Do we not know that,
in whatsoever degree they have troubled or are
troubling us, it is our own half-heartedness that is
most of all to blame? Surely, half-heartedness,
wavering and faltering in faith, or love, or purpose,
the hopeless toil of living two lives,—this is one
chief source, at least, of much of the unhappiness

and unrest, the weariness and overstrain and break-
ing down in modern life. We get so tired with
trying to blend what will not mix; we spend so
much of our strength in vain while we try to work
two ways at once; we make so little progress while
we are always crossing over from the one road to the
other. We know the trouble, the wastefulness, of
half-heartedness; we have often longed, it may be,
for the unity which yet we have not quite courage
enough to grasp and hold and trust. And we know
how hard it is—hard, perhaps, especially in our day
and in this place[1]—to overcome our half-heartedness,
to bring our whole life into one allegiance. But one
thing we can do, please God, with some steady
increase of self-mastery. It may be hard to attain
to such a unity and simplicity of trust as made the
strength of Gordon's life; it may be hard to cast out
the lingering love of worldly gratification, and to
fasten all our affection upon the things of God; but
unity of intention, single-mindedness in aim and
purpose,—this is, God helping us, to a very great
degree within our reach. We can be watchful to
keep a pure and disinterested aim; to allow in our
hearts no plan that we would not avow; to cast out,
to make no terms with self-seeking. This we can do,

---

[1] This sermon was preached in Oxford.

by the grace of God; this in itself is much, and it leads on to more. It may be, indeed, that all through this life we shall never wholly conquer the temptations of half-heartedness; never be secure against the intrusion of the low thought, the mean motive, the feeble looking back, the sordid suspicion, which take the glow out of things well begun; which thrust themselves into the company of whatever generous or righteous purpose we had formed. But if we are resolute to deal firmly with these things when they come; resolute not to let them tell in action or in speech, not to let them pervert judgment; resolute to keep them down with a strong hand, and hold on our way in spite of them; we may find not only that our purpose is growing more single and whole-hearted, and our intention purer and more vigorous; but that in our affection also, and in our trust, there is an ever-increasing unity; that with the freedom of God's service comes the peace that they have who love His Law, and, above all, that blessing of clear-sightedness, of spiritual discernment which is only known as a man escapes from the vacillation and dimness of the double-minded into the strength, the joyful gladness, of the true-hearted— even the blessing of the "pure in heart: for they shall see God."

M

X.

THE IMAGE OF THE LORD.

" Remember that Jesus Christ of the seed of David was
raised from the dead according to my Gospel."

2 Tim. ii. 8.

I. A HEAVY burden had been laid upon the young
disciple to whom St. Paul so wrote. Before he had
reached middle life,[1] Timotheus had been placed as
the Apostle's delegate, with episcopal authority over
the Christian community in Ephesus; and it seems
clear that he was still responsible for that great trust
when this letter was sent to him.[2] It is hard to
realize the strain which at that time such an office
must have put upon a man's robustness of conviction
and tenacity of purpose. It needed, indeed, a clear
head and a steady hand to guide the Church of

[1] Cf. Salmon, "Introduction to the New Testament," p. 501.
[2] Cf. Gore, "The Church and the Ministry," pp. 246-248; Alford's
"Prolegg. to the Pastoral Epistles," pp. 101-103; Shirley, "On the
Apostolic Age," pp. 116, 117.

Christ at Ephesus; it needed, above all else, a heart
that no secret unreality, or bitterness, or self-seeking
had been stealthily enfeebling against the day of
trial. To believe with an unwavering confidence
that the future was Christ's, in spite of all that
pride and splendour of paganism, which nowhere
bore itself more arrogantly than in Ephesus; when
all Asia and the world was thronging to the worship
of Diana, to be always sure that her magnificence was
worse than worthlessness—a hideous and degrading
lie, that must break up and be gone like a bad dream
at the first touch of light; to be quite untroubled by
all the brilliancy and vigour of the social life in
which the claim of Christ was blankly ignored or
cleverly made fun of; to look up at the great temple,
gleaming in the sunlight, famous as the one mansion
worthy of the gods, and then to hold to it constantly
that that little cluster of humble folk, meeting day
by day for their Holy Eucharist, had found a truth
and owned a Lord before Whose glory all that pomp
and strength of idol-worship should be utterly
abolished;—this could not but make for most men
a severe demand on faith. But for Timotheus there
were keener tests of reality and courage than all
these. The language and emphasis of the two letters
addressed to him strongly suggest the impression

that he was not of a very tough, robust, or stubborn temperament. He was not a man who, when things seemed to be going against him or getting into confusion, could shrug his shoulders and refuse to be harassed. Rather, he seems one to whom antagonism, insolence, isolation, would mean sharp suffering; one whose heart might grow sick as he looked at a gathering storm of hostility and danger; one on whose courage and constancy such a storm would break with a severe if not a staggering shock. And certainly there were black and angry clouds coming up over the sky; and things promised a rough time for the Church at Ephesus. The recent persecution under Nero, though its brutalities may have been confined to Rome,[1] had shown what Christians might be called to face whenever policy or passion chanced to prompt a massacre. There were not wanting those who might find it convenient to stir up something of the sort at Ephesus; and the sense that it was always possible could not but tell on the position and outlook of the Church. But graver still was the mischief that was gaining ground within the Church itself; where the restlessness and superstition of some who had seemed to be sincere were corrupting

[1] Cf. Merivale, "History of the Romans under the Empire," vi. 45C.

the faith of Christ, and foisting strange, morbid
fancies into the centre of the Christian teaching;
so that men were drifting off from all reality of
religion, through idle talk and sickly exercises of
perverted cleverness, towards that moral degradation
which, in a place like Ephesus, closed in so readily as
soon as faith had ceased to hold a man above it. Let
us try to measure all these conditions by anything
like the same scale on which we estimate the difficulties of our own day; let us remember how small
and weak and unpromising a movement Christianity
must have seemed to a dispassionate Ephesian critic;
let us add the thought that Timotheus was on the
very point of losing the one man through whose
vivid, penetrating, and inspiring personality he had
drawn the strongest impulse, the constant guidance
and encouragement of his life (since the time of St.
Paul's departure was at hand); and we may probably
feel that things were looking very dark and threatening and terrible to the sensitive and delicate man
who had been placed in charge of the Ephesian
Church.

II. If we were writing to a friend amidst difficulties
so great as these, and especially if we were writing
with the expectation that we might never write to
him again, we should certainly be most careful what

we said. We should do our best to enter thoroughly into his position; we should feel that there was a grave responsibility in being allowed to write to him at such a time; and that we must write nothing which was not absolutely real, and likely to come home to him. And then, I think, this would be a part of our desire as we wrote;—that we might fasten upon his memory, with a deep and clear impression, some thought which seemed to us most likely to emerge into the front of consciousness at the time of peril or despondency, and to rally the wavering forces of the will. We know how one recollection, distinct and dominant in the mind, has often been the decisive force at a critical moment; how upon the battle-field, for instance, or under the almost overpowering pressure of temptation, the thought of a man's country, of his home, of his ancestral traditions, has reinforced as with a fresh tide of strength his faltering heart, and borne him on to victory, whether by success or death. We may recall the scene in one of our African campaigns, where the thought of a man's old school, and the boyish eagerness anyhow to bring it to the front, was the impulse of a splendid courage. Yes; there are images in most men's minds which, if they rise at the right moment, will do much to make them heroes. A word, a glance, some well-known sight, some old, familiar strain of music, may beckon the image out of the recesses of the memory; and, if the man has in him the capacity of generous action, he will use it then.

III. It is on this characteristic of human nature that St. Paul relies, as he writes to Timotheus the words of the text. He would avail himself of this; he would raise it to its highest conceivable employment; he would enlist it as a constant, ready, powerful ally on the side of duty—on the side of God. He may never see Timotheus, never write to him again. Well, then, he will leave dinted into his mind, by a few incisive words, one commanding and sustaining image. For it is not, as it appears in our English version, any event out of the past, however supreme in its importance, however abiding in its results, that St. Paul here fastens upon the memory of his disciple; it is not the abstract statement of a truth in history or theology, however central to the faith, however vast in its consequences; it is a living Person, Whom St. Paul has seen, Whose Form he would have Timotheus keep ever in his mind, distinct, beloved, unrivalled, sovereign: "Bear in remembrance Jesus Christ, raised from the dead."[1] When the hardship which Christ's true soldier must expect is pressing

[1] Cf. A. Plummer, "The Pastoral Epistles," pp. 354–358.

heavily upon you; when the task of self-discipline
seems tedious and discouraging; when the day's work
seems more than you can bear, and when night, it
may be, brings but little rest; when you are sick at
heart to see folly and wilfulness, conceit and treachery,
ruining what years of labour and devotion hardly
reared; then let that ever-living Form stand out
before you: "Bear in remembrance Jesus Christ
raised from the dead." Bear Him in remembrance
as He now is, enthroned in everlasting victory. He
toiled to utter weariness; He pleased not Himself.
He was despised and rejected; He was betrayed by
one whom He had chosen, denied by another,
deserted by all. He suffered more than thought can
compass; and if ever "failure" could be written at
the end of any enterprise, it might have seemed
reasonable to write it of His work, as they took His
Body from the Cross. Well, then, if your tasks and
disappointments seem too much for you, bear Him
in remembrance as He now is.—Never can the
disproportion between advantages and difficulties,
between resources and demands, have seemed to
human eyes wider than when the Galilæan Peasant
came to found a world-wide kingdom; never did an
unreasonable venture seem to end in a more natural
disaster than when the religious leaders of His own

people combined with the representatives of the
Roman government to crush Him with a strong
hand. Well, then, if the strength, the wickedness,
the wealth, the confidence, of paganism at Ephesus
at times appal and stagger you; if there seems
something irresistibly discouraging in the brilliance,
the culture, the self-sufficiency, of the society which
ignores or ridicules you;—bear in remembrance Jesus
Christ, raised from the dead, exalted now to the
Majesty on high.—Yes, bear Him in remembrance,
not only as the supreme and all-illuminating instance
of the victory that overcometh the world; not only
as One Who has erased the word "impossible" out of
the vocabulary that can be used in speaking of God's
work; but also as the ever-living Strength of His
servants, the ever-watchful Guardian of His Church;
as One Who knows your need, and is indeed sufficient
for your help; Who never can forget or fail you;
beneath Whose gaze you serve, and by Whose love
you shall be crowned.

IV. Let us take two thoughts, this Easter morning,
from the counsel which St. Paul thus gives.

(*a*) First, that he is trying to lodge in the heart of
Timotheus' life and work that which has been the
deepest and most effective force in his own.—St. Paul
was convinced that he had seen the Risen Lord; and

the energy, the effect, of that unfading Image throughout his subsequent life might go some way to prove
that the conviction was true. Physical weight is
sometimes measured by the power of displacement;
and in the moral and spiritual sphere we tend, at
least, to think that there must be something solid
and real to account for a change so unexpected, so
unearthly, so thorough, so sustained through every
trial, so vast in its practical outcome, as was the
conversion of St. Paul. No doubt rests on the fact
of the conversion, nor on the greatness of its results;
in regard to both we can appeal to Epistles which the
most trenchant criticism now leaves unquestioned;
and if St. Paul declares that the whole impulse of his
new life came from the sight of One Who had been
crucified and had risen from the dead, we may surely
claim that his witness is a real contribution to the
evidence of Christ's Resurrection. It may be set
aside; it must be, if our knowledge of all things,
actual and possible, enables us to say that there can
be no resurrection of the dead; but that would be
a bold presumption. Or it may be justly said that
no one man's conviction, however commended by its
steadiness under trial and its practical effect, can bear
the weight of so stupendous an inference. But, then,
St. Paul's certainty that he had seen Christ after His

Crucifixion does not stand alone to bear that weight;
it is but one part in a large and various mass of
evidence. Similarly, it may be said with truth that
the convictions of enthusiastic men have produced
immense results, even when they were utterly mis-
taken. But let St. Paul's conviction be taken in its
context; let justice be done to the character it
wrought in him; to the coherence and splendour of
the work it animated; to the penetrating, sober
insight of his practical teaching; to the consistency,
not of expression, but of inmost thought and life,
which is disclosed to any careful study of his
writings; lastly, to the grasp which his words have
laid upon the strongest minds in Christendom through
all succeeding centuries, the prophetic and undying
power which, amidst vast changes of methods and
ideas, men widely different have felt and reverenced
in these Epistles;—let these distinctive notes of St.
Paul's work be realized, together with its incalculable
outcome in the course of history, and it will seem
hard to think that the central, ruling impulse of it all
was the obstinate blunder of a disordered mind.—This
at least, I think, may be affirmed, that if there were
against belief in Christ's Resurrection any such difficulty as the indisputable facts of St. Paul's life and
work present to disbelief, we should find it treated

as of crucial importance; and that, I think, not unjustly.[1]

(*b*) "Bear in remembrance Jesus Christ, raised from the dead." It is the Form which has made him what he is, for life or for death, that St. Paul would with his last words, it may be, leave clenched for ever on the mind and heart of his disciple. The vision of that Form may keep him true and steadfast when all is dark, confused, and terrible around him. May not we do well to take the bidding to ourselves? We know, perhaps, that our hearts are weak, and our wills unsteady; the time in which we should have stored up strength against the day of trial may not have been used as now we wish it had been. For it seems as though life were likely to grow harder as the years go on; as though it might be very difficult to have a right judgment in all things, and to keep loyally in the path of charity and truth. There are signs of trouble and confusion in the air; and some faint hearts begin to fail; and some of us, perhaps, see not our tokens so clearly as we did. But One we may see, as we lift our eyes this Easter Day; "it is He Who liveth, and was dead; and, behold, He is alive for evermore;" He Who cannot fail His

---

[1] Cf. F. W. Farrar, "Life of St. Paul," pp. 114, 115; Milligan, "The Resurrection of our Lord," pp. 40–45.

Church, or leave even the poorest.and least worthy
of His servants desolate and bewildered when the
darkness gathers, and the cry of need goes up; He
Who will be to any one of us what He was to His
Apostles; He, our Strength against all despondency,
and irresoluteness, and cowardice, and sloth; He Who
knows us perfectly, yet loves us—ah, how strange
it is!—yet better than He knows; He Who, if we
have borne with patient courage our few years of
trial in the twilight here, will receive us into that
everlasting light which He both died and rose again
to win for us.

XI.

THE EFFICACY OF THE OLD TESTAMENT THROUGH FAITH WHICH IS IN CHRIST.

"From a child thou hast known the Holy Scriptures, which
are able to make thee wise unto salvation through faith
which is in Christ Jesus."

2 TIM. iii. 15.

I. THERE is a singular and pathetic beauty in the relation between the old man who writes these words
and the young man to whom he sends them. A wide
contrast in natural characteristics, and an entire
fellowship in devotion to one cause, are often the
conditions of a close and affectionate friendship; and
it seems probable that the affection of St. Paul for
Timotheus rested on some such grounds. Unlike in
temperament the two men certainly appear. For,
with whatever hindrances of ill health or nervous
constitution, St. Paul was clearly one whose intensity
of purpose, tenacity of principle, and vehemence of
will made it likely that to any opposition, where his
own judgment was distinct, he would "give place by

subjection, no, not for an hour." Timotheus, on the
other hand, seems to have been by nature one to
whom opposition would always mean distress and
pain,[1] to whom firmness would often be difficult and
expensive—a character deficient somehow in that
useful sort of obstinacy which is an element in some
men's power of endurance, and stands them in good
stead at hard times. The traits of moral beauty on
which St. Paul elsewhere lays stress, in speaking of
Timotheus, are such as might well consist with this
deficiency; they are the attractions likeliest to be
wrought by the grace of God in such a nature.
Eminent unselfishness; the capacity for generous
self-devotion; warm-heartedness and loyalty in personal affection; a spiritual sense which made the care
for others' welfare seem ingenerate and instinctive;—
these are the features which, as we read the First
Epistle to the Corinthians and the Epistle to the
Philippians, appear to supplement the impression of
Timotheus' character which we get from the Pastoral
Epistles. There is often in such men an unfailing
charm of delicacy and gentleness; they seem as
though there had been more summer than winter in
their lives; while, with some characteristics which
may be misnamed effeminate, there is in them a

[1] Cf. Sermon x. p. 164.

really womanly power of patience and self-sacrifice. Surely, if we may form any such idea of Timotheus, we cannot wonder at St. Paul's intense affection for him, as a constant presence of tenderness and sympathy in the midst of much antagonism and disappointment and anxiety. We cannot wonder that St. Paul should have trusted him largely, and believed that he would rightly bear his high charge as Apostolic delegate over the Church of Ephesus;[1] nor yet can we wonder that, as the Apostle thinks of him in the isolation, the perils, the tangled difficulties of his position,[2] as he thinks of the subtlety of error, the restlessness of idle talk, the malignity of moral corruption, the brutality of persecution, all besetting, or likely to beset, that sensitive temperament, a fear should be continually haunting him lest the strain may prove too great; so that he seems never tired of enforcing, with every sanction, every appeal, every encouragement that he can use, the paramount duty of unflinching steadfastness. Again and again that duty is impressed on his disciple's conscience, that it may be safe from all risks of forgetfulness or surprise: "God hath not given us the spirit of fearfulness;" "Be not thou ashamed;"

---

[1] Cf. Gore, "The Church and the Ministry," p. 246.
[2] Cf. Sermon x., pp. 164, 165.

" Take thy share of hardship ; " " Hold fast the form
of sound words ; " " Be strong in grace ; " " Continue,
abide in the things which thou hast learned ; " "Be
instant in season, out of season ; " " Watch thou in
all things ; " " Endure afflictions."—It seems that two
strong motives hold the Apostle's heart and rule his
words as he writes this second letter to Timotheus ;—
his longing to see just once again the face he loves
is only rivalled by his absorbing and persistent
eagerness that Timotheus may be ever steadfast in
unfaltering allegiance to the truth.—That grave,
intense anxiety of one who has not long to live,
that a younger man, whom he has taught and loved,
may not break down or get bewildered in the
increasing perils of the years to come,—surely it has
in it a solemnity and a sadness ever renewed amidst
the unchanging anxieties of a changeful world.

II. In the words of the text, then, St. Paul reminds
Timotheus of one great element and ground of steadfastness in the Christian faith and life. He has been
speaking of the terrible development which he foresees
for the evils already assailing the Church—of the
deepening of darkness and corruption as the days
draw in towards the end ; and he has turned to
plead again with his own dear son, Timotheus, that
when he has to stand alone through all these things,

N

when St. Paul has passed away to wait beyond the veil till Christ shall come and judge the world, he may stand firm and without fear in the one cause for which it is worth while to live and, if it please God, to die. "Abide thou," he says, "in the things which thou hast learned and hast been assured of:" —and then he lays hold of two facts in Timotheus' past history which should help him to be thus steadfast—"knowing," he adds, first, "from whom thou didst learn" the faith of Christ; and secondly, "that from a child thou hast known the Holy Scriptures, which are able to make thee wise unto salvation through faith which is in Christ Jesus." Let us try to enter into the meaning of this second appeal : to see, so far as we can, what is that especial help which St. Paul expects Timotheus now to gain from his all but lifelong training in the books of the Old Testament; and then on what condition, by what power, he may gain it.

(a) The help will lie in that peculiar wisdom which the Holy Scriptures of the Old Testament will engender in Timotheus, if he lets them have their proper work in his inner life. He has known them from early childhood—ἀπὸ βρέφους. They are to him not simply an external object of study, but an inward endowment which has conditioned all his growth;

they are lodged very far back in his heart and mind ; in their presence, under their influence, he has come to be what he is, to realize himself ; he has never known his life without them. He knows them with an intimacy which is more than that of any friendship—an intimacy like that of home ; an intimacy which has, of course, its risks in some cases of unobservantness, of inactivity, of indolence, and of ingratitude, but which certainly gives access to depths of meaning unsuspected by ordinary acuteness and even industry. So knowing the writings of the Old Testament, Timotheus should let them exercise upon his character, his ways of thought and action, the power which properly belongs to them.

And he will find it a power of wonderful efficacy in the time of trial. For it is nothing less than this—that they are able to make him wise unto salvation. They will give him that clearness of insight, that justness of thought, which will keep him in the way that leadeth unto life. St. Chrysostom brings out, with characteristic directness and simplicity, the true force of the words τὰ δυνάμενά σε σοφίσαι εἰς σωτηρίαν. "He who knows the Scriptures as a man ought to know them is offended at nothing that befalls him, but bears all things with a noble endurance." For from the Scriptures he gets "the true canons and standards of judgment." " And what are these ? They are that virtue is good, that vice is evil ; that sickness, poverty, persecution, and the like are things indifferent; that the righteous pass through much tribulation in this world; that the works of God are past finding out; and that no words can tell the difference between His ways and ours." Yes, this is the great power which St. Paul claims for the Old Testament—that it will accustom men to the right way of looking at things, and make them see the meaning of their own life more nearly as God sees it; that it will give them more of that strong and pure and quiet wisdom which poor and simple people often have, and with which they go on, quite clear and unperplexed, amidst all the problems and sophistries which entangle many who are more clever and less spiritual. The shrewdness of the unworldly, the penetrating, steady insight of those whose eye is single, who have done with selfish, secret aims,—this is what men may gain from the Holy Scriptures which Timotheus knew. They may be made wise to understand what the will of the Lord is ; they may take the measure of all earthly things so truly and surely, with so just an estimate, that they may indeed recognize the Crucified as the fulfilment of the world's true hope, and glory in His Cross ; that they may

see how sacrifice both was and is the one true way
of victory in this world, and that there is no strength
like that which hides itself in patience and humility ;
that Christ ought to have suffered these things, and
so to enter into His glory ; that, in the Eternal
Wisdom and by the law of His own perfection, it
became Almighty God, in bringing many sons unto
glory, to make the captain of their salvation perfect
through sufferings.[1]—"Wise unto salvation." They
who are such will trace the ways of God with that
clear insight which only trust and love can gain ;
they will not be offended in their Lord, nor think
it strange concerning the fiery trial that tries His
servants ; they will be ready, when and as He wills,
to bear about in the body the dying of the Lord
Jesus, that the life also of Jesus may be made manifest
in their bodies. " Wise unto salvation." I suppose
there could be no better test or sign of the possession
of that wisdom than this—that a man should really
own, with inner and complete conviction, that the
life of the Beatitudes is indeed the blessed life for
men ; that in that way men may know more of the
very blessedness of God Himself than can be known
in any other way on earth ; and that the poor in
spirit, and they that mourn ; the meek, and they that

---

[1] Cf. B. F. Westcott, "Christus Consummator," pp. 24–27.

hunger and thirst after righteousness; the merciful, the pure in heart, the peacemakers, the persecuted and reviled, are really those whose lives are already in God's sight radiant with the light of heaven, with the glory that shall hereafter be revealed in them.

Brethren, if we might for a moment hold in abeyance the import of the truth that St. Paul was writing under the guidance of the Holy Spirit, would not his words have power still to claim our deference? For he certainly had this wisdom of which he speaks. His whole life, every letter that we read of his, the power he has had, and all the outcome of his work, evince it; it is as clear as any trait which we may know in the character of our nearest friend. And St. Paul certainly knew the Scriptures; he had known them all through his early life; he had carried them with him through the great change of his conversion; he had learnt to read them afresh in the new light that then came to him; he had tried them through years and years of work and joy and suffering in the Church of Christ. Hardly any one could have better credentials than St. Paul for speaking about the power of the Old Testament in the discipline of character, or about the imitation of Christ: and he is speaking here under conditions which would ensure the severest accuracy, the simplest saying what he knows and means. Surely, then, when he tells us that these Scriptures are able to make us wise unto salvation; that they will show us, frail and dim of sight as we may be, both how to live and how to die; even if we were to consider his words only in this narrow and inadequate way, without thinking of their highest sanction, they would in common sense demand for the study of the Old Testament more thought, and hope, and prayer, and love than nine-tenths of us, I fear—than any of us, it may be—have ever given to it.

(*b*) We have tried to see the power which St. Paul assigns to the Old Testament in the formation and maintenance of character; the help which it can yield towards the inner strength of steadfastness and per- severance. But let us mark the condition which he attaches to our finding this help; the means by which alone we can recognize and release, as it were, this power. It can come to us and we can know it only "through faith which is in Christ Jesus:" διὰ πίστεως τῆς ἐν Χριστῷ Ἰησοῦ. "His words"—as Hooker has said—"His words concerning the books of ancient Scripture do not take place but with presupposal of the Gospel of Christ embraced." [1]

The true efficacy of the Old Testament, the Divine

---

[1] "Laws of Ecclesiastical Polity," I. xiv. 4.

energy with which it can penetrate, inform, control the heart of man, can be rightly known only where that faith is, only in proportion as that faith is true and living. It is from his state of union with Christ, and by the light that Christ is to him, that Timotheus must discern, receive, detain, the hidden wisdom that is stored in the Holy Scriptures. By union with Christ he has attained the point from which their various elements are seen in their true relation and significance, each bearing its divinely intended part in the glory, the witness, of the whole. Only in so far as it is not he that lives, but Christ that liveth in him, is he in perfect sympathy, in vital continuity, as it were, with the gradually disclosed but ever dominant principle of the Old Testament; it is one and the same great central truth of the world's history which gives unity to those ancient Scriptures and to his own inner life. And surely here we touch one of the chief reasons which may be felt to underlie the demand for faith in Christ, for union with Him, as the essential secret of access to the depths of changeless meaning, and the springs of strength and light that are in the Old Testament. Archbishop Trench has said, " It is the necessary condition of a book which shall exert any great and effectual influence, which shall stamp itself with a deep impression upon the minds and hearts of men, that it must have a unity of purpose; one great idea must run through it all. There must be some single point in which all its different rays converge and meet." [1] We should all own, I think, that that is true. We can see how it holds good in every field of art. There is no fault that is more readily felt than the lack of such a unity of purpose—felt even by those who may not know the ground of their disappointment, of their sense that there is a failure somewhere, and that they cannot pass through the work into the artist's mind. For it follows, of course, that it is only when we have rightly and distinctly seen what that ruling thought or purpose is, that we can hope to enter into the work, to understand it and to do justice to it; to know the meaning, and to judge of the fitness of its several parts. In general literature it is, I suppose, the characteristic distinction of the true critic that he thus goes straight to the single, central, sovereign idea of a great work, and thence surveys and studies all the tributary details; while another is engrossed, as usefully and happily, it may be, but with obvious risks of disproportion and mis-understanding, in the examination of those details—often on that side of them which is, as it were, turned

[1] "Hulsean Lectures," p. 20.

away from and irrelevant to the central, animating thought. The one is caught up into glad, controlling fellowship with the poet's mind, and sees, though it be but in a glass, darkly, what he saw; the other fastens on the irregularities of construction, or is distressed at the roughness of a verse.—Yes, to know what any work means, to release its inner strength and beauty, to bring ourselves under its influence, we must have grasped the thought that gives it unity.

Ah! but let that thought be not an artist's vision or a speculation in philosophy, but the thought which transfigures life, and turneth the shadow of death into the morning; not the passing fancy or the delicate conception which holds our interest for a few hours, but the thought which meets the lifelong need and hunger of every heart that knows itself; not a thought which merely speaks, however well, of comfort and encouragement, but the thought which is itself the very strength and hope we crave; not a thought of any sinful man like ourselves, but the thought of God Himself, instinct and quick with His own life, and radiant with His everlasting love;—and then, surely, we need something more than any external recognition, any apprehension of it by the intellect alone. We can know that thought only by living in its power; only by committing ourselves to its guidance; only by taking it, with the venture of faith, to be the light of our life. The unity of the Old Testament lies in the gradual disclosure of a certain life for men; and its meaning, its wisdom, its Divineness, can be clear to us only if that life is ours. By faith in Christ, by union with Him, men take their stand, as it were, where that life breaks out and triumphs over death; and as its power renews them, as its brightness streams around them, they look back and see the line of light all through the past growing towards the perfect day. That Divine, eternal thought of love, revealed in all its infinite beauty of compassion when the Word was made flesh, invades and occupies their being; and as they yield themselves to its control, they know what was the reality of hope, the principle of discipline, the central purpose of God's dealings with His people all through those ages of expectation and foreshadowing. The central thought of the Bible is the central power of their life; and round that central thought all the mysteries of the past disclose their hidden wealth of meaning, to make them "wise unto salvation," "perfect, throughly furnished unto all good works."

III. "Through faith which is in Christ Jesus." St. Paul speaks of this as the condition of our knowing

the real power of the Old Testament. We may
learn from him, surely, a great lesson in regard to
an anxiety felt by many in the present day. The
criticism of the Old Testament, the challenge of its
authority, the various questions round about it, are
stirring thoughts of trouble and uneasiness in many
minds.[1] It seems not unlikely that some such wave
as that which we have lately seen receding, thank
God, from its impetuous onset on the books of the
New Testament, may be advancing upon those of the
Old. The disquieting influence of such a movement
is always wide; and it is perhaps most felt by some
who have least considered the real points at issue.
And under this influence men are often in a hurry
to draw lines of limitation; to establish what seems
a scientific frontier; to determine that certain con-
cessions must be made, or certain reserves maintained
against all infringement. But it is always hard and
perilous work to draw such lines; for harm has often
come of their being drawn in the wrong place, too
far either one way or the other. And, surely, there
is a better course by which each one of us may
strengthen his position in regard to the Old Testa-

[1] The writer desires to say that this sermon was preached before
the beginning of the discussion concerning " Lux Mundi," and indeed
before the publication of the book. He has thought it simplest to
leave the words exactly as they stood.

ment; and that is by using every means to make
more real and sure his union with Christ. It is hard
for us to do justice to that which St. Paul meant by
"faith which is in Christ Jesus;" the word "faith"
has been dragged through so many controversies, and
thrust so often into false antitheses. But we can see
that he meant not less than this—the surrender of
one's life to Christ, to be conformed to His example,
guided by the daily disclosure of His will, informed
and strengthened by His grace; the conviction that
for His sake, and by the power of His perfect sacrifice, we can be set free from the sins that hinder and
defile us, and know the miracle of God's forgiveness;
the growing certainty that He Himself, our Blessed
Lord, vouchsafes to come and dwell within us, by
the operation of the Holy Ghost, giving us His own
life, and making us strong to be true, and humble,
and patient, and unselfish; strict with ourselves, as
knowing how much need we have of strictness;
gentle, and making large allowances for others, as
never knowing how sorely they are tried;—enabling
us, in spite of all that is past, to follow the blessed
steps of His most holy life. So may we live by faith,
in living union with Him, seeking continually through
deeper penitence, through the nearer knowledge of
His life, through the less unworthy welcome of His

Eucharistic Presence, to open out our hearts more freely to His love, to enthrone Him in steadier supremacy over all our ways. For thus it may be we shall gain the surest hold upon those words which heralded His coming into the world; a hold which will be firm through all that seems obscure and hard as yet to understand or set in order; a hold which will ensure our seeing things rightly, and being able, if it please God, to help others when the perplexity and unsettlement has abated. There may be new aspects of the truth that press for recognition; there may be need for some restatement of that which cannot change or fail. New thoughts which are strange to us now may prove, indeed, the clues to secrets we have never read. And we may be able to wait, please God, with the frankness and the patience of true insight, if all along we feel, in the certainty of personal experience, that the Holy Scriptures are making us, through God's grace, wiser than we were; and if in them we are learning to discern the forecast glory of the life by which we live—of the example which, as we know more of it, only the more surpasses all our praise and adoration ; of the hope which fills us with thanksgiving to Almighty God, Who, in His love, created us for such an end.

XII.

THE POWER OF AN ENDLESS LIFE.

" Christ being raised from the dead dieth no more."
Rom. vi. 9.

EVEN this present life is full of the rhythm of the
Resurrection; it is ever ready to remind us of the
news of Easter. Time after time, if we will have it
so, as we look at the visible world, as we gain or
recall the lessons of experience, we see some rendering,
as it were, of the glory of this Queen of Feasts, some
parable of the empty tomb and the stone rolled back
and the triumph over death. When the day breaks
and the shadows flee away, and all life stirs and
wakes again; when the long tyranny of winter yields,
and the flowers appear upon the earth, and the time
of the singing of birds is come; when some great
sorrow, or anxiety, or mood of sadness passes from
our hearts, and we rediscover the reality of joy;
when some chastening dimness of faith, it may be,
is taken away, and the light and love of God seem

clearer, dearer, closer to us than ever; when the long days of sickness are forgotten in the new gladness of returning health ;—in all that manifold experience of heaviness enduring for a night and joy coming in the morning, the sequence of Holy Week and Easter is enacted, and the note that sounds out loud on this most blessed day is touched again. All life around us and within displays at times some likeness of a rising from the dead.

But as we think of all these types and parables of the Resurrection, we see one abrupt, decisive failure in them all ; at one point they all halt, unable further to follow the triumph we commemorate on Easter Day. For in all the brightness is but for a while; the voice of joy and health must fail again, we know, in a few years at the most; we cannot stay upon the height of happiness, or bind the light to linger with us; the leaves that to-day are just revealing that ever fresh surprise of beauty which will soon be the glory of the spring must presently be shivering on the trees or scudding along the roads in the November gale; the clouds return after the rain; the morning cometh, and also the night. As nature would prophesy of the Resurrection, and show forth in outward signs what Easter means, her voice, her power, falters ; she can but prophesy in part, for she has no form or type

in all her wealth that will serve to tell of Him Who
"being raised from the dead dieth no more." Winter
and night and death may come more slowly at one
time than at another ; there may be a trace of summer
in the air when St. Luke's Day comes ; there may be
a flush of after-glow when the sun has set; death
may seem near to us, and then, perhaps, draw back
and wait awhile ;—but the summer and the light and
life itself have all their inexorable law. One alone
there is Whose day has no twilight and no night,
Whose glory never fades, and over Whom death hath
no more dominion; since "Christ being raised from
the dead dieth no more."

Yes, here is the unique, distinctive splendour of our
Saviour's triumph ; here He leaves behind Him every
earthly semblance of His Resurrection. "He dieth no
more." To-day the Crucified declares to us, "I am
He that liveth; and I became dead: and, behold, I
am alive for evermore." Of Himself, by the free will
of His great love, He laid down His life for us ; and
now He has taken it again for ever and ever. There
must come the few days of pause before the Ascension ; thenceforth as King and Priest, unchanging and
eternal, He ever reigns and pleads for us, in the
power of an endless life, an "endless morn of light."
His human nature is lifted into the glory which He

o

had with the Father before the world was; perfect
Man, and touched, indeed, with the feeling of our
infirmity, He lives for evermore, above the mist and
clouds of our dying life, above the thought of death
or failure; since by His death He hath destroyed
death, and by His rising to life again hath restored
to us everlasting life.   To-day He met an unconquer-
able hope that was in the hearts of men; He fulfilled
a deep instinct which was astir far and wide.   It has
been truly said that "by a thousand voices and in a
thousand ways the world had been declaring that
it was not made for death—for that dread and alien
thing which, notwithstanding, it found in the midst of
it." [1]   And Christ our Lord caught up that world-wide
hope and made it good; when, as on this day, through
the grave and gate of death He issued forth, not into
any bounded space of time, any longer term of passing
years, but into the ample air of eternity itself—"God
from everlasting, Man for evermore."   The encircling
walls of death were broken through, and humanity
had won a vantage-ground beyond its grasp; since
"Christ being raised from the dead dieth no more."
Life now, not death, is written at the end of human
history.

    But is that all?   Must we wait till the end to find

---

[1] R. C. Trench, "Hulsean Lectures," p. 188.

the difference His victory has made? Nature seems
to have no type, no emblem, of that perfect triumph
over death and darkness; her resurrections are but
for a while; the risen dies again. Is He, then, alone
and distant in His great deliverance? Is He as one
who has crept out by night from a beleaguered city,
and got away in safety, leaving his comrades as they
were, unhelped by his escape; guarded, perhaps, all
the more closely since he broke out and got away?
Are all the gains of earth as insecure as ever? Is
there no rising here save only to fall back again; no
spring that is not transient? Must we wait until
we leave this world to see or know the power of an
endless life?

No, brethren, we can both see and know it here.
It is not far from every one of us. Death can no
longer claim to rule this world; for there are whole
tracts of life which he cannot touch; and there is that
in each which " dieth no more," which has escaped
the great doom of transience.

There is, first of all, the Church of the living God—
the Body of Christ. He Himself is pledged that it
shall not die or fail out of the earth; and through all
that could test the strength and disclose the weakness
of any society of men it has endured and increased.
I suppose there is no solvent or destructive force

which has not at some time tried its power on the
Church of Christ; persecution, scorn, hatred, mis-
representation; favour, ease, power, opulence; soft-
ness, ambition, worldliness, and profligacy, among
laity and clergy alike; infidelity without, and at
times, alas! within as well. It has felt all the subtlety
and violence of evil; and time after time men have
thought and said—at least as confidently as some
may say now—that the Church and the religion of
the Church are coming to an end. And time after
time they have been wrong—absolutely, obviously
wrong. For the inner life of the Church, whether
men assail it from without or betray it from within,
is indeed the endless life of Christ made manifest on
earth; it goes untouched through all the unfaithful-
ness and all the opposition; it abides for the steadfast
light and help of all pure, loving souls; and when the
tyranny or treachery is overpast, it widens out in
ever larger ventures for the glory of God. And in
an age of incalculable changes, when all around seems
shifting and uncertain, it is something to know that
there is one cause which will not betray whatever
faith and love a man may give to it; that whatever
else breaks up and disappears, there is one Body upon
earth which dieth no more. ·

The power of Christ's endless life is here among

us in His Church; it is here among us also in His truth—that truth which, according to St. Paul's great metaphor, the Church upholds among men as a pillar, and sustains as a foundation.[1] "Heaven and earth," our Saviour said, "shall pass away; but My words shall not pass away;" and His Apostle claims for His revelation of God just this very exemption from the law of transience. "For all flesh is as grass, and all the glory of man as the flower of grass. The grass withereth, and the flower thereof falleth away: but the Word of the Lord endureth for ever."[2] And so too the Psalmist shows the one source and assurance of steadfastness in heaven and in earth; the one undying life: "O Lord, Thy Word endureth for ever in heaven; Thy truth also remaineth from one generation to another." From one generation to another; across all the unimaginable changes of the eighteen centuries; through differences of thought, and life, and fashion, and social order so vast that it seems impossible for us to give reality to the pictures of those distant days; through evil report and good report, "both hated and believed," the truth that Jesus of Nazareth stored with His disciples lives still with His own risen life. The huge shiftings of the tide of human thought may modify an indifferent expression

[1] 1 Tim. iii. 15.   [2] 1 St. Pet. i. 24, 25.

here and there, or may prove that the revelation has been stretched to cover ground for which it was not meant; but the truth of God made known in Jesus Christ our Lord, very Man and very God, crucified for us, risen from the dead, ascended into heaven;—this is still, after all the ages of keen and persistent criticism, this is still the steadiest light that gladdens weary eyes and hearts; for this too has its strength of life hidden with God, and therefore dieth no more.

And lastly, in the Christian character, in the character which is formed by Christ's example and sustained by His sacraments, there is that which is not transient—which being raised from the death of sin dieth no more. "The world," says St. John, " is passing away, and the lust thereof : but he that doeth the will of God abideth for ever."—Not that there is any stability at all in us. We are frail, indeed, and faltering, and forgetful, and soon tired; we know ourselves to be capable of the worst; we are always disappointing our Lord, and even ourselves; we resolve and fail, and renew our resolution and fail again; and for all the wealth and might of grace our life is a poor and inconsistent thing. Yet never let us dare to think—no, not when we are weariest of ourselves and of our failures—that this sequence of recovery and relapse, this oscillation to and fro, is the best that we can do, or what God looks for from us, or true to the proper characteristics of the life of grace. No; it is a risen life into which we were welcomed in our Baptism; it is the risen Lord Who comes to us in the Holy Eucharist. However the effects and manifestation of His life may be hindered and obscured by our cowardice and feebleness and sin, in itself it has no limit to its energy, it knows no doom of transience; it has the power of an endless life; it moves not to and fro, between success and failure, but right on from strength to strength, from glory to glory.

So, then, let us try this Eastertide, with freshness of hope, simply to clear away, God helping us, whatever checks the free expansion of the risen life within us; whatever breaks and spoils the work of grace. We have failed, it may be, a thousand times in the years that are past; we have drifted to and fro, and hardly know whether we are any nearer the haven than we were. But it need not be so now; that is not what Christ died and rose again to win for us. We shall not be faultless in the future; but we may do better than we have done, and then better, and better still. Only let us be definite, and let us be humble; let us look right away from ourselves, right up to Him; chastened and sobered by the past, but not degraded

or despondent; dead indeed unto sin, turning our
backs upon it, and resolute never to look round to it
with one hankering glance; but alive unto God—alive
with His own life of love, Who "being raised from the
dead dieth no more;" that

> "So the procession of our life may be
> More equable, and strong, and pure, and free. . . .
> For who indeed shall his high flights sustain,
> Who soar aloft and sink not?   He alone
> Who has laid hold upon that golden chain
> Of love, fast linked to God's eternal throne—
> The golden chain from heaven to earth let down,
> That we might rise by it, nor fear to sink again." [1]

---

[1] R. C. Trench, "Poems," pp. 81, 82 (ed. 1874).   The lines are
slightly altered from their original form.

XIII.

A NEW HEART.

"But Peter and John answered and said unto them, Whether it be right in the sight of God to hearken unto you more than unto God, judge ye. For we cannot but speak the things which we have seen and heard."

ACTS iv. 19, 20.

ON the first Sunday after Easter, with all the thoughts of that surpassing day fresh in our minds we may do well to bring home to ourselves the meaning of those thoughts in the sphere of character; to try to realize some part of that which our Lord's triumph has added to the possibilities of moral change; to think over that intensely real and practical force in human life of which St. Paul speaks as "the power of Christ's Resurrection." We are anxious, all of us, I trust, to grow purer, simpler, stronger, than we are; we feel our own weakness; we cannot forget our frequent and shameful disappointments with ourselves. What should the great truth of Easter do to reinforce the hope which those disappointments may have threatened to impair? How should the Resurrection of Jesus Christ increase in us that strength of expectancy[1] which has, we know, so great a value in our moral and spiritual life? Why does it bid us steadily to aim high?

I. Let us seek a part of the answer to these questions by marking the change which was actually wrought in one to whom our Lord deigned specially to show Himself after He was risen. Let us set in contrast two scenes of St. Peter's life—the one before, the other after, the first Easter Day. And let us measure, in the vast change which had passed over his character, something of the power of Christ's Resurrection and of its fruits to make men other than they have been.

(*a*) And first let us look at the later of the two scenes—that in which St. Peter, with St. John, as they stand before the chief council of the Jews, speaks out to them in the words of the text. And let us try to enter into the character which those words express; the inner life and temper out of which they come.

That short, decisive speech has been called "the watchword of martyrs."[2] There is a ring of strength

---

[1] Cf. Phillips Brooks, "Twenty Sermons," p. 355.
[2] Cf. "The Dictionary of the Bible," vol. ii. p. 802.

and frankness in it which at once attracts us. A great choice is faced, and a distinct resolution made; there is no mistaking what these men mean; and they will not easily be moved from it. In such decisions, when they are rightly formed and loyally held, we feel a dignity and freedom which we should like to make our own; a certain high independence which may be quite consistent with true humility; a clear-sightedness and self-possession which will probably keep a man straight through the big and through the little acts of choice in which character is formed and tried and brought to light.

Thus, I think, the words at once attract us. Men may, indeed, so speak in wilfulness, or blindness, or misunderstanding; and even then there is often something that we cannot help liking in their outspoken courage, their lack of any selfish caution : but when the determination is made with all humility and reverence and thoughtfulness; when the cause is one for which a man ought to make a stand and take the risk of it; then we feel that human nature is mounting, by the grace of God, about as high as it can get in this world.

And, in this case of St. Peter and St. John, there is much to deepen and confirm the first impression which their decision makes on us. Let us try simply

to get the scene before our minds.   The two Apostles
are standing by themselves as prisoners before the
chief council of the Jews.   In front of them, and
on either side of them, in a semicircle, are the
members of the council—about seventy in number—
the most powerful, the most learned, the most famous
men among their nation; men about whom they must
have heard people talking ever since they were boys
in their Galilæan home.   Presiding over the council
are Annas and Caiaphas, two hard and cruel men,
who will have their own way, whatever it may cost.
And here is this whole body, with all its power, and
authority, and cleverness, and strength of will, set
against these two fishermen, St. Peter and St. John;
men without any especial learning or ability, with no
influence, no friends to back them up.—The occasion
of their arrest is this: there has been a great excitement in Jerusalem about their healing a lame man;
every one has heard of it, is talking of it.   There is
no doubt these two men did the miracle; and they
say plainly that it was done by the Name, the power,
of Jesus of Nazareth.   Now, the council hate the
Name of Jesus of Nazareth.   When He was on earth
He would make no terms with their hypocrisy; they
set themselves resolutely against Him, and He in
nothing gave way to them, He showed no fear of

them; and so they "sought how they might kill Him:" they covenanted for His betrayal: they "were instant with loud voices, requiring that He might be crucified," until "Pilate gave sentence that it should be as they required."—And here His Name is coming up again; men say that He is risen; that His presence, His power, is with His followers. The last error is going to be worse than the first; and the council are determined to put it down. They cannot deny the miracle; but, anyhow, they will stop the movement; they will just suppress and silence these two men who are giving them so much trouble; they will simply command them not to speak to anybody at all in the Name of Jesus. There will be no way out of that. And so the commandment is given with a sharp threat to enforce it—with all that power, anger, cruelty, and determination can do to drive it home to these men's hearts, and make them careful to obey it. And the men meet it at once with a very simple answer: "Whether it be right in the sight of God to hearken unto you more than unto God, judge ye. For we cannot but speak the things which we have seen and heard."—"In the sight of God." It is just that which makes the difference; there is an authority higher than that of this great and learned council. The Apostles have made up their minds to

live, as General Gordon used to say, "for God's view
and not for man's;"[1] and they have no doubt what
He would have them do, and no thought of doing
anything else.

(*b*) It is a fine answer; it brings out "the heroism
of faith;" the strength of those who can "endure as
seeing Him Who is invisible." And now let us fasten
our thoughts upon the one of the two men who
answer thus—upon St. Peter;—and let us think how
strange it is to listen to such words as these from his
lips, and then to look back to another scene—to the
last time, so far as we know, that he may have heard
the voice of Annas or Caiaphas. When was that?
So far as the Gospels tell us, it was on the night
before the Crucifixion—that night in which he
thrice denied that he had anything to do with Christ.
What a wonderful contrast it is! Did ever one man
bear himself so differently, and seem so altered in
so short a time—in a few months? Then a maid-
servant's question had frightened him; now the most
peremptory orders of the whole council cannot stir
in him any hesitation or alarm. Then he could not
face the mere thought of having to stand with Christ
in His trial; now he is quite ready to go to death
simply for the Name, the work, of Christ. Then he

[1] C. G. Gordon's Letters to his Sister, p. 30.

broke a solemn promise in his terror; he needs no promise now to keep him steadfast. Then he hurried from one falsehood to another in his eagerness to get off somehow; now he looks straight out, and answers without a quiver of uncertainty, as though it could never cross his mind to say anything but the bare, clear truth, as though there really were no alternative at all to be considered.—Surely it is a most striking and splendid change that has come about in him; and if by chance there was any one there who remembered what had happened in that earlier night, the night of his Master's trial, any one who could recall his shifty, timorous denials, they must have wondered whether it really could be the same man— then so feeble and confused, now so clear and resolute.

II. Can we see at all how the change had come about? In part, I think, we can. We do know of certain events in St. Peter's life during those months which seem to explain why he was so altered. And as they are events which may more or less enter into the experience of every man, and which, whenever they come, are the secret of real strength, I will ask you to look at them for a few minutes, and to try to bear them in mind. They are four in number; they may lead us some way into the meaning of the power of Christ's Resurrection.

First, then, St. Peter had heartily repented of his sins. With bitter tears he had owned how shamefully he had fallen; he had faced his wrong-doing, and hated it, and thrown himself on the pity and the love of God; he had offered up to God the sacrifice of a broken and a contrite heart. He had not hidden or slurred over his misery; he had not made excuses for himself, or tried to get off easily; or said to himself that, after all, the other Apostles, too, forsook Christ and fled; or that Christ would have been crucified anyhow; or that, at least, he had not been as bad as Judas. No; St. Peter had not tried to make himself easy about his sin, or to forget it, or to forget God; he had gone out and wept bitterly.

And then, secondly, St. Peter, as we are reminded to-day, had seen the risen Lord. On the very day of His Resurrection, in the abundance of His love, in the swiftness of His compassion, our Lord had appeared to him. When the two disciples came back from Emmaus late on Easter Day, they found the eleven talking about it, and saying, "The Lord is risen indeed, and hath appeared to Simon." We have no fuller record of that scene; only St. Paul once glances back to it. But we must be sure that two great things were wrought in St. Peter by his Lord's coming to him: that in his penitence he received

forgiveness for all that was past; and that he was
made certain of his Saviour's everlasting love and
care for him—certain of the unseen world, the resurrection of the dead, the power, the watchfulness, the
pleading, of his risen Master and Redeemer. St.
Peter cannot "forget that he has been purged from
his old sins;." and that there is One on high Who
knows him perfectly, and to Whom he can commit
the keeping of his soul.

And, thirdly, St. Peter had been pointed to the
work he had to do; the task that was marked with
his name. His risen Lord had set him his work
in life; and nothing now could matter to him in
comparison with doing it. By the Sea of Tiberias
Christ had charged him, with a threefold bidding, to
feed and tend His flock. Though he had so failed
and disappointed his Master in the past, still he was
not dismissed from His service or degraded in His
ministry. In the Divine long-suffering and gentleness
there was a high and blessed task reserved for him;
and life was worth living, or might thankfully be
laid down, for that task's sake. Life was not dear
to him, any more than to St. Paul, in comparison
with finishing his course with joy, and the ministry
which he had received of the Lord Jesus.

And then, fourthly, St. Peter had received that

P

unspeakable gift for which all this had been the preparation—the shaping and tempering of the vessel to enshrine the treasure. At Pentecost the Holy Ghost had come, the Spirit of counsel and of ghostly strength, to enter in and dwell with him—the Spirit of truth, to make him free indeed; to fill his heart and mind; to abide "by the springs of thought and desire and action;" to teach him what really is and what is not worth caring and contending for; to show the things of this life in the light of that which is to come; to fasten deep into his being the steady conviction that there is nothing in the world so great and high as goodness.

III. Thus had St. Peter's inner life, and all his thoughts about himself and about this world, been changed since the night when he denied Christ; and it is not strange that there should have come with such a change an entire transformation of his outward bearing. He had learnt and used the grace of penitence; he had found the gift of pardon ; he had seen the risen, the ever-living Lord ; from Him he had received his task for life; and then the Spirit of God had come to dwell in him. It was but a fragment in the outcome of all this, that he who had been scared into falsehood by a woman's words should now stand up untroubled, to face, for Christ's sake, the worst that

the great council of the Jews could do to him. He
had something else to think of, care for, live and die
for, now—the joy of the forgiven; the work of Christ;
the peace of God; the dawn and growth and ever-
growing hope of that life which is nothing else than
love. This held his heart beyond the reach of threats;
this may have made it seem to him almost absurd
that the rulers should think that anything which
they could do could come between him and his Lord,
could hinder him from speaking in the Name of
Jesus. Ah! but, where it all comes home to us is in
this—that there is no reason why that which made
him strong and fearless should not make us strong
and fearless too. How many men who make a
figure in the world are a long way off being so
strong and so courageous as they look! And often,
surely, it is some secret sin, unrepented of, indulged,
extenuated, and unpardoned, that is the reason of
their inner weakness, sapping, undermining all their
vigour; some unworthy aim, some hidden unreality,
some moral taint, that is preparing the shameful
failure, the pitiful outburst of selfishness in the time
of trial. Let us, first of all, get our hearts clear with
God, by the pardoning grace of Christ our Lord; let
us fill our minds with this truth, that He, our risen
and ascended Saviour, is ever watching us and

pleading for us; let us be sure that, whatever place we hold, He has a bit of work for us to do, by the example, at all events, of a pure and dutiful and humble life; let us open out our hearts to the power and the guidance of the indwelling Spirit, (remembering again how Gordon said that it is the truth of His indwelling that makes Christianity what it is); and then we shall be gaining quite certainly more and more of that true, deep strength which is among our greatest needs in this world, and of which no man certainly can have too much; we shall be learning the secret of decision and of fearlessness in great things and in small. And so we, in our measure, may realize that new power whereby hearts are changed and characters ennobled; that power whereby many out of weakness have been made strong—even the unending power of our Saviour's Resurrection.

XIV.

THE CONTRASTS OF THIS WORLD.

"Son, remember that thou in thy lifetime receivedst thy
good things, and likewise Lazarus evil things: but now he is
comforted, and thou art tormented."

ST. LUKE xvi. 25.

THERE is something very terrible and disquieting in
the bareness and unexplained brevity of these words.
Simply and abruptly they tell of a vast and twofold
contrast, and then they leave it for us to think over;
they throw on us the responsibility of finding out
all that the contrast means. They are spoken in
that hidden world where the souls of men wait
for the day of judgment; where they receive already
some forecast of the lot which in this life they have
chosen for themselves. Already the hard and stubborn
and relentless selfishness of the rich man is passing
on to its inevitable issue. To the end and in the end
he has cast love away from him; he has destroyed
his own capacity for it; and now the mysterious

terror of everlasting lovelessness is seizing on his heart, and across the great fixed gulf he cries for help. And out of the light and peace that he has ever spurned there comes a voice which throws him back upon the witness of memory. Memory will be heard now; there is nothing now to confuse or drown her voice; he must remember the contrast which in this world was thrust upon him day after day, and ever thrust aside—the contrast between his life on earth and that of the beggar whom he sees far off in the rest of Paradise. "Son, remember that thou in thy lifetime receivedst thy good things, and likewise Lazarus evil things: but now he is comforted, and thou art tormented." It seems to be implied that as he recalls that earlier contrast he will know that the later is by no arbitrary verdict, no merely external law; he will see where he began to be what now he is; how he formed and hardened the character which is now his scourge and torment; how all light and love and life died utterly out of his selfish, pitiless heart.

It is a terrible thought that is thus urged upon us on this First Sunday after Trinity.[1] Perhaps it is meant to teach us, with merciful sternness, to keep

---

[1] On which Sunday this sermon was preached in the Cathedral Church of Christ, in Oxford, at a College Service.

fast hold of that wondrous manifestation, that supreme
and all-transforming gift of love of which we have
been thinking, through the course of the Christian
year up to the height of Whitsuntide. By the fearful
picture of a loveless soul God would teach us something of the greatness of the work of His grace, of
the blessing of His Holy Spirit's presence. Fear may
keep us within the range of love ; that selfishness may
not cast out love, but love in the end may cast out
fear. So let us think of this great contrast, while we
have time to learn whatever lessons it has to teach ;
time to let it tell, as God would have it tell, upon our
lives and characters.

I. (a) "Thou in thy lifetime receivedst thy good
things, and likewise Lazarus evil things." In its
simplest form the abruptness of the contrast comes
before us every day. We can hardly walk out of
Oxford without seeing in its poorer streets, and
down alleys poorer still, the manifold tokens of the
wretchedness in which Lazarus and his like drag out
their comfortless days. Very likely we have grumbled
at the dreariness and uncomeliness of the bit of the
town through which we hurry to the river, or the
hills ; but we have not realized, and perhaps we
have hardly tried to think, what it would be to
spend day after day and year after year, ill·fed and

ill clothed, in the gloom and noise and dirt of an overcrowded house down one of those side courts. To toil on and on at the same monotonous work, with no expectation of any change or brightening of one's lot; to wake morning after morning to the same dragging anxieties, the same hungry needs, the same inevitable vexations; never to have a holiday, never to gain a step, never to know anything like a real intensity of pleasure;—what a tremendous gap there is between such a lot and that which has been given to all of us! Doubtless social science can account for the inequality, and trace its laws; but that does not change the moral significance, the impressiveness, the pathos, of the facts—any more than the lightning loses its grandeur and terror because we were told that the storm was coming across the Atlantic. Doubtless, again, the poor have, by God's grace, most wondrous and beautiful alleviations of their lot; and there are many men who, by idleness, or vanity, or ill-temper, or hypochondria, make themselves far more wretched in their abundance than Lazarus ever was in his want. But still, for all that, there the contrast is; we know that nothing really strips it of its meaning, or warrants our ignoring it: and probably it is by the conditions of our birth that we are on one side rather than the other; it is by no atom of merit on our part that we in our lifetime are receiving our good things, and likewise Lazarus evil things.

(*b*) But the contrast on which the text fastens our thoughts goes far deeper than the outward conditions of the bodily life. It is hard for us, with every opportunity of intellectual development lavished upon us, to think enough of the real suffering that is sometimes borne by those who are cut off from all such opportunities. We can hardly imagine the wistful envy with which some of the poor wonder how we can so much neglect what they so hopelessly covet. Now and then a poor man struggles out through all his hindrances, and the artist, the poet, the naturalist, the mathematician, forces his way above the obscurity and poverty in which he was born, and finds the joy of using the great gift which God has given him. But more often the hope dies down under the grim, exacting demands of the poor man's life. "A first effect of poverty," it has been truly said, "is the confiscation of a man's best time and thought, from sheer necessity, to the task of providing food and clothing for himself and his family."[1] Slowly the vision of that which he knows he might be is darkened by the relentless drudgery for bare life ; the consciousness of power turns, perhaps,

[1] H. P. Liddon's "University Sermons," second series, p. 286.

to fruitless bitterness; the power itself grows weak
and dull; and a mind that, with one-tenth of our
opportunities, might have entered further and mounted
higher far than the best of us into all the glories of
literature or of art, a mind that might have found in
the intellectual life a joy we never dream of, and
enriched and gladdened all men with its work, settles
down into the dreariness of unused gifts, the cruel
restlessness of a misdirected life.   Yes, in the conditions of intellectual growth as well as in those of
bodily comfort we are bound to remember that we
in our lifetime are receiving our good things, and
likewise Lazarus evil things.

(*c*) Ah! but there is yet another sphere of contrast
in comparison with which the opportunity or impossibility of mental culture is a very little thing.
Happily, it is not a sphere in which the same
characters always remain on the same sides of the
contrast.   No; when we come to think of that which
really most of all makes life worth living—when we
come to think of the blessing of home love—we may
often find that Lazarus is richer far than Dives.
And yet there are especial risks besetting the growth
of love and gentleness in the crowded homes of the
very poor; it is not easy, it is sometimes terribly
difficult, for them to guard those delicate, ennobling,

purifying, hallowing influences to which we owe, perhaps, by God's mercy, whatever is best and most hopeful in our characters. But, at all events, whether we think of rich or poor, there is this tremendous and all-affecting contrast in men's lives—that some live in the abundance of love and friendship, while others hardly, it may be, know one face that grows brighter when they come, one voice that has a glad or a tender tone reserved for them, one heart that would feel desolate if they were taken away. Yes, these are the poor indeed, those are really rich beyond all words ; and this is the strangest inequality in all the unequal distribution of good and evil in this world. What have we ever done, that we should know that highest theme of thanksgiving—

> "Blessings of friends, which to our door
> Unask'd, unhoped, have come ;
> And choicer still, a countless store
> Of eager smiles at home "?[1]

Surely it is a chastening thought that here too, while we are thus enriched, there are others who, in their lonely or darkened lives, hardly find one touch of friendship or of love.

II. "Son, remember that thou in thy lifetime receivedst thy good things, and likewise Lazarus evil

---

[1] J. H. Newman, " Verses on Various Occasions," p. 42.

things." As we try to enter into the great, deep contrasts of the several conditions under which men pass through this world to that which is beyond, can we see at all what bearing this thought should have on our life? It bears, of course, the obvious lesson of humble and sincere thanksgiving for all that has been given us to enjoy; and it also plainly demands that we should be ever watchful and eager to do all we can to help and cheer in any possible way those who lack so much that gladdens our days. But it should have, I think, another and perhaps a wider influence on our minds and our hearts. Let me try to speak of it.—These astounding contrasts, these vast inequalities, after all that we can do or say to alleviate or to account for them, remain as a great and ultimate fact in human life. They have their place side by side with sorrow, with suffering, with death. They are among the solemn presences, as it were, before which we have to play our part. We may forget them, or ignore them, or explain them away, or disparage their importance, if we will; we have that fatal power of inattention; we can accustom ourselves to any strangeness of neglect, as the soldiers in the Crimea learnt to sleep beside the guns that were being fired. Dives used that power of inattention; he refused to think about facts which threatened to make an unwelcome demand on him ; and because he deliberately wished it, the facts receded, probably, from his mind in this world; but only to meet him again in the day of reckoning. For of every great fact in our life this is true: " Neglectum sui ulciscitur."—But, on the other hand, we may, God helping us, steadily and faithfully and humbly face these strange, inexplicable, silent witnesses of our life; we may now, " while we have time," remember; we may bear in mind these pathetic contrasts as characteristic features of the scene in which we have to do what good we can for a few years. And then quite surely they will tell upon our character, upon our estimate of life, our conception of its meaning, our use of the present, our purpose in the future. They will make it impossible for us to think of this world as a place laid out for our amusement or self-display ; they will help us, as we become men, to put away childish things ; they will, as tragedy of old was said to do, purify in us the passions of pity and of fear ; teaching us, at all events, not to be too ready to pity ourselves, and not to fear when fear is vile or cowardly.[1] They will show us the real vulgarity of a luxurious life ; they will defy us to go on living only for pleasure

[1] Cf. note [2] on p. 64.

when others are living—as it might almost seem—
only for pain; to go on loitering or trifling in a
world that is so grim and stern for others. We shall
grow more reverent, more humble, more anxious and
strenuous to do all we can of whatever work Almighty
God has given us to do ; and then, perhaps, He may
show us more to do, and, it may be, give us more to
suffer in this world. And so, since with Him all things
are possible, He may save us out of all the perils of
a life that lacks the unchosen discipline of want, the
severity of undisguised compulsion ; and hereafter
we may remember, with wonder and abasement, but,
by His mercy, without utter terror and confusion, that
in this life we had so many privileges, and so strange
a wealth of the opportunities for happiness.

XV.

HUMILITY AND ASPIRATION.[1]

"What is man, that Thou art mindful of him? and the son of man, that Thou visitest him?"

Ps. viii. 4.

To live, or even to stay for a week or two, in a remarkable place, ought not to be without some effect upon one's character, one's ways of thought and conduct. A man must be, for instance, grievously absorbed either in himself or in his work, to be wholly unchanged by his first visit to London or to Rome; to receive into his inner life, to work into his own views and habits, nothing out of all that is distinctively wonderful, or glorious, or pathetic in such cities—in their present aspect or their past history. The inmost depths of character, the efforts and struggles through which it is moving in one

[1] This sermon was preached at Oxford, in the Cathedral, at a service attended by many of the University Extension Students during their summer meeting.

direction or another, growing better or growing
worse, cannot, indeed, be determined or controlled
by any such external influence; a man who habitually
pleases himself will become continually more selfish
and sordid even among the most noble and beautiful conditions which nature, or history, or art can
furnish; and, on the other hand, any one who will
try each day to live for the sake of others, will grow
more and more gracious in thought and bearing,
however dull and even squalid may be the outward
circumstances of the soul's probation. So Tito Melema
sinks lower and lower amidst all the glory and the
delicacy of Florence at its height of beauty; and so
Thomas à Kempis rises ever nearer to the perfect life
in the monotony of his seventy years at one poor
monastery, amidst the hard features and the dull
plains of Holland. No outward conditions can touch
the divergence of such lives. But if we, by God's
grace, are willing, famous cities may do something
for us, just as music may; they may bring great
thoughts before us, and speak to us with a strong
appeal; they may bear into our hearts some faint,
indefinite suggestion of the greatness, the sincerity,
the generosity, the faith of those who made them
what they are; they may, perhaps, make us ashamed
of ourselves; they may leave with us a picture, a

translation, as it were, into a new language, of that inner quality, that moral excellence, which their outward beauty or dignity may seem to resemble, or even to express. So, then, let us try to think of a certain influence, perhaps the chief and the most helpful influence, which Oxford might exert on those who live in it, and on those who visit it with something deeper than a hurried curiosity.

I. It has been well said by a great writer that "in the course of his history man has by turns depreciated and exaggerated his true importance among the creatures of God. Sometimes he has made himself the measure of all things, as though his was the sovereign mind, and the Creator a being whose proceedings could be easily understood by him. Sometimes," on the other hand, "man has appeared to revel in self-depreciation, placing himself side by side with or below the beasts that perish, insisting on his animal kinship with them, and anxiously endeavouring to ignore or deny all that points to a higher element in his life."[1] We can trace, I think, these two contrasted tendencies of thought in the theories which have been formed about man's nature, and his place in the universe. But to most of us the same contrast may come home more vividly and

[1] H. P. Liddon, " Christmastide Sermons," p. 129.

Q

practically in two strangely diverse temptations to
think wrongly about ourselves and our work in life.
Surely we are apt to be very inconsistent in the view
we take of our place and purpose in the world; in
some ways vastly exaggerating our importance, and
in others failing of the reverence we owe to ourselves.
Sometimes a man seems to think of the whole world
as revolving round his life, and measures everything
with reference to his own wishes and opinions; and
sometimes he is content to drift along as though he
had no distinct power of choice and will—as though
he could only go where the current and the eddies
carry him.   Sometimes he seems unable to imagine
that the lives, the feelings, the convictions, of others
can possibly mean as much to them as his do to him;
and sometimes he hardly seems to have a conviction
in him, but yields to any pressure that is on him, and
calls himself the victim of circumstances.   Sometimes
he speaks as though his knowledge were certain and
his decisions infallible; sometimes as though he could
know nothing at all of that on which all knowledge
depends.   Sometimes he seems to himself remarkable,
exempt from the obvious defects he sees in others,
and incapable of their blunders and misdoings; at
other times he practically takes the poorest view of
his own endowments; he thinks that it is of no use

for him to aim high, or to attempt a noble life ; that
he may make himself easy on a low level, or a down-
grade; that there are temptations which he cannot
withstand, and sins which he will never overcome;
that people must take him as he is, and not expect
too much of him.—Surely it is a curious and not
uncommon inconsistency; and perhaps we all, in some
degree, in some aspects of our life, fall into it: we
think of ourselves both more highly and more meanly
than we ought to think.

II. To think of one's self at once too highly and
too meanly, to be at once too confident and too faint-
hearted, at once to exaggerate and to ignore one's
own importance,—there should be, I think, in Oxford
helpful influences against both elements in this
complex temptation. For, first, it ought surely to
be difficult to think one's self remarkable, to think
that one has attained any right to rest on one's
achievements, or to be self-confident in such a place
as this. The surpassing beauty, the quiet nobleness,
the venerable antiquity of Oxford ought to check
us like a living and a reverend presence; it might
make us lower, as it were, the tone of our voices, if,
in the din of a competitive age, we have grown apt
to talk too positively; it might remind us sometimes that we "speak under. correction."—For there

has been so much of greatness here. The succession of great founders and builders and benefactors that comes before us as we pass from college to college; the great statesmen who have been trained here; the great teachers who from Oxford have moved men's hearts and minds, and turned the broad stream of human thought; the great students who, as was said of one of the greatest and most modest of them, have searched into all learning, and come to nothing that was too hard for their understanding;[1] the great master-minds that have seen and grasped the truth, where others could only grope among details; and, above all, the " holy and humble men of heart; " —these confer on Oxford something which seems to lift the standard of life and work, and to silence the words of praise and confidence which we are apt to use so lightly.—Ah! but then, it would be a poor result if we stopped there; if the greatness of the past served only to dwarf the present; if the impression of distinction and grandeur simply made us feel how very poor and rudimentary and feeble are our best efforts and our utmost attainments; if the only outcome of visiting the Bodleian Library were to realize the truth that one has virtually read nothing at all. But while the influence of Oxford ought, indeed, to

[1] Clement VIII., concerning Hooker, in Walton's " Life of Hooker."

chasten us and to repress all rising of self-confidence, certainly it should also quicken us; it should rebuke all our faint-heartedness and failure of aspiration. For our lives are enriched by all this labour and bounty of the past; and therefore we must use them reverently, with a high standard of unselfish effort. More or less, directly or indirectly, consciously and unconsciously, we all are using day after day that which the great workers of past ages won and stored for us. In the material surroundings of our life; in the knowledge of nature's laws and the power which that knowledge gives; in the thoughts that glow with an unfading brightness; in the visible forms of beauty and the recorded examples of goodness;—in all these ways we are helped forward and urged upward by the greatness that has been. Oxford may well call us to remember how, as Dr. Whewell finely said, our education rests on " the results of ancient triumphs of man's spirit over the confusion and obscurity of the aspects of the external world; and even over the waywardness and unregulated impulses of his own nature, and the entanglements and conflicts of human society." [1]

There is hardly any duty which we may not do the better for realizing that great inheritance of

---

[1] " Lectures on Education," p. 19.

which Oxford may especially remind us. For some of the commonest faults of thought and work are those which come from thinking too poorly of our own lives, and of that which must rightly be demanded of us. A high standard of accuracy, a chivalrous loyalty to exact truth, generosity to fellow-workers, indifference to results, distrust of all that is showy, self-discipline and undiscouraged patience through all difficulties,—these are among the first and greatest conditions of good work; and they ought never to seem too hard for us if we remember what we owe to the best work of bygone days.

III. "Lord, what is man, that Thou art mindful of him? and the son of man, that Thou visitest him?" Thus may a great historic city point us, if we are willing and humble, just a little way towards the true answer to that deep question; thus may it, perhaps, suggest to us some thought both of the littleness and of the greatness of our separate lives.[1] But it cannot take us very far; it cannot do much to keep us in order, or to control our vanity and wilfulness and self-pleasing. We know that; and Oxford has, it must be feared, like other great places, seen enough both of self-assertion and of indolence, both of empty pride and of wasted opportunities, to forbid our ever thinking

[1] Cf. J. H. Newman's "Sermons for the Seasons," p. 341.

that even the most gracious of external influences can discipline men's characters or guard a great heritage from their misuse. We need, indeed, something far more penetrating and arresting than historical associations and visible beauty. We need the knowledge of God, and of that which He made us to be, and has made possible for us; we need, if we are really to understand and to employ our lives aright, the grace and truth that came by Jesus Christ. All that is noblest in history and art may be lavished, often has been lavished, in the circumstances of a life that has only seemed to sink the faster into the depths of misery, the decadence of vanity and sloth. It is only as we take to our hearts that astounding disclosure which God has made to us of Himself, and of His will and love for us, that we may really overcome the temptation to think too highly or too poorly of our lives. We can trace the two great lines of that disclosure of man's true place with increasing clearness in the Old Testament; they are seen at once in the record of creation, where he who is formed of the dust of the ground is yet made in the image of God; they meet in the question of the text. For as the Psalmist looks at the magnificence, the purity, the splendour, of the starry heavens, as he thinks of the glorious majesty of their Creator, as he realizes

in immeasurable contrast the littleness and poverty
and feebleness of man, he yet knows that this is only
half the truth ; since human life is lifted out of all its
outward insignificance by the Creator's love and care;
since in His wondrous mercy He is mindful of the
sons of men, and visits them in tenderness and blessing.　As man seems to sink towards nothingness
before the infinite greatness of Almighty God, he is
raised again and ennobled beyond all thought or hope
by the assurance that God loves and pities him, and
has a purpose and a work for his frail, fleeting life.
—But it is only in the fulness of time, only in the
Incarnation of the Eternal Son, that the true place
and worth of every human soul is perfectly revealed.
For then at length is seen the glory of God; since
all the marvels of creation, all the splendour and
surprise of earth and sky, far less disclosed His glory
than did the Cross of Christ; since in His willing
death we may see at length the greatness of God's
love.　"God so loved the world:" there is the true
unveiling of Himself; there, where "the love o'ertops
the might."　And we have far, far more cause to feel
our meanness, our base ingratitude, our blank and
shameful failure, before that disclosure of perfect
love and holiness and self-surrender than in all the
splendour of the greatest pageant that art or nature

can display; since in contrast with that sight the misery of our selfish hearts breaks in on us at last. Ah! but with that sharp conviction comes another voice of truth to banish all despondency and faint-heartedness; for it is to draw us to Himself that He hangs there: "He loved me, and gave Himself for me." His Death and Resurrection are not only the revelation, they are also the triumph, of His love; that love which His grace is ever ready to bear even into our unworthy hearts, that we may find, in humbly following the blessed steps of His most holy life, the true greatness of that nature which He deigned to wear on earth—that human nature which He has exalted now to the right hand of the Majesty on high.

XVI.

THE RESPONSIBILITY OF INHERITANCE.

"Freely ye have received, freely give."
ST. MATT. x. 8.

I. THE first reference of these words seems to be to the supernatural gifts of healing power which the twelve Apostles had received from our Blessed Lord. He, to Whom the Father had eternally given "to have life in Himself," had imparted to His chosen servants that life-giving energy which was His essentially. "He gave them power against unclean spirits, to cast them out, and to heal all manner of sickness and all manner of disease." This transcendent grant they had received freely; they had in no way earned it or achieved it for themselves; it had come to them as spontaneously as the rain falls upon the drooping plant; and it must be used as it had come—spontaneously, ungrudgingly, without demand or expectation of a recompense. There must be no exacting insistence upon merit or upon gratitude; they must not look upon the powers they had received as conferring greatness or importance on themselves, or as convertible into so much of thanks and popularity and influence, or as enabling them to enforce their own particular views of what men and women ought to be. Freely they had received, and freely they were to give; with a pure regard to the will of God; with a humble care not to thrust in their own claims between the work of His mercy and the thankfulness of those to whom they were allowed to bear it. Doubtless the warning was needed then: how greatly needed we may feel, if we venture to wonder what use Judas Iscariot made of the beneficent powers he had freely received. It had been needed constantly in the past; and the neglect of it had shut out Moses from the promised land, because at Meribah "he spake unadvisedly with his lips," and did not sanctify the Giver of all good in the eyes of the children of Israel. It is needed at all times, even in its first and plainest application; for I suppose that there has never been a period when even the highest and most mysterious gifts that issue from the love of God have been safe from the abuse of greed and wilfulness, of lust for praise or power.

But the words are general in form; they have a bearing far beyond the sphere of those distinctive gifts which God entrusts to the stewards of His mysteries. And one plain lesson which they teach us all is this—that a great duty rests on us in regard to our use of all that manifold heritage which has come to us so freely and so generously, unearned, unasked, from the toil, and patience, and wisdom, and bounty of past ages. It is a lesson of which we ought to think at the beginning of a week still nominally concerned with the commemoration of founders and benefactors.[1] Let us for a few minutes fasten our thoughts upon it.

II. "Freely ye have received." Directly or indirectly very many of us are debtors to the splendid generosity of those who long ago devoted their wealth to the glory of God in the advancement of religion and learning. Some of us may feel that through every stage in our life since childhood we have owed some privilege to their liberality; and most of us, perhaps, either for ourselves, or through the help, the training, the deeper thoughts and higher aims that others have received in school or college life, have had some share from the bounty of the past. And whatsoever has thus come to us we have received as a free gift. Men gave of old with large-hearted, unexacting

[1] This sermon was preached at Oxford, in the Cathedral, on "Commemoration Sunday."

liberality; they cared and planned and spent for those who might never think of them, who could never show them gratitude or make them any recompense, save by their prayers. From some who have " left a name behind them, that their praises might be reported;" and from some who have no memorial, whose names are forgotten where their work lives on—the broad stream of bounty has come down to us.—There seems a curious contrast between the almost morbid restlessness with which many men are anxious to be or to seem quit of any obligation to a living benefactor, and the uninquiring acquiescence with which they will settle down to enjoy the splendid gifts of those who have passed away. It would be difficult to measure how much harder, poorer, darker, our lives would be if men had been in bygone ages narrow or cold in giving; if the great builders had stayed their hands at that which would do for their own need or last out their days; if all had been timidly bounded by

> "The lore
> Of nicely-calculated less or more;"[1]

if the enthusiasm of a great conception had not been allowed its liberty. Freely we have received; nothing

[1] Wordsworth's Ecclesiastical Sonnets, "Inside of King's College Chapel, Cambridge."

was asked of us as we entered into all this heritage of help and beauty; we found the homes of worship, the facilities and encouragements of learning, ready for our use. Freely we have received; and our Saviour teaches us how to show our gratitude for this ungrudged and unconditioned largess. We, in our turn, must freely give. Without looking for requital, without making bargains, without any thought of recognition or gratitude, we must bear our part in that great chain of giving which binds age to age, that tradition of generosity which looks like the sunny side of the road in the course of human affairs. Freely we must give, for the good of those whom we shall never see, and who will never know of our existence; those for whom, in distant lands or ages, our gifts may, perhaps, help to do something like what the gifts of the past have done for us. Surely the best "commemoration of founders and benefactors," here or elsewhere, is to ask ourselves what we can do, with some approach to their ungrudging and un-bargaining spirit, for those who as yet have been left destitute of the wealth that has so freely come to us. And if, amidst the expense and pleasure of this week, it occurs to any one that a Latin speech, not always listened to or understood by all, is rather a poor acknowledgment of all that Oxford owes to the great givers of former generations, then the words of the text may point to a clear way of commemorating them more worthily:—"Freely give:" try to learn more of their bountiful temper, their far-sighted, open-handed care for others; see what you can do to keep up their work.

Freely we have received our opportunities of education: what are we doing in our turn for the education of the poor? Freely we have received these "monuments of love divine," our churches and cathedrals, rich with the living thoughts, the lingering prayers, of bygone times: what are we doing to provide even the simplest buildings that are needed for God's service in the quickly spreading suburbs of our huge, grim towns? Freely we have received the tradition of revealed truth: what are we doing for the proffer of that truth to those who, at home and abroad, are living, sinning, suffering, and dying without any knowledge of the love of God made manifest in the Incarnate Son? It is in those who are really caring for such works as these that the wise and generous temper of our founders and benefactors lives among us still; it is they who are true to the traditions of the past, and to the best part of all that Oxford means. In ventures and efforts such as those of the Universities' Mission to Central Africa, the

Oxford Mission to Calcutta, the Oxford House in Bethnal Green, the Christ Church Mission at Poplar, the spirit from which we ourselves so freely have received still struggles on to deal, in the hopefulness of faith, with the vast needs of the present, and to make such scanty provision as it can for the incalculable demands and difficulties of the future. Yes; and surely it may come to pass, in the swift changes through which history works out the will of Him Who " putteth down one and setteth up another," that, when the greatness of Oxford is a mere story of the past, the high purpose of our founders may be living still, and their devotion to God's glory may be bearing its true fruit in some distant field, in India or elsewhere, as the Church of Christ rises in the old way, by the self-sacrifice of those who love not their life even unto death.

III. "Freely ye have received, freely give." We must not limit our application of the words to such benefits as have been placed within our reach, or brought indirectly to bear on our lives, out of the liberality of founders and benefactors. In far wider ways we owe more than we can ever tell to the large-heartedness of our forefathers. Other men have laboured, and we have entered into their labours. Think of all the toil, and patience, and self-discipline, and perseverance of artists and students and artificers in age after age, that have gone to make possible or conceivable the things that we may take for granted; the most ordinary comforts or adornments of our lives. Think of the vast suffering that went before the discovery of the simplest laws by which our health is guarded or regained. Or think of that which has been finely described as "the cost of moral movement;" "the immense cost, the appalling severity of the effort which has been spent on lifting men's spiritual faculties from the state of the savage to the condition in which we find them in ourselves to-day."[1] Freely we have received the outcome of all this; and if there is any sense of chivalry or of justice in us, we cannot realize at how vast a cost we have been thus endowed, enabled, taught, and then let the giving halt at our unproductive, comfortable lives.—But, above all, let us try to imagine what others may have had to bear that the faith of Christ and the ministry of His sacraments might be handed on to us in unimpaired integrity. We are always talking of the difficulties, the anxieties, the perplexities of our day in matters of religion. And doubtless our difficulties are real and serious; they are likely to test our strength of character and our

[1] H. S. Holland, "Logic and Life," p. 79.

R

patience, likely to prove what we are made of, before we have done with them. But, can we imagine that it ever was an easy thing to be a Christian ? Surely all the generations of the past have had their trials of faith; their difficulties, practical or theoretical, to deal with; their especial exercise for trust in God, for loyalty through dark times, for resolute tenacity of truth, even when it has looked fragmentary and disappointing. There has never been a time when doubts had not a fair chance of wresting the faith of Christ out of the grasp of the prayerless, the faint-hearted, the impatient, the double-minded, and the undisciplined. But by the strong grace of God, in one generation after another, His servants have been of a widely different character; they have endured as seeing Him Who is invisible; they have fought the good fight against all that, within them or without, threatened to drag them back from their Redeemer; and so the faith has come down to our age. Freely we have received what all that moral effort has preserved; and can we shrink, ungenerous, soon wearied, or soon frightened, from the demand that the maintenance of our own faith may make in our day ? It is but the old demand in a new form ; and there will have been grave fault somewhere if, when we should freely give to those who come after us, freely give the heritage which we received, we have to say that, somehow, it has slipped from our hold. Let us see to this, at least, that that which has come down to us through centuries of such endurance shall not, by any lack of prayer, of trust, of self-control, self-sacrifice, and patience on our part, be wasted in our hands; and then, we may thankfully believe, Almighty God will see to it that we shall not have less to give than that which we have, by His unspeakable mercy, received through the patience of the saints and the steadfast wisdom of the Spirit-bearing Church.

XVII.

THE RESPONSIBILITY OF STRENGTH.

"We then that are strong ought to bear the infirmities of the weak."

ROM. xv. 1.

I. LET us try to enter into the position which has been under St. Paul's consideration when he writes these words.

(a) The peace and welfare of the Church at Rome had been imperilled by the divergence of two groups of Christians in certain details of practice. It was a divergence such as might naturally result when a new principle, telling with incalculable energy for change on thought and conduct, had been welcomed by a number of men who differed widely in calibre and temperament and training. The revelation of Jesus Christ and of the grace and truth that came by Him held within it a power to make all things new; and as the touch of faith released that power, it must often have been found that the acceptance of Christianity involved far more than had been at first disclosed. To be a Christian; to believe that the Eternal and Almighty Son of God had taken to Himself a human nature, and lived and died on earth and risen from the dead; to go about one's work each day in constant reliance on His strength, knowing that He was looking on, wondering whether that very day He might come back to judge the world, to judge one's self;—this could not but affect profoundly the meaning of all earthly things, the drift and intensity of all hopes and fears and cares and efforts. And as the Holy Spirit bore deeper and more fully into a man's soul the life of Christ, with all its surprising consequences of conviction and of duty, many forces which had claimed some influence or lordship over him would fall back, relaxing their hold and relinquishing their pretensions. We may know how conventional axioms are swept aside in moments of sudden passion or enthusiasm; we may know how passions stronger than any conventionality may yield up their tyranny in those rare cases when a man knows, with undimmed and unenfeebled intellect, that he has but a few hours more to live. But it was with a broader, calmer, surer onset, that the truth of Christ advanced to vindicate its empire, and to free the hearts of men from all narrow, timid deference to merely outward rules. For the motive force, the guiding light, of the Christian life left no place or meaning for such soulless precautions : they would look like street-lamps left burning by mistake at midday ; they could add nothing to the amplitude of radiance which Christ was pouring into the new-born souls of His redeemed.

(*b*) But to part with outward rules, however unspiritual and however conventional they may be, requires a certain force of character, a certain power of self-realization, which is not found in all men. For outward and particular rules, if sometimes they are irksome, are often comfortable and reassuring : they seem to save men trouble, to leave less room for uncertainty, to lighten the burden of responsibility at a moderate cost: men are told what is asked of them, and can, if they will, be sure that they have rendered it.   What the strong may feel as a restriction the weak may welcome as a safeguard ; and there is need of courage and enterprise to venture beyond the tutelage of external directions into the higher sphere of life, where the challenge of God's infinite love is the one principle of guidance, and His absolute perfection is the source and strength of every law.   And so, as the call to substitute the obedience of faith for attention to rules came home to the conscience of Christians individually, it brought to light some dee

differences of character and temperament; men fell
apart from one another according as they were or
were not able to welcome such a call, to commit themselves to such a venture, to trust themselves, God
helping them, in the liberty wherewith Christ had
made them free. There were some who, in the sanctified independence of a strong character, sprang at
once to realize the privilege and the demand of the
new life: risen with Christ, they looked to Him alone;
from Him, from Him alone, by whatsoever influence,
through whatsoever channels of communication He
might be pleased to use, must come the law whereby
they must be judged, even the royal law of liberty;
to them the narrow and unquickening rules by which
men crept about the world seemed somewhat as our
roads and railways may look to the swallow while, in
obedience to the impulse God has given him, he wings
his way through the broad spaces of the sky towards
the ever-growing light and warmth he loves. But
there were others who had not strength of character
or firmness of self-realization to renounce all deference
to those laws whose limit of demand they could
exactly measure, and with which they could conform
so perfectly as to feel a sense of security if not of
self-satisfaction. It does not seem that these weak
brethren in the Church at Rome denied any truth

which the strong believed; they were not like the Judaizers of the Galatian Church; but belief meant less to them, because, if one may so speak, they meant less to themselves; they had not the moral vigour to enter on their heritage of liberty; they were like the timid convalescent who shrinks from the ventures to which his doctor encourages him, and keeps up the precautions and the dietary of his illness long after they have become, to say the least, wholly unnecessary for him. Whether it was from dread of even the slightest pollution by any unconscious contact with a heathen sacrifice, or from an idea of some intrinsic unfitness in certain kinds of food, or from a scrupulous anxiety to secure the merit of being on the safe side, we cannot tell; but there were Christians at Rome who persisted in. carefully submitting their life to rules which they had learnt elsewhere than in the school of Christ, and in hanging back from the liberty to which He called them. And so there had arisen that divergence and contrast, that danger of mutual misunderstanding, with which St. Paul deals in the fourteenth chapter of this Epistle: one man believed that he might eat all things; another, who was weak, ate only herbs: one man esteemed one day above another; another man esteemed every day alike.

II. Such is the difficulty before St. Paul, and he

deals with it on principles of wide and lasting import.
He has, you will remember, a word of warning for
each of the two divergent groups : " Let not him that
eateth despise him that eateth not : and let not him
which eateth not judge him that eateth." He, on
the one hand, whose swiftness of apprehension and
strength of grasp and moral energy enable him to
realize how a single and absolute allegiance to Christ
lifts a man above the reach of this world's arbitrary
and traditional rules, must have no thought of scorn
or ridicule for the backward but well-meaning brother
who, with perhaps an equal desire to devote himself
wholly to Christ's service, is still of opinion that such
rules ought not to be disregarded. And he, on the
other hand, as he keeps his rules and eats his dinner
of herbs, must not be thinking any hard things of
those who with an unhesitating conscience live a less
restricted life. The reason for the latter part of this
counsel, for the Apostle's warning to the weak, is
simple. That unnecessary censure of other men's
ways is an ignorant and irreverent meddling with the
Divine prerogative of judgment; it is an intrusion of
ill-informed opinion where only the unerring voice
of Christ should speak : " Who art thou that judgest
another man's servant ? To his own Master he
standeth or falleth."

The principle here is clear for us all, however reluctant we may be in realizing it; however hard it may be to recollect that one's impertinent fault-finding with one's neighbours simply adds to one's own unsightliness before the Judge of all. But for the strong, for him who has insight and confidence to commit himself wholly to the law of liberty, St. Paul has a more complex task, involving that great and characteristic principle of Christianity which is enunciated in the text: and it is of this task, of this principle, that I would try especially to speak.

His words recall the closely parallel passage in the First Epistle to the Corinthians. The strong, he recognizes, may be rightly free from any scruples of his own; but the very love which gives him freedom binds him to be considerate for the scruples of the weak. The weak man is like one with a delicate constitution who may easily be encouraged to imprudence; and the strong must use for his sake a care which he need never use for his own. "For," it has been well said, "there is a tyranny which even freedom may exercise, when it makes us intolerant of other men's difficulties." [1] And weakness itself is a source of real difficulties, and a claim therefore for

---

[1] B. Jowett, "St. Paul's Epistles to Thessalonians, Romans, and Galatians," ii. 345.

forbearance and for considerateness. The weak and scrupulous brother may be distressed and wounded by the inconsiderate display of liberty; or he may be led on by the force of example, if not of ridicule, to venture beyond the sanction of his own conscience, and thus made bold to do what in itself may be indifferent but for him is wrong, since all the while his moral sense is witnessing against it. Well, then, if one is strong, to be always clutching one's liberty, to look at it as a prize to be held tight, a right to be asserted, a flag to be displayed at all hazards and all times; to forfeit sympathy that one may evince superiority; to prove one's own advance at the expense of others' welfare, is a preposterous inversion of the whole order of a Christian life. Strength and freedom are indeed great gifts; and when a man has realized that they are his, and has thanked God for them, let him turn them to a really great use. Let him exercise and prove them by stooping down and taking upon himself the burdens of the weak; putting himself in the place of the weak; going back, as it were, to take his stand with them, to stay with them till he can help them onward; divesting himself, not indeed of the very strength and freedom which belong to him as a member of Christ, but of the assertion and mani-

festation and enjoyment of them : controlling and
humbling himself for the sake of others (yes, it is the
one sufficient task for the strong and free), controlling
and humbling himself so to live as though, in these
regards, his freedom and his strength were bounded
by the limits of their weakness. So may he make
known to them the reality of that grace which makes
him free, and will in due time free them also : so may
his life be used to help them, as God bears into their
hearts the beauty and the strength of love, teaching
them through His servant's humility and unselfishness
what is the central splendour of that life, of which
the liberty that men discuss is but an incidental trait.
For the kingdom of God—that invasion and conquest
and transfiguration of this life by the powers of the
life to come—does not consist, and is not realized and
displayed, in setting men free from this or that external rule, however justly such freedom may belong
to the children of the kingdom ; but in righteousness
and peace and joy ; in a reverent and generous recognition of one's *duty* towards others ; in that *tranquil-
lity* which love is for ever tending to increase around
and in the soul it rules ; and in that quiet and steadfast glow of *joy* which neither pain, nor poverty, nor
weariness, nor injustice can overwhelm—the joy which
in its triumph over anxiety and sin tells from whence

it comes. In these things let the strong evince the reality of his life of faith; thus let him employ and prove that freedom which he has found only that he may exercise it in self-surrender, that he may bring to the work of God and the service of man the offering of a free heart.

III. "We then that are strong ought to bear the infirmities of the weak." Let me briefly speak of three points in regard to the ethical principle which is thus, in its widest form, declared.

(*a*) First, let us realize how great and how unlike the ordinary ways of men is the demand it makes. There is nothing which seems to try men's patience and good temper more than feebleness: the timidity, the vacillation, the conventionality, the fretfulness, the prejudices of the weak; the fact that people can be so well-meaning and so disappointing,—these things make many men impatient to a degree of which they are themselves ashamed. But it is something far more than patience and good temper towards weakness that is demanded here. It is that the strong, in whatsoever sphere their strength may lie, should try in silence and simplicity, escaping the observation of men, to take upon their own shoulders the burdens which the weak are bearing; to submit themselves to the difficulties amidst which the weak are stumbling on; to be, for their help's sake, as they are; to share the fear, the dimness, the anxiety, the trouble and heart-sinking through which they have to work their way; to forego and lay aside the privilege of strength in order to understand the weak and backward and bewildered, in order to be with them, to enter into their thoughts, to wait on their advance; to be content, if they can only serve, so to speak, as a favourable circumstance for their growth towards that which God intended them to be.[1] It is the innermost reality of sympathy, it is the very heart and life of courtesy, that is touched here: but like all that is best in moral beauty, it loses almost all its grace the moment it attracts attention. It is noblest when it is least conscious, when another's load, another's limitations, another's trials are assumed quite naturally, as a mother takes her children's troubles for her own, by the straightforward instinct of her love; it is impaired whenever the disfiguring shadow of self-consciousness has begun to creep about it; it is ruined utterly, it ceases to have any semblance of its former self, when once it has been tainted by any insolent complacency in condescension. But when it is pure and true and self-forgetful; when it

---

[1] Cf. "The Gifts of the Child Christ," in "Stephen Archer, and other Tales," by G. MacDonald.

is guarded by a real hatred of praise, a real joy in hiddenness; when it has no motive and no goal save love;—then, indeed, it may be the distinctive glory of the Christian character.

In strangely different ways we try sometimes to prove to others or to ourselves that we are strong: by self-assertion and positiveness, by getting our own way, by vehemence or wilfulness or diplomacy, or by. standing aloof in an attitude of critical reserve. Let us try our strength where St. Paul would have it exercised, in making others' trials our own: and perhaps our first reward may be the wholesome and necessary discovery that our strength is less than we imagined. For it has been truly said that "there is no strain so continuous as that of helping the weak friend to climb. Every footstep has to be steadied as he laboriously ascends; he gets fatigued, he gets giddy, he disdains the use of the rope; perhaps he slips and falls; his constant stumbles seem to imperil our very existence; he keeps us back, he makes our progress slow; we cannot enjoy the prospect by the way, nor the delight of climbing."[1] That parable points us, I think, to the hardest task, the highest privilege that true strength of character can find. In God's service, we are taught, is perfect

[1] W. C. E. Newbolt, "The Fruit of the Spirit," pp. 58, 59.

freedom; and the ancient prayer from which those words are taken seems to say even more—that to serve Him is to reign. But there is yet a higher dignity to be found in service than either royalty or freedom, since to serve others is to help them to be free.

(*b*) Yes; for, in the second place, there is no sure way of helping others save that to which St. Paul directs us. It is an impressive part of the witness that comes to Christianity from the sphere of ethics, that if we have courage to let it lead us apart from all that we think natural and hopeful, we find that it has put us in the way to reach an end beyond our hopes, and to realize a higher nature than that which men usually call human. Christ tells us, for instance, that the meek shall inherit the earth; and we begin to see, as life goes on, that there are indeed no victories so real and sure as those which meekness wins. We are taught that we must be made perfect through suffering; and we put a very scanty meaning into the words, until some day we see a human soul ascend through pain to a dignity and beauty before which we stand abashed. "He that followeth Me shall not walk in darkness:"—there are no words which admit of more conclusive verification by experience than those. And so in the case of which we have been thinking: the guidance which crosses our natural impulse as to the use of strength points us to the very secret of its worth and safety and increase. We shall not much help others to advance till we have taken our stand with them, and made their task our own. We know that well in regard to education. The man of learning, who is so engrossed in his own investigations, or so dazzled by his own brilliancy, or so anxious to make his own standpoint clear, that he forgets or fails to enter at all into his hearers' minds, may possibly impress but hardly educate them. His teaching may show, indeed, how far on he has got, and it may quicken aspiration in those who are nearest to him; but it will leave many whom he might help just where they were. To "bear the infirmities of the weak;" to learn how things may seem to them; to realize how naturally they may see but little meaning in words and arguments which study has made full of force to the teacher; to measure the possibility of misunderstanding or the range of prejudice; to recollect how easily an untrained mind confuses the relative importance of its data;—we are familiar with these conditions of all excellence in the ministry of teaching. And surely we know how in those deeper and more anxious difficulties through which we may have to fight our way, in the trials of the moral and spiritual life, if any help can come to us from others, it can only be

s

from those who see our troubles, not from without but from within; who with the wisdom, the simplicity, the strength of love, will come out of the sunshine to be with us in the gloom and dimness; who touch our wounds as tenderly as though their own nerves throbbed for them; who measure our fears and hindrances and sorrows not by the cold estimate of an external critic, but as they are to the heart which really has to bear them. We may be unreasonable enough in our fears, our anxiety, our faint-heartedness, our despondency, our slowness of belief; but if we are to be helped at all, it will not often be by one who stands far off and calls to us to be as rational and robust as he is; but by some one who never seems to pity us just because he stands so close beside us; some one in whom the quiet radiance of love scarcely suffers us at first to see the sustaining massiveness of strength; some one whom we can gladly trust with the knowledge of our infirmities because he never thrusts on us his own exemption from them, because when he is with us he turns all his strength and insight to the task of taking on himself the burden of our weakness.

(*c*) Lastly, let us lift our eyes to look towards Him Who is for evermore our One Supreme Example in the task thus set to love and strength. " We that are

strong ought to bear the infirmities of the weak."
Yes, how can we evade or wonder at the claim, since He
Himself took, our infirmities, and bare our sicknesses;
since, though He was rich, yet for our sakes He became
poor; since we "owe everything to the self-abnegation
of a Redeemer," Who, "being in the form of God,"
"did not cling with avidity to the prerogatives of His
Divine Majesty," "but divested Himself of the glories
of Heaven," and "made Himself of no reputation, and
took upon Him the form of a Servant"? He (as has
been said by a great historical and theological teacher
in this University)—He accepted within the human
sphere on which He entered by becoming Man "restriction, subjections, obscurations, pertaining to the position
of a servant;" "as Man, He willed to live compassed
with sinless infirmities, and in dependence, as to His
soul's life, on the word, the will, the presence of His
Father—a dependence, be it always remembered, not
scenic, but genuine and actual."[1] There could be
indeed "no sin in Him to become that spring of
evil," which our sins so often are to us; but save in
this He took His stand with us, that He might lead
us to be with Him where He is. How, then, can
we hang back òr cling to thoughts of pride and care

[1] W. Bright, "The Incarnation," p. 277. Cf. Bishop Lightfoot on
Phil. ii. 5–11.

for self, if He will let us help to lead the least of all He saved a little nearer to His light by humbly trying to bear with them the burden of their weakness ? It is true that His vast condescension wrought a work we cannot touch; and true again that the example of it comes to us across a great gap; for the utmost difference that there can ever be between two sinful men is as nothing in comparison with the infinite difference which for love's sake He spanned when He was made man, and hid His glory and omnipotence in weakness and in hunger, in shame and weariness, in suffering and death. Yet still across the gap we look to Him; and surely anything like self-assertion, anything like anxiety for the display and acknowledgment of our powers and position, seems a strange infatuation when we think what He forewent, how He was pleased to live for our sakes on earth. We wonder at the words He spake—words such as no other ever spake; but what can we say about the wonder of His silence, about the patient, gentle holding back of that He had to say, because men could not bear it yet ? " Whence hath this Man this wisdom ? " —so men asked as they listened to His teaching; but neither they nor we could ever tell the love and might of self-restraint which checked the beams of His Divine omniscience, that being very Man He

really grow in wisdom as in stature.[1]   We mark how
His almighty power issued forth to quell the storm,
to heal the sick, to raise the dead; but we must not
miss the majesty of hidden strength, the marvel and
the teaching of His patient self-repression, as He
keeps in calm abeyance that which could not but
belong to Him as the Eternal and Co-equal Son of
God.

> "He might have reared a palace at a word,
>   Who sometimes had not where to lay His head :
>   Time was, and He Who nourished crowds with bread
>   Would not one meal unto Himself afford :
>   Twelve legions girded with angelic sword
>   Were at His beck, the scorned and buffeted :
>   He healed another's scratch, His own side bled,
>   Side, feet, and hands, by cruel piercings gored.
>   Oh, wonderful the wonders left undone !
>   And scarce less wonderful than those He wrought.
>   Oh, Self-restraint, passing all human thought,
>   To have all power, and be as having none !
>   Oh, Self-denying Love, which felt alone
>   For needs of others, never for its own !"[2]

---

[1] Cf. Hooker, V. liv. 6.   H. P. Liddon, "Bampton Lectures," p. 464.
[2] Archbishop Trench, "Poems," p. 142.

XVIII.

OLD AND YOUNG.

"I write unto you, little children, because your sins are
forgiven you for His Name's sake. I write unto you, fathers,
because ye have known Him that is from the beginning. I
write unto you, young men, because ye have overcome the
wicked one. I write unto you, little children, because ye
have known the Father. I have written unto you, fathers,
because ye have known Him that is from the beginning. I
have written unto you, young men, because ye are strong, and
the Word of God abideth in you, and ye have overcome the
wicked one."

1 St. John ii. 12-14.

I. WHEREVER we look in the wide scene of human
life we seem to mark two elements or factors working
out the Will of God. The ceaseless drama of history,
however great or humble may be the stage on which
we see it played, constantly betrays in its course
the presence of two forces, animating the action,
meeting in its critical points. Let us try, speaking
broadly, to distinguish them.—On the one hand there
is the force of such convictions, affections, antipathies,
associations, habits of mind as belong to those who

have already given their distinctive impress to a
period which is now passing away. It is not that
their work, or even the greater part of their work,
is done; it well may be that "they shall bring forth
more fruit in their age;" and perhaps in the years
that remain to them their influence may be, if they
will have it so, stronger than it ever has been before.
But the stage of life which bears their stamp, and in
which their characteristic powers told most freely
and evidently, is receding further and further into
the past; and to their eyes, at all events, the retro-
spect of their life looks more than the prospect in
this world.—Then, on the other hand, there is the
force of their convictions or intentions whose distinctive work lies for the most part before them, or
is but just beginning. They are looking forward to
a time in which they shall win out of the new
conditions of their age a new triumph because of the
truth: a time which shall be characterized by the
ideas that seem to them the noblest and most just,
even as the past was either characterized or redeemed
by the truth their fathers saw; a time in which they
shall find their scope, achieve their task, say what
they have to say, and dedicate what they have to
spend. For with them there is, or should be, the
gladness and confidence of morning; and with what-

ever thankfulness and reverence and admiration
they may look back to the victories of the past, the
victories which have won for them the very ground
on which they stand, still they know that it is only
in sham fights that men can simply mimic former
victories; that it is on other fields, amidst other
difficulties, and, it may be, with other weapons that
their battle must be fought, and their service rendered
in the cause of God and of His truth.

Such are, I think, roughly stated, the two great
tendencies or currents of influence which are always
telling in the course of human life. Still more
roughly it might be said that they are the tendencies
generally characteristic of the old and of the young:
the elements which they respectively contribute to
the development of history. The distinction is such
as one can often see, real and deep, though not
marked by any sharp, precise line. Differences of
training and temperament often take the place of
difference in age. The boundary is indefinite, and
there is constant interaction over it; for the scenes
of history succeed one another like dissolving views,
and the lineaments and colours of that which is
passing away can be traced long after that which is
coming in has begun to gather strength and clearness.
Hard outlines are seldom true to nature; yet when

we stand back a little and try to get a broad view, we can scarcely doubt, I think, that two such currents are acting on the affairs of men; and as we watch the surging tide of change, whether in the leaping waves or in the multitude of swirling eddies, we see that human history is for the most part τόπος διθάλασσος, a place where two seas meet.

II. Surely, then, if it be true that at point after point in the world's course, in its preparation for the second coming of Christ, there are these two forces to be felt telling on the way things take: if the two groups of characters and convictions which I have tried to describe are always present in that silent and unconscious conference of mind with mind, where the drift of human thought and opinion is decided—then we may be confident that there must always be a work for each to do, a gift for each to bring, towards the fulfilment of the Will of God. He maketh the outgoings of the morning and of the evening to praise Him; so long as it is day we must work the works of God, each according to the powers he has gained, the light that he has seen, the experience that has trained his judgment, and disciplined his will. So long as it is day each must do all he can of that which he can do best, and it may be that no man knows when he can do most, when the gift that it is his to bring may tell most for the cause of God and for the good of man. But we can be sure that there is a true part for us all to bear at every stage of life, whether we be young or old: a contribution that we have to make, being what and where we are, to the welfare of the world: an offering which God, Who has placed it in our power, looks to us to bring. And we can see, I think, how large a part of the worth and happiness of a man's work, both in his earlier and in his later years, depends on his bearing towards that tide of life, that drift of feeling and conviction which is not his own. The relation between the generation that is passing away and that which is coming on is always full alike of difficulties and of opportunities on both sides; and there is a deep pathos in the frequency with which the opportunities are missed and the difficulties aggravated. Let us keep our minds back from any thought of judging where the blame should fall; let us only think how pitiful it is when those who might enrich and gladden and invigorate each other's lives (each bringing what the other lacks, each thankfully welcoming from the other's hand what lay beyond his own reach), instead of this stand off and look askance with mutual distrust or fear, or even scorn, letting themselves fall back, after only a half-hearted effort towards

sympathy, into that despondency, or impatience, or
suspicion, which blocks with an ever-increasing barrier
all the ways of mutual understanding and influence.
We may recall the great disasters which in bygone
ages have been thus wrought; but to some extent
we may see the same dreary misconception and misuse
of the relation between old and young going on in
many fields of life. We may see it in the history
of a nation, or of the Church; it has been prominent
among the causes of religious discord and divisions;
and I venture to think that it has sometimes cost
much waste of time and strength in our academic and
collegiate life.[1]   And often, surely, the same tragedy
is going on in the life of many a home : and nowhere
perhaps is it more pathetically played; as father and
son, or mother and daughter grow conscious, sometimes with silent pain and sometimes with scarcely
veiled resentment, of an ever-widening severance, a
perpetual and almost irrevocable ebbing of sympathy
and trust.   I think that there can hardly be a sadder
thought to realize than that; for all the while the
years are passing by so swiftly, and the help that
each needs from the other, the joy that each might
minister to the other, is wasting away unused, un-

[1] This sermon was preached in the University Church of Great
St. Mary's, Cambridge.

sought, until it is hopelessly too late to seek it ; wasting like water that sinks into the desert sand, while but a few yards off the traveller lies down despairingly to die of thirst. Is it not true, brethren, that there is no relation of life in which men have greater need of help and guidance and self-discipline than in this of which I have been trying to speak : the relation between that which is passing away and that which is coming forward ; between that which the young are apt to call old-fashioned and that which the old are apt to call new-fangled ? It is difficult indeed. But the grace of God is given for the hallowing, the illumination, of every relation of life ; and it is the very work of grace to transform difficulties into opportunities. So let us try to see how this difficulty is touched by the light of the Christian faith.

III. In the passage which I read for my text, St. John is, as has been well shown,[1] halting for a moment and calling vividly before his mind the characters and positions of those to whom he writes. He is about to close one part of his letter with a great appeal for unworldliness; and he stays to consider on what grounds he can presume a readiness for that appeal in those to whom he sends it. Twice

---

[1] Cf. Bishop Westcott *in loco.*

do they seem to stand before his gaze: each time he
sees them first as one group, then as parted into two;
each time he marks first a warrant for his confidence
that is common to them all, and then the special
warrant that he has for making his appeal to the
older among them, and to the younger. "I write
unto you, little children, because your sins are forgiven you for His Name's sake"—there is his first
ground of hope about them all, both old and young;
but in each of those two classes he marks a distinctive note that promises an answer to his words
"I write unto you, fathers, because ye know Him
that is from the beginning;" "I write unto you,
young men, because ye have overcome the evil one."
Again he seems to see them standing all together,
old and young alike his little ones in Christ: "I have
written unto you," he says, changing the tense, it
may be, as he resumes his writing after some inter-
ruption, "I have written unto you, little ones, because
ye know the Father," and then, just as before, he
turns first to the old and afterwards to the young:
he repeats to each the peculiar claim on which before
he had rested his appeal: "I have written unto you,
fathers, because ye know Him that is from the
beginning;" "I have written unto you, young men
because"—and here he lingers on his former words,

and amplifies them, as though with something like that special love and eagerness with which a parish priest thinks of those who are giving to their Lord the full vigour of their early manhood—"because ye are strong, and the Word of God abideth in you, and ye have overcome the evil one."

Let us try briefly to gather up the teaching of this passage: necessarily foregoing the consideration of many points of very suggestive detail. And first let us mark the thoughts that rise in St. John's mind as he regards separately the elder and the younger among those to whom he is appealing.

(a) Each class, then, stands before the Apostle bearing its distinctive gift, characterized by the peculiar power which lifts the standard of its hope and effort, and binds it to hear and to obey Christ's bidding. There is first the matured discernment and experience, the steady penetration of the old. They " know Him that is from the beginning." Faith has made them clear-sighted, and experience has deepened and confirmed their intuition : they have learnt what it is that is really going forward under all the apparent confusion and disorder of the world, and Who it is that through the strife and din ever has been, ever is, carrying on the work of love ; and knowing Him they have found the clue to life, and

grown surer of its meaning, and less likely to be led
aside from the true aim of effort and self-concentration. Others may be impatient of the twilight,
others may lose heart when hopes prove false, or
may sacrifice the greater to the nearer object; but
he who knows Him that is from the beginning will
endure as seeing the Invisible—

> "He holds on firmly to some thread of life—
> (It is the life to lead perforcedly)
> Which runs across some vast distracting orb
> Of glory on either side that meagre thread,
> Which, conscious of, he must not enter yet—
> The spiritual life around the earthly life :
> The law of that is known to him as this,
> His heart and brain move there, his feet stay here." [1]

And then, on the other hand, in the young there is
the glad enthusiasm of consecrated strength, the glow
of victory and enterprise. "They are strong, and the
Word of God abideth in them, and they have overcome
the evil one." The natural vigour of their age is
lifted up and hallowed and assured in the warfare
to which Christ has called them : they will not "faint
and be weary," for they "renew their strength" in
abiding communion with the Eternal Word; and in
the thrilling sense of conquest they are sure that
greater is He that is in them than he that is in the

---

[1] R. Browning, vol. iv. p. 193, ed. 1888.

world. The fresh and bracing air of triumph fills their hearts with hope : they rejoice in this, that the spirits of evil are subject unto them; they are confident of mastery in Christ's Name "over all the power of the enemy."

(*b*) Thus, then, in the prerogative graces of the old and of the young, St. John sees ground for making his appeal with a good hope. He looks to that which God the Holy Ghost has made of their age and of their youth, and he is not afraid to bid them to further ventures for Christ's sake. As they stand apart he has been insisting on their distinctive powers : each has that which will give penetration and definiteness to the appeal as it falls upon his ears ; each has something of his own, something in his own experience and consciousness which quickens a distinct receptive faculty, something which will wake and stir at the Apostle's words. But beyond and above these separate gifts there are the two great master truths to which he points as dominant alike in the experience of all; the truths that, high and steadfast as the arch of heaven, span from end to end the Christian life : those strong supreme convictions which are the light and strength of every age, availing most of all, wherever they are ruling a man's heart, to guard him from the things

which make us slow to hear God's voice, and dull to
see His way in the various relations of this earth.
" Your sins are forgiven you for His Name's sake,"
and " Ye know the Father." These are the all-
controlling, all-transforming truths for every period
and every task in life; in their light the Christian
course begins, they give the strength of perseverance,
they sustain the glow of eventide; many things
change around a man as he advances in his journey
through this world, but as he draws near its close,
weary and travel-stained, he lifts his eyes to those
same heights on which they rested as he set out in
the freshness of the morning. No change has told on
them; only it may be, by the Divine mercy, he sees
a little clearer now the forgiveness of sins and the
Fatherhood of God. And thus it is that when he
speaks of these St. John makes no distinction between
old and young; these are truths whose power he
presumes in all who are Christ's; truths in whose
ever-remembered presence all must stand and work
together, as forgiven and as children.

IV. The forgiveness of sins: the Fatherhood of God.
Can it be, brethren, that in the constant recollection,
the advancing realization of these truths, we may
find the help we need in that frequent difficulty of
which we have been thinking? Is it thus that we

T

may learn to do our true work in every stage of life, and to be wise and just and generous towards those whom the broad difference of age or temperament may tempt us, if we are careless or wilful, to think irreconcilably and impenetrably unlike ourselves ? It is so easy, on either side, to acquiesce in such differences as insuperable; it is so hard at once to bear one's own witness to the truth of which one's self is sure, and yet to persevere in courageous generosity and trustfulness towards those whose thoughts and ways belong to another generation than one's own. It may be that from those two great truths, in whose light St. John forgets the difference of age and youth, some help may come; help, perhaps, only the deeper and surer for coming indirectly; for telling rather on ourselves than on our difficulties. In our own hearts, or in the history of the past, we may discover some of the faults that darken counsel and make men prone to misunderstand and to suspect each other; such faults as pride, impatience, wilfulness, despondency; or, issuing more or less from these, that fear of being beaten which makes men withhold the opposition which they should have offered; the dread of being wounded or of seeming slighted; the exaggeration of fragments till they seem the whole truth; the disinclination to keep judgment in suspense; the failure to allow for that

which may be hidden in the unexplored; the love of
symmetry, or paradox, or epigram; reluctance or pre-
varication in acknowledging one's blunders. Surely
we may be stronger to resist such things as these if
we realize the seriousness and urgency that is disclosed in human life since Christ was crucified that
man might be forgiven, and the strength of hope
that should abound in those who know the Fatherhood
of God. "Your sins are forgiven you for His Name's
sake:" the words recall to us our deepest need, our
uttermost unworthiness; but they recall us also to
the Cross; and there falls on life an awe in which
the thoughts of self-esteem and self-assertion, of
vanity and petulance, die down for very shame. "Ye
know the Father:" infinite in power and in wisdom
and in goodness: ever watching over this world, and
working out in many ways the will of love:—how,
then, is it possible to be faint-hearted or despondent,
or to doubt that in the coming years His glory shall
appear as in the ages that are past? Let us fasten
our thoughts upon the Cross of Christ and lift our
hearts to our Father Which is in heaven; and we may
find it easier with reverence and self-distrust simply
to do what work we can, to be patient under the
discipline of incompleteness and obscurity, and to
hope that much which we think strange and un-

promising, much even which, so far as we can judge, we feel bound in duty to resist, may have its hidden purpose and value in His sight. And as the evening of life falls on us, He will guard us from the true sadness of old age : from

> " The inward change
> On mind and will and feelings wrought ;
> The narrowing of affection's range,
> The stiffness that impedes the thought ;
> The lapse of joy from less to less,
> The daily deepening loneliness." [1]

He will save us from all this ; and, if it please Him, give us grace to say our Nunc Dimittis with unfading hope : thankful to believe that our eyes have seen His salvation, and that He Who has shown us, unworthy as we are, some fragment of His work, may grant to those who shall come after us to see His glory.

V. I was led to speak of these things by the thought of him in whose stead I have been suffered to come here to-day.[2] We are slowly learning at Oxford as this term goes on what we have lost by Aubrey Moore's death. We knew how rare a mind his was,

---

[1] W. Bright, "Iona and other Verses," p. 148.

[2] The Rev. Aubrey L. Moore, Hon. Canon of Christ Church, Oxford, Tutor of Magdalen and of Keble College, who was to have preached the University Sermon on the Sunday on which this sermon was preached. He died on January 17, 1890.

how true and resolute and fearless and delightful he
had always been ; but we hardly realized, I think, at
how many points we should find ourselves longing
in vain to hear his voice : and to some of us it
seems as though Oxford can never be to us as it was
while he was there, to bring clearness and courage
into all perplexities, and to enrich all interests and
hopes.

God gave us many blessings through his life. But
in nothing, perhaps, was he more singular and noble
than in the power he had of delighting with equal
generosity, equal helpfulness, in the best qualities, the
distinctive excellences, of men of all ages. I doubt
whether any one entered so thoroughly into minds
so widely diverse. It seemed as though his vivid
and penetrating intellect was lifted by great moral
qualities to a level where it could work in steady
victory over the faults and blunders which so often
spoil the worth and limit the beneficence of mental
brilliancy. Thoroughness, reverence, consistency,
humility, patience, unworldliness,—these seemed, by
God's grace, ever growing in him; these made the
keenest mind that I have ever known to be always
bringing help and gladness alike to old and young.
His love for truth was, I think, like that which
Francis of Assisi bore to poverty : he would always

go where truth led: for truth, he knew, could not betray him: and it seemed in his work as though indeed his love for truth had cast out fear. May God, from Whom all good gifts come, grant to His Church in the needs that now are on us and in those which seem swiftly to be drawing near, some who will work for her as Aubrey Moore was working: in steadfastness and self-control, in courage and simplicity and love.

XIX.

SIN AND LAW.

"The sting of death is sin; and the strength of sin is the law."

1 Cor. xv. 56.

THE first aspect of these words is clear and vivid. They come before us and demand attention with a power to which neither the simplest nor the most critical mind can be insensible. There is something deep in them which goes straight to something deep in us. The rough lad who hears them read at his father's funeral in the village church may know where they touch him, and what it is they ask of him; the priest who reads them may be feeling how no familiarity changes in the very least the sharpness and penetration of their challenge; the most thoughtless may be finding that for once he cannot choose but stay to think. "The sting of death is sin;"—we may say what we will, we may almost do or think what we will; but while we live, and know that we must die, those words will keep, please God, some power to get at us and to recall us to ourselves.

I. The warning and the challenge, then, with which we are at once confronted, may be plain enough. But a change comes as soon as we begin to look into the words—to try to frame a definite conception of the truth which was filling St. Paul's mind and ruling all his thoughts as he wrote. We cannot be content with discovering expressions more or less analogous in his other letters : for here the words fall within the strong inclusive hold of a great purpose ; and parallel passages elsewhere may be suggestive, but can hardly be decisive in regard to their dominant and inmost meaning. And as we try to keep our minds fixed upon them, as we labour to think out into clearness and reality some answer to the question in what sense is sin the sting of death, and the law the strength of sin, we may feel that we are touching truths which we can never grasp; that behind the words we use are vast, mysterious presences, whose import and issues and interdependence we can only know in part; and that the fragment we discern shades off into depths and distances far beyond our ken. What sin and death and law may in the fulness of their meaning be, we cannot tell ; and that partial apprehension which, if we are

faithful and obedient, suffices amply for the guidance
of life, the discipline of character, and the increase
of light, will not suffice us if we want at once to
round our thoughts into a system or to answer all
the questions we can ask. "The sting of death is
sin;"—it would be hard to say how far St. Paul is
thinking of that unnatural power which accrued to
death [1] when man fell and sin entered into the
world; when, as one has said,[2] "by sin death became
a king, and got him a dominion, pale, hideous, terrible;" when "he clothed himself with terrors, and
made himself a palace of mankind." Again, it would
be hard to say how far the Apostle is thinking of
that more awful scene which lies beyond the day of
death; how far, as he speaks of death, he links with
it that certainty of the judgment to come which
could shake even the mean and lustful heart of
Felix with a terror that he could not hide. And
then, "the strength of sin is the law:" here again
many lines of thought are suggested when one reflects
that probably about twelve months after he wrote
these words St. Paul was writing the Epistle to the
Romans; though I venture to think that such suggestions must be treated as subordinate to the de-

[1] Cf. St. Athanasius, "De Incarnatione Verbi," iii.-v.
[2] Cf. Bishop Milman, "The Love of the Atonement," p. 38.

mands of the passage in which the words here stand
and to their close connection with the preceding
clause;—so that we must not lose hold upon the
thought that in some especial way it is to be the
sting of death that sin is made strong by the law.
Thus many avenues of meditation open out before
us as we gaze into the depths beyond the words: and
each, it may be, looks as though it stretched further
than our utmost strength of penetration. It is with
consciousness of this that I would try to speak this
morning only of one fragmentary thought, which
seems to rise out of the words, and which at times,
perhaps, may bring, by God's grace, something of
their force to bear on our lives.

II. " The sting of death is sin; and the strength of
sin is the law." Yes: for " sin is lawlessness." [1]
Those words of St. John's carry us to the inner and
unvarying character of sin: whatever outward form
it wears this is the common, constant quality of it;
this we shall find at the heart of it. It is, says the
Bishop of Durham, " the assertion of the selfish will
against a paramount authority. He who sins breaks
not only by accident or in an isolated detail, but
essentially the ' law ' which he was created to fulfil." [2]

---

[1] St. John iii. 4.
[2] Cf. Bishop Westcott on the Epistles of St. John, *in loco.*

It may be "the law of his own personal being, or the law of his relation to things without him, or the law of his relation to God:" for we may distinguish these three, though all alike proceed from God, as rays from the central light of His Eternal Law, and though none can be broken without infringement upon all. But whether it be primarily against his own inner life and health and growth that a man sins, or against the society in which he lives, or against Almighty God Who is waiting to have mercy on him—whether it be the love of God, or the love of man, or the true unselfish love of self, that he disregards and casts aside in sloth or wilfulness or passion; in every case the ultimate, the characteristic note of his sin is still the same: it is lawlessness: it is the abuse of will, thrusting away the task, declining from the effort, refusing the sacrifice wherein lay the next step towards the end of life, the man's one *raison d'être:* it is the distortion of faculties, the wrenching aside of energy, the perversion of a trust from the purpose marked upon it, from the design which conscience seldom, if ever, wholly ceases to attest, to a morbid use, to a senseless squandering, a listless, wasteful, indolent neglect, a self-chosen and self-centred aim. Whether the sin be quiet or flagrant, brutal or refined, secret or

flaunting, arrogant or faint-hearted, its deep distinctive quality, its badness and its power for havoc
lie in this—that the man will not have law to reign
over him; that he will do what he wills with that
which is not in truth his own; that he is acting, or
idling, in contempt of the law which conditions the
great gift of life, and is involved in his tenure of it.

(*a*) "Sin is lawlessness:" and to persist in any sin
is to go on, with ever-increasing ease and senselessness it may be, beating off the everlasting Law,
ignoring or defying the essential rules of moral
health and spiritual growth, rejecting in the Law
the Lawgiver Who created us to find in its ways
our joy and strength. So do men go on who sin
against the law of their own personal being. For
instance, let us mark for a moment that dull rebellion
of lawless thoughts; the perverseness, the ever-deepen-
ing disorder of a mind that swerves from its true calling
wilfully to loiter or to brood about the thoughts of
sin; about thoughts of sensuality, or of jealousy, or
of self-conceit. The high faculties of memory, reflection, fancy, observation, are dragged down from their
great task: day by day the field for their lawful
exercise is spread out before them: all the wonder,
the beauty, the mystery, the sadness, the dignity
and wretchedness, the endless interests and endless

opportunities of human life and of the scene which
it is crossing—these are ever coming before the
mind which God created to enter into them, to find
its work and training and delight and growth amidst
them: while over all His creatures, He Himself, the
Most High God, is ready to lead on the mind from
strength to strength, preparing it for that surpassing
sight in which it may hereafter find its ceaseless
exercise and perfect rest—the sight of His uncreated
glory. Such is its lawful course: such are the good
works which God has prepared for it to walk in:
whatever may by nature be its strength or weakness,
He will enable it by grace for such an end as this.
And yet, all the while, in the dismal lawlessness of
sin, it stays to grovel among the hateful thoughts
of mean, degrading vices; or turns day after day to
keep awake the memory of some sullen grudge, some
fancied slight; to tend the smoky flame of some dull,
unreasonable hatred: or to dwell on its own poor
achievements, its fancied excellences, the scraps of
passing praise that have been given to it, the dignity
that its self - consciousness is making laughable.
Surely it is terrible to think that a man may so go
on, and so grow old, continually stumbling further
and further from the law of his own joy and health.

(b) Let us mark, again, in the case of luxury, how

a man may refuse year after year to listen to the law
of his relation to his fellow-men; how he may be
ever putting off until the end of this life the day of
reckoning with that law which God fastened into his
very nature when He framed him for the privilege,
the happiness, the responsibilities of a social being.
To gather round one's self, in ever-growing plenty
and elaboration, all the means of comfort and
pleasure which civilization brings within one's
reach; to shelter, and enrich, and decorate, and soothe
one's daily life with the outcome of others' toil and
ingenuity; to take whatever one can get of all that
has been won by the labour, the experience, the
inventiveness, the suffering of the past and of the
present;—to let all this flow towards one for the ease,
the pride, or the pleasantness of one's own lot, and
then to make no real contribution to the work of
one's own day;—to shirk one's share of hardship and
fatigue, to bear no part, with whatever gifts one has,
in the painful efforts, the unselfish ventures, the
exacting strain of mind or body to their utmost
strength, through which the social order, that makes
all this comfort possible, may move on its slow,
costly course of progress towards a better, juster,
happier, more peaceful state:—how can a life like
this seem other than a continual lawlessness; a plain

abuse of the conditions of one's place among mankind; an unnatural absorption of that which one is
suffered to receive only in order that, only so far as,
it may make one better able to repay one's due and
thankful tribute to the welfare of others? It may
be possible for some of us to thrust off that demand,
to keep that law of social life at arm's length, as it
were, year after year; it is possible for most of us
to meet it with miserable inadequacy, with glaring
disproportion between that which we receive and
all that in any way we give. But conscience witnesses that wilful luxury is lawlessness; and that
those who go on fancying that more and more is
necessary or reasonable for themselves, while they
think less and less of what is certainly necessary for
others, must somehow have to meet the Nemesis of
violated law. For "the poor shall not alway be
forgotten: the patient abiding of the meek shall not
perish for ever"—and "the Helper of the friendless"
cannot in the end let man have the upper hand.

(c) Or think again of the lawlessness of a prayerless life: the disorder, the disproportion, the atrophy
and wasting that must come when the faculty for
communion with God is never used, and love, the
first law of our relation to Him, is never stirred by
the realization of His Presence, the recollection of

His Love. The nature that is endued with the capacity for prayer, the soul that can be filled with the disclosure of His Goodness, the life that was meant to find its highest exercise, its point of illumination, its way to rise, in seeking Him, cannot without hurt refuse all this. Prayer is, for spiritual beings, a law of health—a law which we may put back and ignore persistently in this life if we will, but which we cannot change. The desire to pray may disappear, just as for a lazy man there may cease to be any pleasure in the healthy use of his limbs: like him, we may find it hard, distasteful work at first to take up again what we have long abandoned. But if we yield to that distaste, if we acquiesce in our inertness, we are withholding the effort which an essential law of our life demands from us; silently and sluggishly, or in impatience and vexation, we are saying that we will not have law to reign over us. God bids the soul press on to claim its goodly heritage; and the soul of the prayerless thinks scorn of that pleasant land and gives no credence to His Word. And so that which was made for Him is imprisoned in the world; that which should hunger and thirst after His Righteousness is set to make what it can of the substitutes which this life offers; that which can receive the

Infinite and the Eternal Love is silenced with the things of sense and time.

III. Our own personal being, our relation to society, our relation to Almighty God; each has, we know, its law: and great is the peace that they have who love that law; and those who seek it, walk at liberty. But while this life lasts, for its few precarious years, we can, if so we will, dispute, reject, evade, ignore the law. But not for ever; we must meet and own it some day: for lawlessness is sin; and sin, if we are not trying now by the grace of God to deal with it, must be the sting of death. For, surely, when we try to think what the moral law is, and where, as men in every age have owned, it lives and has its being, it is hard to see how we can demur to words like these: "Those things that are held within the vault of heaven, cannot flee from heaven save by drawing near to it; for howsoever far they go from the one part of heaven, by so much do they approach the other part. And even so, though a man will not be obedient to the Divine will and ordinance, yet can he not flee from it; for if he sets himself to flee from under the will that bids, he runs under the will that punishes."[1] We cannot think, if we try to think

[1] Cf. St. Anselm, "Cur Deus Homo," I. xv. Also Hooker, "Of the Laws of Ecclesiastical Polity," I. iii. 1, and note; St. Thomas Aquinas, S. Th. 1ma 2^{dae} xciii. 6.

at all, that the soul, when it has done with this
world, can go on trifling with the laws that it has
slighted here : we know that sooner or later, somehow or other, that essential demand, "Fast linked as
Thy great Name to Thee, O Lord," must needs be
reckoned with ; and that the career of wilfulness
must have an end. And Death, as it comes among
us, ought to make us think of this. For it is the
great, indisputable witness of the arrest of wilfulness, the folly of a lawless will. In its awful steadfastness, its refusal of all compromise, resource,
appeal, evasion, it shadows forth, as nothing else in
this world, the ultimate certainty of law. No man,
however rich, or powerful, or insolent, or ingenious,
can for one instant say it nay, or make the smallest
difference in the way it deals with him ; the traveller
might as well attempt to check the avalanche that
is already thundering upon the fields of ice and snow
above the ledge of rock on which he stands. We
may come to terms with many of our troubles :
almost all bodily pain may now be more or less alle-
viated, though not quite all ; when sorrow comes, some
of us may perhaps be able to divert our minds from
it, or to harden our hearts ; we may refuse to face the
difficulties of our day, and make up phrases to con-
ceal its miseries ;—and civilization has made many

inventions for prolonging the comfort of a selfish
life; but there is no way of making terms with
Death; and when he comes, the utmost wealth has
nothing to offer which he is not already clutching.
Abruptly the sheer certainty of law breaks in among
our confusions, and half-heartedness, and crooked
ways: away go all the subterfuges, the half-truths,
the means of forgetfulness whereby men get off facing
facts; and the puny, lawless, wilful heart is brought
to book. Even if it could mean nothing more than
this, that we are left to be for evermore what we have
chosen to become, how could we bear to think of it?

IV. It is amidst such thoughts as these that we
may come to know the meaning and the power of
the Cross of Christ, and the exceeding great love of
our Master and only Saviour dying for us. You will
remember what are the words that follow those of
which we have been thinking, " The sting of death is
sin; and the strength of sin is the law. But thanks
be to God, Which giveth us the victory through our
Lord Jesus Christ."—St. Paul had known that grace
of repentance, that power of renewal which the
astounding Love of God had sent into the world.
For him, old things were passed away, and all things
were become new; he had found that penetrating
reality of pardon which changes the whole look of

life and death; and amidst the things of time his conversation was in heaven. And so he springs in an instant from the awful thoughts of sin and death to the unhindered gladness of thanksgiving. Thousands since then have known, in part at least, what he knew of God's victorious and pardoning grace; and we, in His infinite compassion, may know it too: for us, too, He has stored within His Church the means of that great deliverance, the power of that glad renewal. Yes, for all the past, for all our lawlessness and shame and backwardness, St. Paul's thanksgiving may be ours yet. Only it is good, it is necessary, for us to remember what was the life, the habit of mind and work, out of which those thankful and triumphant words arose in the very face of death. It was the life of one who lived by the faith of the Son of God; as the slave of all men, constrained by the love of Christ; in weariness and painfulness, and in much patience; as poor, yet making many rich, as having nothing and yet possessing all things: one who counted not his life dear unto himself, that he might finish his course with joy, and the ministry which he had received; and who, having suffered the loss of all things that he might win Christ, still in all simplicity and truth could only judge himself to be the chief of sinners.

XX.

A GOOD EXAMPLE.

BISHOP ANDREWES: HIS TIME AND WORK.

THERE are many ways, I think, in which we may be helped by the study of those passages in the history of the English Church which seem to have been characterized by especial elements of difficulty and distress. For so we may be taught to take a truer measure of the troubles and imperfections and anxieties of our own day; to see how hopefully a man may try to deal with them, and to do his work in spite of much that he would fain have otherwise; refusing to let the wholesome sense of urgency degenerate into the weakness of panic or fretful impatience. Again, we may thus deepen our loyalty and our love towards the Church, which in such trials has evinced her God-given power of endurance and advance, and, holding her course through the dimness and the storm, has emerged with surer strength of experience and self-realization for whatever still remains to be undertaken or endured. But we may also learn a lesson which will bear more directly on our own conduct, helping us to bestow aright whatever of effort, labour, service, and self-sacrifice we may have to contribute to the setting forward of God's cause in our own age. For plainly every one of us may, if he will, do something, be it much or little, towards making that which will be the history of our generation; and the abiding worth of whatever he can do will depend, perhaps, mainly on his just discernment of the chief issues that are being either decided or kept open in his day; on his correcting in his own mind the misplaced emphasis of common talk and controversy; on his throwing whatever strength he has into the real, and not the merely apparent crisis of the perpetual conflict between truth and error, between good and evil, or between the better and the less good. It needs some insight and calmness and independence to see clearly and steadily what matters most in one's own day; and men have, for instance, said sometimes that the Church was in danger, without apparently suspecting that by their own worldly anxiety and partisanship, and their own neglect of simple duties, they were, indeed, doing more to endanger their real trust than any political opponent ever could have done. It is a safeguard against all such misdirection of vehemence and solicitude, it may help us to give to the real task of our day whatever energy or influence we have to dedicate, if, from time to time, looking back to past ages of especial trial and confusion, we single out in the *mêlée* of the fight those whom time, the great arbiter of all blunders, has approved as the men who were not misled; who saw for what they must contend, and held to that; who were strong enough to do without the encouragement of easy triumphs, fighting neither with small nor great, but only with the antagonist whose onset was making for the true centre of their position—the men who not only meant well, but went right. As we watch them, standing apart somewhat from the throng of their contemporaries, misunderstood, perhaps, or distrusted by many on their own side in the struggle, quietly and chivalrously holding fast the principle, the right which they had seen to be the secret of freedom, integrity, and hope; foregoing for its sake obvious advantages and tempting compromises; we may, perhaps, be able to gain a little more of the faith and patience of that quiet insight which enabled them to guard intact the truth or liberty which later ages prized aright as it disclosed its latent strength and fruitfulness.

It is with the hope of some such gain that I would ask you to look back to-night across just three centuries; and from the eventful scene of London in the later years of Elizabeth's long reign, to single out one figure; and to try to form some estimate of the service which Lancelot Andrewes rendered to his generation and for the good of those who have come after him.

I. Three hundred years ago. Let us try to bring before our minds, with as few words as may be used, the anxieties which seem likely to have been foremost in the thoughts of any thoughtful man who in 1589 was caring, working, praying, for the Church of England. He would be conscious that a certain change for the better had passed over the aspect of her affairs within the last twelve months; that an imperious and engrossing fear had been, though not dispersed, yet greatly lightened and moderated. The ruin of the Spanish Armada had not only thrilled men's hearts with the sense of a national deliverance which may well have seemed unique; it had also told upon the course and temper of religious thought.[1] The dread lest the supremacy of Rome should be enforced in England was not so near and huge on the horizon at the end of 1588 as it had been at the

---

[1] Cf. Keble's Preface to Hooker's Works, sec. 35.

beginning; and in the relief thus gained some were
entering upon larger and worthier ways of thought,
and laying aside the hesitation and reserve with
which under the stress of fear they had spoken of
their heritage. But, however thankfully an English
Churchman in 1589 may have recalled the events of
the preceding year, however gladly he may have felt
the abatement of one great hindrance to the Church's
freedom in realizing her prerogative, in developing
her resources, in putting forth her strength, in grap-
pling with her task; still the reasons for alarm, the
excuses for faint-heartedness, were neither few nor
slight. A strong and resolute party, including some
who were learned and able, and many who were
earnest and unworldly, was bent upon setting up in
England the discipline and government which Calvin's
masterfulness had made paramount at Geneva. Some
who were thus minded had seceded from the Church's
worship; others, more numerous, more weighty, and
more dangerous, were endeavouring, while they
retained their positions and exercised their ministry,
to intrude the Genevan system, silently and steadily,
into the English Church; and, with the help of two
men of very real power, a plan had lately been
devised by which this alien structure might be
quietly built up within the Episcopal, and athwart

its lines, so as gradually to supersede it.[1] And
then beyond the range of tacit secession and of
conformity for innovation's sake, there were sects
clamorous and active—one tampering with the basal
principles of Christianity, and, it was alleged, of all
morality also;[2] the other, with far more power and
result, lifting the great banner of independence,
taunting and upbraiding those who let "I dare
not" wait upon "I would," crying for "reformation
without tarrying for any,"[3] and calling upon the
"Queen to forbid and exterminate within her
dominions all other religious worship and ministers"
than their own.[4] And as three hundred years ago a
quiet man was thinking of these things, and wondering what would come of it all, he would grow sick
at heart as he saw from time to time the gross and
ribald nonsense that was being poured out in abusive
pamphlets from the secret presses; and he would
grow yet more wretched and despondent when the
Church's cause was dishonoured by an attempt to
answer such pamphlets in their own style. He well

[1] Cf. Neal's "Puritans," vol. i. pp. 204, 205: 265, 266: 303-305 ;
Fuller's "Church History," ix. 103, 142.

[2] Cf. Archbishop Sandys' "Sermons," p. 130.

[3] Robert Browne in 1582.

[4] H. Barrow's "Platform," quoted by Gardiner, "History of
England," vol. i. p. 37.

might say, as one great layman did about that time, " Two principal causes have I ever known of atheism, curious controversies and profane scoffing. Now that these two are joined in one, no doubt that sect will make no small progression;"[1] and he would hardly wonder that some were venturing to assert, as they saw this travesty of controversy, that the religion which men thus degraded was itself but a shrewd device for keeping society in order.[2] But nothing, perhaps, would make his heart so heavy and apprehensive as the apparent inability of many among the clergy to meet in any way the needs and perils which beset them; the slowness with which they were emerging out of the disorder and neglect disclosed in the earlier years of Elizabeth's reign;[3] the ignorance, and incapacity, and sloth, and worldliness with which in many places they were still so senselessly provoking the victorious onset of any antagonist who could wield against them the rightful and unfailing strength of a high purpose, a pure life, and a truth sincerely trusted.[4]

[1] Lord Bacon, " An Advertisement touching the Controversies of the Church of England." Probably written about 1590.

[2] Cf. Hooker, V. ii. 2–4.

[3] Cf. the returns elicited in 1561 : quoted from Strype's " Parker," by Perry, " English Church History," p. 277.

[4] Cf. Hooker, V. lxxxi. 1.

Such may have been among the thoughts which rose in a man's mind three hundred years ago as he watched the course of Church affairs and tried to guess their likely outcome; such were some of the conditions under which Lancelot Andrewes sought and found his work.

II. If a Londoner had been asked in 1589 who were the most remarkable preachers in the City, the answer would probably have included three names that soon were very famous throughout England. One certainly would be the name of Richard Bancroft, rector of St. Andrew's Holborn, treasurer of St. Paul's, and chaplain to Sir Christopher Hatton, the Lord Chancellor of England. For Dr. Bancroft had lately come to the front of discussion and conflict by a sermon preached at Paul's Cross early in the year [1] — a sermon in which many have traced the first public utterance of that more adequate and courageous defence of the Church's ancient order and discipline which seems to have been released by the destruction of the Armada. It would have been characteristic of Bancroft to be the first to say what many had been thinking; and he was probably, at the time we are recalling, still busy with the assailants

[1] Reprinted in Hickes's "Bibliotheca Scriptorum Ecclesiæ Anglicanæ."

whom his impetuosity had provoked.[1] But there was a greater man than Bancroft preaching every Sunday morning in the Temple Church; neither popular nor happy there, but with strength and diligence and learning of the rarest splendour, working steadily at a great book which should outlive all the controversies that had made his fame and spoilt his peace. For Richard Hooker was still Master of the Temple, though he was longing to regain the blessings of obscurity in a country parish; and while some men thought his sermons tedious and obscure, and others who had sided with his now silenced adversary, Travers, bore a grudge against him for the past, still men could not be unmoved by his massive thought and knowledge, by the power of his patience and holiness, and by the memory of those exciting Sundays, when there were almost as many writers as hearers in the Temple Church, and the gravest Benchers were busy morning and afternoon taking notes of the discourses through which the Master and the Lecturer argued out their differences.[2] And then, with Hooker and Bancroft, Lancelot Andrewes surely would be recalled, as prominent among the younger men who were closing with the

[1] Cf. Strype's " Life of Whitgift," i. 559, *seq*.
[2] Cf. Fuller's " Church History," bk. ix. §§ 49-62.

difficulties of the day. For, junior to Hooker by two years, to Bancroft by eleven, he had at the age of thirty-four already taken his place in the strongest work of his day. Let us glance back over the earlier stages of his career.—He had hardly entered boyhood when the enthusiasm of the true student came on him; and there is something pathetic in the picture of the lad at Merchant Taylors' School needing to be driven out into the playground from the books he loved—the books for which he rose at four in the morning and lingered far into the night. He, like Hooker, owed much to the watchfulness and insight of his schoolmasters, first at the Coopers' Free School and then at Merchant Taylors'; whence in 1571 he went to Pembroke Hall at Cambridge, holding one of the eight Greek scholarships newly founded by Thomas Watts, the Archdeacon of Middlesex, and further helped in 1573, (as Hooker, too, was helped more than once,) by Robert Nowell, a great lawyer in London, wise and large in his bounty.[1]

I have the copy of Demosthenes which Andrewes used at Cambridge; in the title-page he has written with his own name that of his benefactor, the Archdeacon; and if the beautiful and elaborate Latin

[1] Cf. "The Towneley Nowell Manuscripts," edited by Dr. Grosart, p. 184.

annotations in the margin of the volume are indeed
his, they illustrate the scholarly diligence and precision which made him, it is said, "one of the rarest
linguists in Christendom," knowing more than twenty
languages, and "so perfect in the grammar and criticism," "as if he had utterly neglected the matter,"
and yet "so exquisite and sound in the matter," "as
if he had never regarded the grammar."[1] It is not
strange that in 1576 he was elected a Fellow of his
college, receiving soon after the distinction of an
Honorary Fellowship at the new foundation of Jesus
College, Oxford. To this period of his life belongs,
I think, his earliest published work, a wondrous
monument of painstaking and conscientious toil.

A great French Bishop of this century has told us
that for many years he wrote at full length all his
catechizings; and his biographer says that ten
volumes of manuscript attest that dutiful and hidden
labour.[2] Lancelot Andrewes in the same stage of
his life seems to have taken like pains over a task
not very different. "The custom of catechizing in
church was, in those days" (says a recent historian
of Cambridge), "systematic and general. . . . While

---

[1] Bishop Buckeridge, in the sermon preached at Bishop Andrewes'
funeral.
[2] F. Lagrange, Vie de Mgr. Dupanloup, i. 82.

not one minister in ten was permitted to preach, all were expected to catechize. With the view, therefore, of rendering those in the University who were destined for the clerical profession more competent to the discharge of this primary duty, Andrewes initiated at Pembroke a series of Saturday and Sunday afternoon catechetical lectures, designed to serve to some extent as illustrations of the best method of teaching the elements of Christian belief." He soon had gathered round him a large class, both from the University and from among the neighbouring clergy; and we are even told that a man "was scarcely reputed a pretender to learning and piety in Cambridge" (at that time) "who had not made himself a disciple of Andrewes by diligent resorting to his lectures; nor he a pretender to the study of divinity who did not transcribe his notes, which ever after passed from hand to hand in many hundred copies."[1] It appears that after his death inaccurate and incomplete reproductions of these notes were published, till in 1675 his own papers were elaborately edited, in a folio of five hundred pages.[2]

He does not stand alone in having prepared himself

[1] Mullinger's "History of the University of Cambridge," vol. ii. pp. 487, 488.

[2] "The Pattern of Catechistical Doctrine at Large" (Preface to the Reader).

for the most complete tasks by taking immense pains over the simplest; so illustrating the peculiar efficacy of the work that does not show, and the wide range of the great law, that "he that is faithful in that which is least is faithful also in much."

We have little knowledge of his earlier work in Holy Orders, save that he was singled out for special trust and encouragement by the Earl of Huntingdon and by Sir Francis Walsingham, travelling with the former to the north, and there evincing, it is said, those controversial powers which he afterwards employed with reluctance and with distinction. In 1589, it seems, the year to which we have especially been looking back, a threefold charge was given to his care: he was made Vicar of St. Giles's, Cripplegate, a Residentiary Canon of St. Paul's, and Master of his old college, Pembroke Hall, at Cambridge. The first of his printed sermons, which was preached before the Queen, bears date in this same year.

So, then, we may think of him as now prominent and active in the central life of England—a student still, as he was to the end of his laborious days; jealously guarding for this duty the forenoon; so that it has been said that "the rare exceptions to his usual sweetness and gentleness of temper were provoked by those who disturbed" his morning hours.

They were no true scholars," he used to say, " who came to speak with him before noon."[1] But now the external activity of his life was considerable, and the demands of a conspicuous position were beginning to come upon him. On most Sundays he would preach twice to his parishioners, though we are told in the sermon preached at his funeral that "he ever misliked often and loose preaching without study of antiquity, and he would be bold with himself and say, when he preached twice a day at St. Giles's, he prated once."[2] Nor, it seems, did he neglect the quiet round of daily duties in his parish; for the "Manual of Directions for the Sick," which was published after his death, is said to have been "conceived and used by him in his ordinary Visitation of the sick, when he was Vicar of St. Giles's, Cripplegate." At St. Paul's he read the divinity lecture thrice a week in term time ; and he is described as "walking about the aisle, ready to give advice and spiritual counsel to any who sought it ;" for, we are told, he was "deeply seen in cases of conscience."[3] Nor, for all he had to do in London, was his work at Cambridge neglected. "As an administrator" (writes one

[1] Cf. R. W. Church, in "Masters in English Theology," p. 63.
[2] Bishop Buckeridge in "Andrewes's Sermons," p. 295 of vol. v.
[3] H. Isaacson: cf. Fuller's "Abel Redevivus."

concerned especially with his University work)—"as
an administrator he was no less successful than as
a teacher.   He found his college in debt ; he left it "
(thanks to his care in business and to his personal
generosity) " not only with the debts paid off, but
with a reserve fund of £1000 at its command." [1]   In
1601 he was made Dean of Westminster ; and there,
as in the old days of his catechizing at Pembroke,
the true teacher's love of teaching came out in spon-
taneous painstaking.   "He did often supply," says
a Westminster scholar, "the place of both head
schoolmaster and usher for the space of a whole
week together, and gave us not an hour of loitering
time from morning to night . . . And all this without any compulsion of correction ; nay, I never
heard him utter so much as a word of austerity
among us." [2]

But austere he could be when need was : strict and
firm enough to refuse two bishoprics in Elizabeth's
reign, because he could not accept them without con-
niving at some plunder of Church property : [3] grave
says Fuller, with a certain patristic gravity, which
" in a manner awed King James, who refrained from

[1] Mullinger, *ubi supra*, p. 488.
[2] Cf. Mullinger, *ubi supra*, p. 487, note 3.
[3] Cf. Bishop Buckeridge's Sermon.

that mirth and liberty in the presence of this prelate which otherwise he assumed to himself." [1] It is striking to combine with this the assurance that " all evidence attests the lovableness of his nature; " [2] and that "of all those whose piety was remarkable in that troubled age, there was none who could bear comparison for spotlessness and purity of character with the good and gentle Andrewes." [3] For thus we see in him that singular union of tenderness and decision which seems to be the distinctive beauty of a life of prayer. All the chief elements of strength may seem to have met in him—learning, ability, power of work, facility of expression, charm of manner, purity of purpose, courage, holiness; so that it is not strange that great honours came to him unsought, and did him no harm. Elizabeth made him one of her Chaplains-in-Ordinary; James, soon after his accession, made him Bishop of Chichester, and thence translated him first to Ely, and afterwards to Winchester. He was, moreover, Almoner, Dean of the Chapel, and a Privy Councillor to James and to Charles I., in the second year of whose reign he passed away, at the age of seventy-one. The

---

[1] Book xi. sec. 46.
[2] R. W. Church, *ubi supra*, p. 67.
[3] Gardiner, ii. 33, quoted by R. W. Church.

manner of his life has been summed up by the Dean of St. Paul's in a few vivid words: "When he was called into public employment he lived, as great Church officers did in those days, through a round of sermons, Court attendances, and judicial or ecclesiastical business, varied by occasional controversies and sharp encounters, on paper or face to face, with the numberless foes and detractors of the English Church and State; from great Cardinals, like Bellarmine and Du Perron, to obscure sectaries, like Barrow and Mr. Traske. . . . It was the life of many men of that period. What is specially to be noticed in his case, is the high standard which was recognized both in his learning and his life."

So he lived, in constant converse both with the great scholars, philosophers, statesmen of his own day, and with the great saints and doctors of the past; resolute, laborious, consistent, sympathetic, effective, amidst the things of this world, just because so large a part of all his time and care and love was spent upon the things unseen. The manner of his death is told in the sermon preached at his funeral by the Bishop of Ely, his successor as Vicar of St. Giles's—told in words which touch so dominant a note of all his life that I will venture to quote them at length :—

"After the death of his brother, Master Thomas Andrewes, in the, sickness time, whom he loved dearly, he began to foretell his own death before the end of summer or before the beginning of winter. And when his brother Master Nicholas Andrewes died, he took that as a certain sign and prognostic and warning of his own death; and from that time till the hour of his dissolution he spent all his time in prayer, and his prayer-book, when he was private, was seldom seen out of his hands, and in the time of his fever and last sickness, besides the often prayers which were read to him, in which he repeated all the parts of the Confession and other petitions with an audible voice, as long as his strength endured, he did—as was well observed by certain tokens in him—continually pray to himself, though he seemed otherwise to rest or slumber; and when he could pray no longer with his voice, yet by lifting up his eyes and hands he prayed still, and when both voice and eyes and hands failed in their office, then with his heart he still prayed, until it pleased God to receive his blessed soul to Himself."[1]

His body was buried in the little chapel which, till its destruction in 1830, stood at the east end of the Lady Chapel of St. Saviour's Church, in South-

[1] Bishop Buckeridge in Andrewes's Sermons, vol. v. p. 297.

wark. At that date it was removed to the Lady Chapel, and his name was often mentioned in the struggle which saved that chapel from being also demolished a few years later.[1] Wherever he rested in his life his unfailing generosity left its trace. It is pitiful to think how the irreverence and neglect of later generations have dealt with the place of his burial. It is a reproach which now, I trust, is soon to be, so far as it is possible, put away.

III. I have reserved but very scanty time in which to speak of that which, most of all, I wish that I could duly bring before you—namely, the character of his especial service to the Church of England, the secret of his work's effective value; the conviction which guided him to see what were the real issues of his day, where lay the great strength of the Church's cause, and what were the principles never to be let go, never to be trifled with. It is hard to speak briefly of these things; and I must speak from only a fragmentary knowledge of his writings, with large indebtedness to those who have more worthily studied them. But this, I think, is clear. His place is in that great line of English theologians who, beginning in the later Elizabethan period, carried

[1] Cf. W. Taylor, "Annals of St. Mary Overy," and "Papers relating to St. Saviour's, Southwark," in Bodleian Library.

forward the realization, and elicited the energy and worth of those essential elements of vitality and strength which the Church of England had, in the providence of God, carried through all the struggle and confusion of the sixteenth century. The great safeguards of continuity, the pledges of renewal, had been preserved by those who hardly seem, in some instances, to have understood the worth of the treasure they were defending—its worth, that latent and unending power of fruitfulness which it disclosed in the hands of their successors, and is disclosing still. There are splendid names along that line; but I doubt whether we can owe to any among them much more than to those two who stand close together near the beginning of the series, Hooker and Andrewes. For it seems that they especially developed and secured for the Church of England the strength which lay in her power to appeal to two great witnesses of her authority and truth—to reason and to history. A recent writer has finely said, " I believe, with a conviction the strength of which I could hardly express, that it is the vocation of the English Church to realize and to offer to mankind a Catholicism which is Scriptural, and represents the whole of Scripture; which is historical, and can know itself free in face of historical and critical science; which is rational and constitutional in its claim of authority."[1]

These three great elements of strength and courage had been carried unimpaired through the work of reformation: the first had been vivid in the consciousness and work of its earlier agents; but the second and the third, guarded no less really, present no less certainly, waited for the touch which should release their potency and blessing. And as Hooker, in his great treatise, maintained, against the faithlessness of Puritan distrust and scorn, the place and dignity of human reason, " aided with the influence of Divine grace "—showing that " the way to be ripe in faith " is not necessarily to be " raw in judgment "[2] —so Andrewes, outliving Hooker by a quarter of a century, deployed, as it were, upon the field of thought and controversy the force that issues from the strongholds of history.[3] He realized and trusted and displayed the strength of an historic Church; he was fearless when he felt that history was with him, and careless about apparent advantages which history encouraged him to disregard. In a vigorous passage of his answer to Bellarmine he heartily accepts, and

[1] C. Gore, in Preface to last edition of " Roman Catholic Claims."
[2] III. viii. 18, 4.
[3] Cf. R. W. Church, in " Masters in English Theology," pp. 105, 106, whence the thought of this comparison is taken.

wields as one familiar with his weapon, the famous
canon of the Catholic faith—that it is that which
has been believed always and everywhere and by all.[1]
He meets Du Perron at point after point of his attack ;
frankly accepting the verdict of antiquity, even where
the English Church had not spoken explicitly, as in
regard to prayers for the dead,[2] frankly untroubled
by any criticism which has not history behind it.
And the same profound belief in the future of the
Church that can fearlessly appeal to the witness of
the past, the same unqualified reliance on the strength
of a continuous history, makes him apparently indifferent to advantages which men less sure of their
footing are apt somewhat restlessly to desire. Indifferent, for instance, to present and obvious completeness. "I doubt," says the Dean of St. Paul's,
"whether Andrewes cared much for that intellectual
completeness of theory which we make much of."
And this strong patience in unfinishedness seems
characteristic of one who was always resting on the
witness of the past. For history, I suppose, would
certainly not teach him that the purest truth had
always been embodied in the compactest system.
There never was a scheme more perfect in logical

---

[1] "Responsio ad Apologiam," p. 20, ed. 1610.
[2] "Stricturæ," p. 9, ed. 1629.

coherence and finish than the scheme of Calvin at
Geneva—a scheme so perfect and disastrous that it
well might serve for a perpetual warning against the
attractions of completeness. And as the resolute
faithfulness of his appeal to history made Andrewes
content to do without the luxury of theoretic neat-
ness—a luxury which we can hardly hope to have
in this fragmentary world save at some expense of
truth—so also did it strengthen him against all
hankering for peace where it involved the blurring
of principles or the forgetting of facts. " We wish
not," he writes to Du Moulin, " we wish not a concord
that is but pieced and patched up, but an entire,
absolute agreement without piecing and.patching ; "
and while he prays for the union of all reformed
Churches, it is, he is careful to tell Du Moulin, that
they may be united in that form of government, that
bond of polity which traces its origin from the very
cradle of the Church ; against which he who sets himself sets himself against all antiquity—that government which (with whatever considerateness he may
speak of defects which he is willing to attribute
to the iniquity of the times) he never hesitates to
uphold as of Divine right.[1]

So he laboured and contended ; so he preached,

[1] *Vide* " Responsiones ad Petri Molinæi Epistolas Tres," ed. 1629.

ever striving to uplift and quicken men by the power of a religion in which the communion of saints was felt as a reality—a religion " which claimed kindred with all that was ancient and all that was universal in Christianity; which looked above the controversies and misunderstandings of the hour to the larger thought and livelier faith and sanctified genius of those in whom the Church of Christ has recognized her most venerated teachers."[1]   And so, above all else, he prayed ; and it may be doubted whether any uninspired words have done more to teach men how to pray in truth, and purity, and generosity, and self-abasement than that manuscript on which he never thought that other eyes than his would fall: "the manuscript that was scarce ever out of his hands and that was found worn by his fingers and blotted with his tears."[2]—The distinctive lesson of such a life as his is neither hard to find nor easy to fulfil. For it never has been and it never will be easy to forego the power, the readiness, the security, the certainty, which seem to be promised us by any system that is complete and rounded-off and logical. There is a true instinct in us which desires perfectness; but it is a false, impatient craving which would

---

[1] R. W. Church, *ubi supra*, pp. 97, 98.
[2] Bishop Horne, in Preface to " Private Devotions," p. 8.

demand it in this world. Nor, again, will the thought of concord and reunion ever lose its rightful beauty, ever cease to command our aspiration. It is a true instinct in us which desires peace; we cannot doubt it when we remember Who is the Author of peace and Lover of concord. But here, again, it is a faithless haste that for the sake of agreement and co-operation disregards the witness of history and imperils the strength of an inviolate consistency by surrendering or obscuring in some popular compromise, some pleasant semblance of generosity, principles by which the Church, in spite of all the sins and perils of the past, has still maintained her continuity and renewed her strength.

It would be a true and fitting thought to take from Bishop Andrewes's work that there is no such strength as that of patience; the patience that prefers truth to symmetry and facts to logic; the patience that makes men brave to say that there is much which they do not know, that there are many questions which will never be answered in this life, many wants and blemishes and troubles that the Church may have to bear so long as she is militant; the patience with which great men have been content to live on even to the end in seeming weakness in weary conflict, if only they might so hand down to their successors an undiminished heritage of light and hope and opportunity; the patience which Bishop Andrewes learnt, perhaps, in no other way so surely as in prayer.

PRINTED BY WILLIAM CLOWES AND SONS, LIMITED, LONDON AND BECCLES.

A Catalogue of Works

IN

THEOLOGICAL LITERATURE

PUBLISHED BY

Messrs. LONGMANS, GREEN, & CO.

39 Paternoster Row, London, E.C.

Abbey and Overton.—THE ENGLISH CHURCH IN THE EIGHTEENTH CENTURY. By Charles J. Abbey, M.A., Rector of Checkendon, Reading, and John H. Overton, M.A., Rector of Epworth, Doncaster, Rural Dean of Isle of Axholme. *Cr. 8vo. 7s. 6d.*

Adams.—SACRED ALLEGORIES. The Shadow of the Cross —The Distant Hills—The Old Man's Home—The King's Messengers. By the Rev. William Adams, M.A. *Crown 8vo. 5s.*

The Four Allegories may be had separately, with Illustrations. *16mo. 1s. each. Also the Miniature Edition. Four Vols. 32mo. 1s. each;* in a box, 5s.

Aids to the Inner Life.

Edited by the Rev. W. H. Hutchings, M.A., Rector of Kirkby Misperton, Yorkshire. *Five Vols. 32mo, cloth limp, 6d. each; or cloth extra, 1s. each. Sold separately.*
Also an Edition *with red borders,* 2s. each.

OF THE IMITATION OF CHRIST. By Thomas à Kempis. In Four Books.

THE CHRISTIAN YEAR: Thoughts in Verse for the Sundays and Holy Days throughout the Year.

THE DEVOUT LIFE. By St. Francis de Sales.

THE HIDDEN LIFE OF THE SOUL. From the French of Jean Nicolas Grou.

THE SPIRITUAL COMBAT. Together with the Supplement and the Path of Paradise. By Laurence Scupoli.

Andrewes.—A MANUAL FOR THE SICK ; with other Devotions. By Lancelot Andrewes, D.D., sometime Bishop of Winchester. With Preface by H. P. Liddon, D.D. *24mo. 2s. 6d.*

Augustine.—THE CONFESSIONS OF ST. AUGUSTINE. In Ten Books. Translated and Edited by the Rev. W. H. HUTCHINGS, M.A. *Small 8vo.* 5s. *Cheap Edition.* 16mo. 2s. 6d.

Bathe.—Works by the Rev. ANTHONY BATHE, M.A.

A LENT WITH JESUS. A Plain Guide for Churchmen. Containing Readings for Lent and Easter Week, and on the Holy Eucharist. *32mo,* 1s.; *or in paper cover,* 6d.

WHAT I SHOULD BELIEVE. A Simple Manual of Self-Instruction for Church People. *Crown 8vo.* 3s. 6d.

Bickersteth.—Works by EDWARD HENRY BICKERSTETH, D.D., Bishop of Exeter.

THE LORD'S TABLE; or, Meditations on the Holy Communion Office in the Book of Common Prayer. *16mo.* 1s.; *or cloth extra,* 2s.

YESTERDAY, TO-DAY, AND FOR EVER : a Poem in Twelve Books. *One Shilling Edition,* 18mo. *With red borders,* 16mo, 2s. 6d. *The Crown 8vo Edition* (5s.) *may still be had.*

Blunt.—Works by the late Rev. JOHN HENRY BLUNT, D.D.

DICTIONARY OF DOCTRINAL AND HISTORICAL THEOLOGY. By various Writers. Edited by the Rev. JOHN HENRY BLUNT, D.D. *Imperial 8vo.* 21s.

DICTIONARY OF SECTS, HERESIES, ECCLESIASTICAL PARTIES AND SCHOOLS OF RELIGIOUS THOUGHT. By various Writers. Edited by the Rev. JOHN HENRY BLUNT, D.D. *Imperial 8vo.* 21s.

THE BOOK OF CHURCH LAW. Being an Exposition of the Legal Rights and Duties of the Parochial Clergy and the Laity of the Church of England. Revised by Sir WALTER G. F. PHILLIMORE, Bart., D.C.L. *Crown 8vo.* 7s. 6d.

A COMPANION TO THE BIBLE : Being a Plain Commentary on Scripture History, to the end of the Apostolic Age. *Two vols. small 8vo. Sold separately.*

THE OLD TESTAMENT. 3s. 6d.   THE NEW TESTAMENT. 3s. 6d.

HOUSEHOLD THEOLOGY : a Handbook of Religious Information respecting the Holy Bible, the Prayer Book, the Church, the Ministry, Divine Worship, the Creeds, etc. etc. *Paper cover,* 16mo. 1s. Also the Larger Edition, 3s. 6d.

Body.—Works by the Rev. GEORGE BODY, D.D., Canon of Durham.

THE SCHOOL OF CALVARY ; or, Laws of Christian Life revealed from the Cross. A Course of Lectures delivered in substance at All Saints', Margaret Street. *Crown 8vo.*

THE LIFE OF JUSTIFICATION : a Series of Lectures delivered in substance at All Saints', Margaret Street. 16mo. 2s. 6d.

THE LIFE OF TEMPTATION : a Course of Lectures delivered in substance at St. Peter's, Eaton Square ; also at All Saints', Margaret Street. 16mo. 2s. 6d.

Boultbee.—A COMMENTARY ON THE THIRTY-NINE ARTICLES OF THE CHURCH OF ENGLAND. By the Rev. T. P. BOULTBEE, formerly Principal of the London College of Divinity, St. John's Hall, Highbury. *Crown 8vo.* 6s.

Bright.—Works by WILLIAM BRIGHT, D.D., Canon of Christ Church.

LESSONS FROM THE LIVES OF THREE GREAT FATHERS: St. Athanasius, St. Chrysostom, and St. Augustine. *Crown 8vo.* 6s.
THE INCARNATION AS A MOTIVE POWER. *Crown 8vo.* 6s.
IONA AND OTHER VERSES. *Small 8vo.* 4s. 6d.
HYMNS AND OTHER VERSES. *Small 8vo.* 5s.
FAITH AND LIFE: Readings for the greater Holy Days, and the Sundays from Advent to Trinity. Compiled from Ancient Writers. *Small 8vo.* 5s.

Bright and Medd.—LIBER PRECUM PUBLICARUM EC-CLESIÆ ANGLICANÆ. A GULIELMO BRIGHT, S.T.P., et PETRO GOLDSMITH MEDD, A.M., Latine redditus. [In hac Editione continentur Versiones Latinæ—1. Libri Precum Publicarum Ecclesiæ Anglicanæ ; 2. Liturgiæ Primæ Reformatæ ; 3. Liturgiæ Scoticanæ ; 4. Liturgiæ Americanæ.] *Small 8vo.* 7s. 6d.

Browne.—AN EXPOSITION OF THE THIRTY-NINE ARTICLES, Historical and Doctrinal. By E. H. BROWNE, D.D., formerly Bishop of Winchester. *8vo.* 16s.

Campion and Beamont.—THE PRAYER BOOK INTER-LEAVED. With Historical Illustrations and Explanatory Notes arranged parallel to the Text. By W. M. CAMPION, D.D., and W. J. BEAMONT, M.A. *Small 8vo.* 7s. 6d.

Carter.—Works edited by the Rev. T. T. CARTER, M.A., Hon. Canon of Christ Church, Oxford.

THE TREASURY OF DEVOTION: a Manual of Prayer for General and Daily Use. Compiled by a Priest. *18mo.* 2s. 6d. ; *cloth limp,* 2s. ; *or bound with the Book of Common Prayer,* 3s. 6d. *Large-Type Edition. Crown 8vo.* 5s.

THE WAY OF LIFE: A Book of Prayers and Instruction for the Young at School, with a Preparation for Confirmation. Compiled by a Priest. *18mo.* 1s. 6d.

THE PATH OF HOLINESS: a First Book of Prayers, with the Service of the Holy Communion, for the Young. Compiled by a Priest. With Illustrations. *16mo.* 1s. 6d. ; *cloth limp,* 1s.

THE GUIDE TO HEAVEN: a Book of Prayers for every Want. (For the Working Classes.) Compiled by a Priest. *18mo.* 1s. 6d. ; *cloth limp,* 1s. *Large-Type Edition. Crown 8vo.* 1s. 6d. ; *cloth limp,* 1s.

[continued.

Carter.—Works edited by the Rev. T. T. CARTER, M.A., Hon.
Canon of Christ Church, Oxford—*continued.*
SELF-RENUNCIATION. From the French. *16mo. 2s. 6d. Also the
Larger Edition. Small 8vo. 3s. 6d.*
THE STAR OF CHILDHOOD; a First Book of Prayers and Instruc-
tion for Children. Compiled by a Priest. With Illustrations. *16mo. 2s. 6d.*

Carter.—MAXIMS AND GLEANINGS FROM THE WRIT-
INGS OF T. T. CARTER, M.A. Selected and arranged for Daily
Use. *Crown 16mo. 2s.*

Compton.—THE ARMOURY OF PRAYER. A Book of Devotion. Compiled by the Rev. BERDMORE COMPTON, M.A. *18mo. 3s. 6d.*

Conybeare and Howson.—THE LIFE AND EPISTLES OF
ST. PAUL. By the Rev. W. J. CONYBEARE, M.A., and the Very
Rev. J. S. HOWSON, D.D. With numerous Maps and Illustrations.
LIBRARY EDITION. *Two Vols. 8vo. 21s.*
STUDENT'S EDITION. *One Vol. Crown 8vo. 6s.*

Crake.—HISTORY OF THE CHURCH UNDER THE
ROMAN EMPIRE, A.D. 30-476. By the Rev. A. D. CRAKE, B.A.
Crown 8vo. 7s. 6d.

Creighton.—HISTORY OF THE PAPACY DURING THE
REFORMATION. By the Rev. CANON CREIGHTON, M.A., LL.D.
8vo. Vols. I. and II., 1378-1464, 32s. *Vols. III. and IV.,* 1464-1518, 24s.

Devotional Series, 16mo, Red Borders. *Each 2s. 6d.*
BICKERSTETH'S YESTERDAY, TO-DAY, AND FOR EVER.
CHILCOT'S EVIL THOUGHTS.
CHRISTIAN YEAR.
DEVOTIONAL BIRTHDAY BOOK.
HERBERT'S POEMS AND PROVERBS.
KEMPIS' (À) OF THE IMITATION OF CHRIST.
ST. FRANCIS DE SALES' THE DEVOUT LIFE.
WILSON'S THE LORD'S SUPPER. *Large type.*
*TAYLOR'S (JEREMY) HOLY LIVING.
* ———   ———   HOLY DYING.
These two in one Volume. 5s.

Devotional Series, 18mo, without Red Borders. *Each 1s.*
BICKERSTETH'S YESTERDAY, TO-DAY, AND FOR EVER.
CHRISTIAN YEAR.
KEMPIS' (À) OF THE IMITATION OF CHRIST.
WILSON'S THE LORD'S SUPPER. *Large type.*
*TAYLOR'S (JEREMY) HOLY LIVING.
* ———   ———   HOLY DYING.
These two in one Volume. 2s. 6d.

IN THEOLOGICAL LITERATURE. 5

Edersheim.—Works by ALFRED EDERSHEIM, M.A., D.D., Ph.D., sometime Grinfield Lecturer on the Septuagint, Oxford.

THE LIFE AND TIMES OF JESUS THE MESSIAH. *Two Vols.* *8vo. 24s.*

JESUS THE MESSIAH : being an Abridged Edition of ' The Life and Times of Jesus the Messiah.' *Crown 8vo. 7s. 6d.*

PROPHECY AND HISTORY IN RELATION TO THE MESSIAH : The Warburton Lectures, 1880-1884. *8vo. 12s.*

TOHU-VA-VOHU ('Without Form and Void') : being a collection of Fragmentary Thoughts and Criticism. *Crown 8vo. 6s.*

Ellicott.—Works by C. J. ELLICOTT, D.D., Bishop of Gloucester and Bristol.

A CRITICAL AND GRAMMATICAL COMMENTARY ON ST. PAUL'S EPISTLES. Greek Text, with a Critical and Grammatical Commentary, and a Revised English Translation. *8vo.*

1 CORINTHIANS. 16s.

GALATIANS. 8s. 6d.

EPHESIANS. 8s. 6d.

PASTORAL EPISTLES. 10s. 6d.

PHILIPPIANS, COLOSSIANS, AND PHILEMON. 10s. 6d.

THESSALONIANS. 7s. 6d.

HISTORICAL LECTURES ON THE LIFE OF OUR LORD JESUS CHRIST. *8vo. 12s.*

Epochs of Church History. Edited by the Rev. CANON CREIGHTON, M.A., LL.D. *Fcap. 8vo. 2s. 6d. each.*

THE ENGLISH CHURCH IN OTHER LANDS. By the Rev. H. W. TUCKER, M.A.

THE HISTORY OF THE RE-FORMATION IN ENGLAND. By the Rev. GEO. G. PERRY, M.A.

THE CHURCH OF THE EARLY FATHERS. By the Rev. ALFRED PLUMMER, D.D.

THE EVANGELICAL REVIVAL IN THE EIGHTEENTH CENTURY. By the Rev. J. H. OVERTON, M.A.

THE UNIVERSITY OF OXFORD. By the Hon. G. C. BRODRICK, D.C.L.

THE UNIVERSITY OF CAM-BRIDGE. By J. BASS MULLINGER M.A.

THE ENGLISH CHURCH IN THE MIDDLE AGES. By the Rev. W. HUNT, M.A.

THE CHURCH AND THE EASTERN EMPIRE. By the Rev. H. F. TOZER, M.A.

THE CHURCH AND THE ROMAN EMPIRE. By the Rev. A. CARR.

THE CHURCH AND THE PURI-TANS, 1570-1660. By HENRY OFFLEY WAKEMAN, M.A.

HILDEBRAND AND HIS TIMES. By the Rev. W. R. W. STEPHENS, M.A.

THE POPES AND THE HOHEN-STAUFEN. By UGO BALZANI.

THE COUNTER-REFORMATION. By ADOLPHUS WILLIAM WARD, Litt. D

WYCLIFFE AND MOVEMENTS FOR REFORM. By REGINALD L. POOLE, M.A.

THE ARIAN CONTROVERSY. By H. M. GWATKIN, M.A.

Fosbery.—Works edited by the Rev. THOMAS VINCENT FOSBERY, M.A., sometime Vicar of St. Giles's, Reading.

VOICES OF COMFORT. *Cheap Edition. Small 8vo.* 3s. 6d.
The Larger Edition (7s. 6d.) may still be had.

HYMNS AND POEMS FOR THE SICK AND SUFFERING. In connection with the Service for the Visitation of the Sick. Selected from Various Authors. *Small 8vo.* 3s. 6d.

Garland.—THE PRACTICAL TEACHING OF THE APO-CALYPSE. By the Rev. G. V. GARLAND, M.A. *8vo.* 16s.

Gore.—Works by the Rev. CHARLES GORE, M.A., Principal of the Pusey House ; Fellow of Trinity College, Oxford.

THE MINISTRY OF THE CHRISTIAN CHURCH. *8vo.* 10s. 6d.

ROMAN CATHOLIC CLAIMS. *Crown 8vo.* 3s. 6d.

Goulburn.—Works by EDWARD MEYRICK GOULBURN, D.D., D.C.L., sometime Dean of Norwich.

THOUGHTS ON PERSONAL RELIGION. *Small 8vo, 6s. 6d.* ; *Cheap Edition,* 3s. 6d.; *Presentation Edition, 2 vols. small 8vo,* 10s. 6d.

THE PURSUIT OF HOLINESS : a Sequel to 'Thoughts on Personal Religion.' *Small 8vo.* 5s. *Cheap Edition,* 3s. 6d.

THE CHILD SAMUEL : a Practical and Devotional Commentary on the Birth and Childhood of the Prophet Samuel, as recorded in 1 Sam. i., ii. 1-27, iii. *Small 8vo.* 2s. 6d.

THE GOSPEL OF THE CHILDHOOD : a Practical and Devotional Commentary on the Single Incident of our Blessed Lord's Childhood (St. Luke ii. 41 to the end). *Crown 8vo.* 2s. 6d.

THE COLLECTS OF THE DAY : an Exposition, Critical and Devotional, of the Collects appointed at the Communion. With Preliminary Essays on their Structure, Sources, etc. *2 vols. Crown 8vo.* 8s. *each.*

THOUGHTS UPON THE LITURGICAL GOSPELS for the Sundays, one for each day in the year. With an Introduction on their Origin, History, the Modifications made in them by the Reformers and by the Revisers of the Prayer Book. *2 vols. Crown 8vo.* 16s.

MEDITATIONS UPON THE LITURGICAL GOSPELS for the Minor Festivals of Christ, the two first Week-days of the Easter and Whitsun Festivals, and the Red-letter Saints' Days. *Crown 8vo.* 8s. 6d.

FAMILY PRAYERS compiled from various sources (chiefly from Bishop Hamilton's Manual), and arranged on the Liturgical Principle. *Crown 8vo.* 3s. 6d. *Cheap Edition,* 16mo. 1s.

Haddan.—APOSTOLICAL SUCCESSION IN THE CHURCH OF ENGLAND. By the Rev. ARTHUR W. HADDAN, B.D., late Rector of Barton-on-the-Heath. *8vo.* 12s.

Hatch.—THE ORGANIZATION OF THE EARLY
CHRISTIAN CHURCHES. Being the Bampton Lectures for 1880.
By EDWIN HATCH, M.A., D.D. *8vo.* 5*s.*

Hernaman.—LYRA CONSOLATIONIS. From the Poets of
the Seventeenth, Eighteenth, and Nineteenth Centuries. Selected and
arranged by CLAUDIA FRANCES HERNAMAN. *Small 8vo.* 6*s.*

Holland.—Works by the Rev. HENRY SCOTT HOLLAND, M.A.,
Canon and Precentor of St. Paul's.

CREED AND CHARACTER : Sermons. *Crown 8vo.* 7*s. 6d.*

ON BEHALF OF BELIEF. Sermons preached in St. Paul's Cathedral.
Crown 8vo. 6*s.*

CHRIST OR ECCLESIASTES. Sermons preached in St. Paul's
Cathedral. *Crown 8vo.* 3*s. 6d.*

GOOD FRIDAY. Being Addresses on the Seven Last Words, delivered
at St. Paul's Cathedral on Good Friday. *Small 8vo.* 2*s.*

LOGIC AND LIFE, with other Sermons. *Crown 8vo.* 7*s. 6d.*

Hopkins.—CHRIST THE CONSOLER. A Book of Comfort
for the Sick. By ELLICE HOPKINS. *Small 8vo.* 2*s. 6d.*

James.—COMMENT UPON THE COLLECTS appointed to
be used in the Church of England on Sundays and Holy Days
throughout the Year. By JOHN JAMES, D.D., sometime Canon of
Peterborough. *Small 8vo.* 3*s. 6d.*

Jameson.—Works by Mrs. JAMESON.

SACRED AND LEGENDARY ART, containing Legends of the Angels
and Archangels, the Evangelists, the Apostles, the Doctors of the Church,
St. Mary Magdalene, the Patron Saints, the Martyrs, the Early Bishops,
the Hermits, and the Warrior-Saints of Christendom, as represented in
the Fine Arts. With 19 etchings on Copper and Steel, and 187
Woodcuts. *Two Vols. Cloth, gilt top,* 20*s. net.*

LEGENDS OF THE MONASTIC ORDERS, as represented in the
Fine Arts, comprising the Benedictines and Augustines, and Orders
derived from their Rules, the Mendicant Orders, the Jesuits, and the
Order of the Visitation of S. Mary. With 11 etchings by the Author,
and 88 Woodcuts. *One Vol. Cloth, gilt top,* 10*s. net.*

LEGENDS OF THE MADONNA, OR BLESSED VIRGIN MARY.
Devotional with and without the Infant Jesus, Historical from the
Annunciation to the Assumption, as represented in Sacred and
Legendary Christian Art. With 27 Etchings and 165 Woodcuts.
One Vol. Cloth, gilt top, 10*s. net.*

THE HISTORY OF OUR LORD, as exemplified in Works of Art,
with that of His Types, St. John the Baptist, and other Persons of the
Old and New Testaments. Commenced by the late Mrs. JAMESON ;
continued and completed by LADY EASTLAKE. With 31 etchings and
281 Woodcuts. *Two Vols. 8vo.* 20*s. net.*

Jennings.—ECCLESIA ANGLICANA. A History of the Church of Christ in England from the Earliest to the Present Times. By the Rev. ARTHUR CHARLES JENNINGS, M.A. *Crown 8vo. 7s. 6d.*

Jukes.—Works by ANDREW JUKES.

THE NEW MAN AND THE ETERNAL LIFE. Notes on the Reiterated Amens of the Son of God. *Crown 8vo. 6s.*

THE NAMES OF GOD IN HOLY SCRIPTURE: a Revelation of His Nature and Relationships. *Crown 8vo. 4s. 6d.*

THE TYPES OF GENESIS. *Crown 8vo. 7s. 6d.*

THE SECOND DEATH AND THE RESTITUTION OF ALL THINGS. *Crown 8vo. 3s. 6d.*

THE MYSTERY OF THE KINGDOM. *Crown 8vo. 2s. 6d.*

Keble.—MAXIMS AND GLEANINGS FROM THE WRITINGS OF JOHN KEBLE, M.A. Selected and Arranged for Daily Use. By C. M. S. *Crown 16mo. 2s.*

SELECTIONS FROM THE WRITINGS OF JOHN KEBLE, M.A. *Crown 8vo. 3s. 6d.*

Kennaway.—CONSOLATIO; OR, COMFORT FOR THE AFFLICTED. Edited by the late Rev. C. E. KENNAWAY. *16mo. 2s. 6d.*

Knox Little.—Works by W. J. KNOX LITTLE, M.A., Canon Residentiary of Worcester, and Vicar of Hoar Cross.

THE CHRISTIAN HOME. *Crown 8vo.*

THE HOPES AND DECISIONS OF THE PASSION OF OUR MOST HOLY REDEEMER. *Crown 8vo. 3s. 6d.*

THE THREE HOURS' AGONY OF OUR BLESSED REDEEMER. Being Addresses in the form of Meditations delivered in St. Alban's Church, Manchester, on Good Friday, 1877. *Small 8vo. 2s.; or in Paper Cover, 1s.*

CHARACTERISTICS AND MOTIVES OF THE CHRISTIAN LIFE. Ten Sermons preached in Manchester Cathedral, in Lent and Advent 1877. *Crown 8vo. 3s. 6d.*

SERMONS PREACHED FOR THE MOST PART IN MANCHESTER. *Crown 8vo. 7s. 6d.*

THE MYSTERY OF THE PASSION OF OUR MOST HOLY REDEEMER. *Crown 8vo. 3s. 6d.*

THE WITNESS OF THE PASSION OF OUR MOST HOLY REDEEMER. *Crown 8vo. 3s. 6d.*

THE LIGHT OF LIFE. Sermons preached on Various Occasions. *Crown 8vo. 7s. 6d.*

SUNLIGHT AND SHADOW IN THE CHRISTIAN LIFE. Sermons preached for the most part in America. *Crown 8vo. 7s. 6d*

Lear.—Works by, and Edited by, H. L. SIDNEY LEAR.

CHRISTIAN BIOGRAPHIES. *Crown 8vo. 3s. 6d. each.*
> MADAME LOUISE DE FRANCE, Daughter of Louis XV., known also as the Mother Térèse de St. Augustin.

FOR DAYS AND YEARS. A Book containing a Text, Short Reading, and Hymn for Every Day in the Church's Year. *16mo. 2s. 6d. Also a Cheap Edition, 32mo. 1s.; or cloth gilt, 1s. 6d.*

FIVE MINUTES. Daily Readings of Poetry. *16mo. 3s. 6d. Also a Cheap Edition. 32mo. 1s.; or cloth gilt, 1s. 6d.*

WEARINESS. A Book for the Languid and Lonely. *Large Type. Small 8vo. 5s.*

THE LIGHT OF THE CONSCIENCE. *16mo. 2s. 6d. Also the Larger Edition. Crown 8vo. 5s.*

A DOMINICAN ARTIST: a Sketch of the Life of the Rev. Père Besson, of the Order of St. Dominic.

HENRI PERREYVE. By A. GRATRY.

ST. FRANCIS DE SALES, Bishop and Prince of Geneva.

THE REVIVAL OF PRIESTLY LIFE IN THE SEVENTEENTH CENTURY IN FRANCE.

A CHRISTIAN PAINTER OF THE NINETEENTH CENTURY.

BOSSUET AND HIS CONTEMPORARIES.

FÉNELON, ARCHBISHOP OF CAMBRAI.

HENRI DOMINIQUE LACORDAIRE.

DEVOTIONAL WORKS. Edited by H. L. SIDNEY LEAR. *New and Uniform Editions. Nine Vols. 16mo. 2s. 6d. each.*

FÉNELON'S SPIRITUAL LETTERS TO MEN.

FÉNELON'S SPIRITUAL LETTERS TO WOMEN.

A SELECTION FROM THE SPIRITUAL LETTERS OF ST. FRANCIS DE SALES.

THE SPIRIT OF ST. FRANCIS DE SALES.

THE HIDDEN LIFE OF THE SOUL.

THE LIGHT OF THE CONSCIENCE.

SELF-RENUNCIATION. From the French.

ST. FRANCIS DE SALES' OF THE LOVE OF GOD.

SELECTIONS FROM PASCAL'S THOUGHTS.

Library of Spiritual Works for English Catholics. *Original Edition. With Red Borders. Small 8vo. 5s. each. New and Cheaper Editions. 16mo. 2s. 6d. each.*

OF THE IMITATION OF CHRIST.

THE SPIRITUAL COMBAT. By LAURENCE SCUPOLI.

THE DEVOUT LIFE. By ST. FRANCIS DE SALES.

OF THE LOVE OF GOD. By ST. FRANCIS DE SALES.

THE CONFESSIONS OF ST. AUGUSTINE. *In Ten Books.*

THE CHRISTIAN YEAR. *5s. Edition only.*

Liddon.—Works by HENRY PARRY LIDDON, D.D., D.C.L., LL.D., late Canon Residentiary and Chancellor of St. Paul's.

THE DIVINITY OF OUR LORD AND SAVIOUR JESUS CHRIST. Being the Bampton Lectures for 1866. *Crown 8vo. 5s.*

ADVENT IN ST. PAUL'S. Sermons bearing chiefly on the Two Comings of our Lord. *Two Vols. Crown 8vo. 5s. each. Cheap edition in one Volume. Crown 8vo. 5s.*

CHRISTMASTIDE IN ST. PAUL'S. Sermons bearing chiefly on the Birth of our Lord and the End of the Year. *Crown 8vo. 5s.*

PASSIONTIDE IN ST. PAUL'S. Sermons bearing chiefly on the Passion of our Lord. *Crown 8vo. 5s.*

EASTER IN ST. PAUL'S. Sermons bearing chiefly on the Resurrection of our Lord. *Two Vols. Crown 8vo. 5s. each. Cheap Edition in one Volume. Crown 8vo. 5s.*

SERMONS PREACHED BEFORE THE UNIVERSITY OF OXFORD. *Two Vols. Crown 8vo. 5s. each. Cheap Edition in one Volume. Crown 8vo. 5s.*

THE MAGNIFICAT. Sermons in St. Paul's. *Crown 8vo. 2s. 6d.*

SOME ELEMENTS OF RELIGION. Lent Lectures. *Small 8vo. 2s. 6d. ; or in Paper Cover, 1s. 6d.*
The Crown 8vo Edition (5s.) may still be had.

SELECTIONS FROM THE WRITINGS OF H. P. LIDDON, D.D. *Crown 8vo. 3s. 6d.*

MAXIMS AND GLEANINGS FROM THE WRITINGS OF H. P. LIDDON, D.D. Selected and arranged by C. M. S. *Crown 16mo. 2s.*

Littlehales.—Works Edited by HENRY LTTLEHALES.
A FOURTEENTH CENTURY PRAYER BOOK : being Pages in Facsimile from a Layman's Prayer Book in English about 1400 A.D. *4to. 3s. 6d.*

THE PRYMER OR PRAYER-BOOK OF THE LAY PEOPLE IN THE MIDDLE AGES. In English, dating about 1400 A.D. Part I. Text. *Royal 8vo. 5s.*

Luckock.—Works by HERBERT MORTIMER LUCKOCK, D.D., Canon of Ely.

AFTER DEATH. An Examination of the Testimony of Primitive Times respecting the State of the Faithful Dead, and their Relationship to the Living. *Crown 8vo. 6s.*

THE INTERMEDIATE STATE BETWEEN DEATH AND JUDGMENT. Being a Sequel to *After Death. Crown 8vo. 6s.*

FOOTPRINTS OF THE SON OF MAN, as traced by St. Mark. Being Eighty Portions for Private Study, Family Reading, and Instructions in Church. *Two Vols. Crown 8vo. 12s. Cheap Edition in one Vol. Crown 8vo. 5s.*

[continued.

Luckock.—Works by HERBERT MORTIMER LUCKOCK, D.D., Canon of Ely—*continued.*

THE DIVINE LITURGY. Being the Order for Holy Communion, Historically, Doctrinally, and Devotionally set forth, in Fifty Portions. *Crown 8vo.* 6*s.*

STUDIES IN THE HISTORY OF THE BOOK OF COMMON PRAYER. The Anglican Reform—The Puritan Innovations—The Elizabethan Reaction—The Caroline Settlement. With Appendices. *Crown 8vo.* 6*s.*

THE BISHOPS IN THE TOWER. A Record of Stirring Events affecting the Church and Nonconformists from the Restoration to the Revolution. *Crown 8vo.* 6*s.*

LYRA APOSTOLICA. Poems by J. W. BOWDEN, R. H. FROUDE, J. KEBLE, J. H. NEWMAN, R. I. WILBERFORCE, and I. WILLIAMS; and New Preface by CARDINAL NEWMAN. 16*mo.* 2*s.* 6*d.*

LYRA GERMANICA. Hymns translated from the German by CATHERINE WINKWORTH. *Small 8vo.* 5*s.*

MacColl.—CHRISTIANITY IN RELATION TO SCIENCE AND MORALS. By the Rev. MALCOLM MACCOLL, M.A., Canon Residentiary of Ripon. *Crown 8vo.* 6*s.*

Mason.—Works by A. J. MASON, D.D., formerly Fellow of Trinity College, Cambridge.

THE FAITH OF THE GOSPEL. A Manual of Christian Doctrine. *Crown 8vo.* 7*s.* 6*d.* *Large-Paper Edition for Marginal Notes.* 4*to.* 12*s.* 6*d.*

THE RELATION OF CONFIRMATION TO BAPTISM. As taught by the Western Fathers. A Study in the History of Doctrine. *Crown 8vo.*

Mercier.—Works by Mrs. JEROME MERCIER.

OUR MOTHER CHURCH: being Simple Talk on High Topics. *Small 8vo.* 3*s.* 6*d.*

THE STORY OF SALVATION: or, Thoughts on the Historic Study of the Bible. *Small 8vo.* 3*s.* 6*d.*

Moberly.—Works by GEORGE MOBERLY, D.C.L., late Bishop of Salisbury.

PLAIN SERMONS. Preached at Brighstone. *Crown 8vo.* 5*s.*

THE SAYINGS OF THE GREAT FORTY DAYS, between the Resurrection and Ascension, regarded as the Outlines of the Kingdom of God. In Five Discourses. *Crown 8vo.* 5*s.*

PAROCHIAL SERMONS. Mostly preached at Brighstone. *Crown 8vo.* 7*s.* 6*d.*

SERMONS PREACHED AT WINCHESTER COLLEGE. *Two Vols.* *Small 8vo.* 6*s.* 6*d. each.*

Mozley.—Works by J. B. MOZLEY, D.D., late Canon of Christ Church, and Regius Professor of Divinity at Oxford.

ESSAYS, HISTORICAL AND THEOLOGICAL. *Two Vols.* 8vo. 24s.

EIGHT LECTURES ON MIRACLES. Being the Bampton Lectures for 1865. *Crown* 8vo. 7s. 6d.

RULING IDEAS IN EARLY AGES AND THEIR RELATION TO OLD TESTAMENT FAITH. Lectures delivered to Graduates of the University of Oxford. 8vo. 10s. 6d.

SERMONS PREACHED BEFORE THE UNIVERSITY OF OXFORD, and on Various Occasions. *Crown* 8vo. 7s. 6d.

SERMONS, PAROCHIAL AND OCCASIONAL. *Crown* 8vo. 7s. 6d.

Mozley.—Works by the Rev. T. MOZLEY, M.A., Author of 'Reminiscences of Oriel College and the Oxford Movement.'

THE WORD. *Crown* 8vo. 7s. 6d.

LETTERS FROM ROME ON THE OCCASION OF THE ŒCUMENICAL COUNCIL 1869-1870. *Two Vols. Cr.* 8vo. 18s.

Newbolt.—Works by the Rev. W. C. E. NEWBOLT, Canon Residentiary of St. Paul's.

THE FRUIT OF THE SPIRIT. Being Ten Addresses bearing on the Spiritual Life. *Crown* 8vo. 2s. 6d.

THE MAN OF GOD. Being Six Addresses delivered during Lent 1886, at the Primary Ordination of the Right Rev. the Lord Alwyne Compton, Bishop of Ely. *Small* 8vo. 1s. 6d.

COUNSELS OF FAITH AND PRACTICE. Being Sermons preached on Various Occasions. 8vo. 7s. 6d.

THE VOICE OF THE PRAYER BOOK. Being Spiritual Addresses bearing on the Book of Common Prayer. *Crown* 8vo. 2s. 6d.

Newnham.—THE ALL-FATHER : Sermons preached in a Village Church. By the Rev. H. P. NEWNHAM. With Preface by EDNA LYALL. *Crown* 8vo. 4s. 6d.

Newman.—Works by JOHN HENRY NEWMAN, B.D. (Cardinal Newman), formerly Vicar of St. Mary's, Oxford.

PAROCHIAL AND PLAIN SERMONS. *Eight Vols. Cabinet Edition. Crown* 8vo. 5s. *each. Popular Edition. Eight Vols. Crown* 8vo. 3s. 6d. *each.*

[continued.

Newman.—Works by JOHN HENRY NEWMAN, B.D. (Cardinal Newman), formerly Vicar of St. Mary's, Oxford—*continued.*

SELECTION, ADAPTED TO THE SEASONS OF THE ECCLE-SIASTICAL YEAR, from the 'Parochial and Plain Sermons.' *Crown 8vo. 5s.*

FIFTEEN SERMONS PREACHED BEFORE THE UNIVERSITY OF OXFORD, between A.D. 1826 and 1843. *Crown 8vo. 5s.*

SERMONS BEARING UPON SUBJECTS OF THE DAY. *Crown 8vo. 5s.*

LECTURES ON THE DOCTRINE OF JUSTIFICATION. *Crown 8vo. 5s.*

*** *For the Catholic Works of Cardinal Newman, see Messrs. Longmans & Co.'s Catalogue of Works in General Literature.*

THE LETTERS AND CORRESPONDENCE OF JOHN HENRY NEWMAN DURING HIS LIFE IN THE ENGLISH CHURCH. With a Brief Autobiographical Memoir. Arranged and Edited by ANNE MOZLEY. *Two Vols. 8vo. 30s. net.*

Osborne.—Works by EDWARD OSBORNE, Mission Priest of the Society of St. John the Evangelist, Cowley, Oxford.

THE CHILDREN'S SAVIOUR. Instructions to Children on the Life of our Lord and Saviour Jesus Christ. *Illustrated. 16mo. 3s. 6d.*

THE SAVIOUR-KING. Instructions to Children on Old Testament Types and Illustrations of the Life of Christ. *Illustrated. 16mo. 3s. 6d.*

THE CHILDREN'S FAITH. Instructions to Children on the Apostles' Creed. *With Illustrations. 16mo. 3s. 6d.*

Oxenden.—Works by the Right Rev. ASHTON OXENDEN, formerly Bishop of Montreal.

THE PATHWAY OF SAFETY; or, Counsel to the Awakened. *Fcap. 8vo, large type. 2s. 6d. Cheap Edition. Small type, limp. 1s.*

THE EARNEST COMMUNICANT. *Common Edition. 32mo. 1s. New Red Rubric Edition. 32mo. 2s.*

OUR CHURCH AND HER SERVICES. *Fcap. 8vo. 2s. 6d.*

FAMILY PRAYERS FOR FOUR WEEKS. First Series. *Fcap. 8vo. 2s. 6d.* Second Series. *Fcap. 8vo. 2s. 6d.*

LARGE TYPE EDITION. Two Series in one Volume. *Crown 8vo. 6s.*

COTTAGE SERMONS; or, Plain Words to the Poor. *Fcap. 8vo. 2s. 6d.*

THOUGHTS FOR HOLY WEEK. *16mo. 1s. 6d.*

DECISION. *18mo. 1s. 6d.*

[*continued.*

Oxenden.—Works by the Right Rev. ASHTON OXENDEN, formerly Bishop of Montreal—*continued.*

THE HOME BEYOND ; or, A Happy Old Age. *Fcap. 8vo.   1s. 6d.*

THE LABOURING MAN'S BOOK. *18mo, large type, cloth.   1s. 6d.*

CONFIRMATION. *18mo, cloth. 9d. ; sewed, 3d. ; or 2s. 6d. per dozen.*

COUNSELS TO THOSE WHO HAVE BEEN CONFIRMED ; or, Now is the Time to serve Christ. *18mo, cloth. 1s.*

THE LORD'S SUPPER SIMPLY EXPLAINED. *18mo, cloth. 1s. Cheap Edition. Paper. 6d.*

PRAYERS FOR PRIVATE USE. *32mo, cloth. 1s.*

WORDS OF PEACE ; or, The Blessings of Sickness. *16mo, cloth. 1s.*

Paget.—Works by the Rev. FRANCIS PAGET, D.D., Canon of Christ Church, and Regius Professor of Pastoral Theology.

THE SPIRIT OF DISCIPLINE : Sermons. *Crown 8vo.*

FACULTIES AND DIFFICULTIES FOR BELIEF AND DIS-BELIEF. *Crown 8vo. 6s. 6d.*

THE HALLOWING OF WORK. Addresses given at Eton, January 16-18, 1888. *Small 8vo. 2s.*

PRACTICAL REFLECTIONS. By a CLERGYMAN. With Prefaces by H. P. LIDDON, D.D., D.C.L. *Crown 8vo.*

> Vol. I.—THE HOLY GOSPELS. *4s. 6d.*
> Vol. II.—ACTS TO REVELATION. *6s.*
> THE PSALMS. *5s.*

PRIEST (THE) TO THE ALTAR ; Or, Aids to the Devout Celebration of Holy Communion, chiefly after the Ancient English Use of Sarum. *Royal 8vo. 12s.*

Pusey.—Works by the late Rev. E. B. PUSEY, D.D.

MAXIMS AND GLEANINGS FROM THE WRITINGS OF EDWARD BOUVERIE PUSEY, D.D. Selected and Arranged for Daily Use. By C. M. S. *Crown 16mo. 2s.*

PRIVATE PRAYERS. With Preface by H. P. LIDDON, D.D. *32mo. 2s. 6d.*

PRAYERS FOR A YOUNG SCHOOLBOY. Edited, with a Preface, by H. P. LIDDON, D.D. *24mo. 1s.*

SELECTIONS FROM THE WRITINGS OF EDWARD BOUVERIE PUSEY, D.D. *Crown 8vo. 3s. 6d.*

Richmond.—CHRISTIAN ECONOMICS. By the Rev. WILFRID RICHMOND, M.A., sometime Warden of Trinity College, Glenalmond. *Crown 8vo.* 6s.

Sanday.—THE ORACLES OF GOD : Nine Lectures on the Nature and Extent of Biblical Inspiration and the Special Significance of the Old Testament Scriptures at the Present Time. By W. SANDAY, M.A., D.D., LL.D. *Crown 8vo.* 4s.

Seebohm.—THE OXFORD REFORMERS—JOHN COLET, ERASMUS, AND THOMAS MORE : A History of their Fellow-Work. By FREDERICK SEEBOHM. *8vo.* 14s.

Stephen.—ESSAYS IN ECCLESIASTICAL BIOGRAPHY. By the Right Hon. Sir J. STEPHEN. *Crown 8vo.* 7s. 6d.

Swayne.—THE BLESSED DEAD IN PARADISE. Four All Saints' Day Sermons, preached in Salisbury Cathedral. By ROBERT G. SWAYNE, M.A. *Crown 8vo.* 3s. 6d.

Tweddell.—THE SOUL IN CONFLICT. A Practical Examination of some Difficulties and Duties of the Spiritual Life. By MARSHALL TWEDDELL, M.A., Vicar of St. Saviour, Paddington. *Crown 8vo.* 6s.

Twells.—COLLOQUIES ON PREACHING. By HENRY TWELLS, M.A., Honorary Canon of Peterborough *Crown 8vo.* 5s.

Wakeman.—THE HISTORY OF RELIGION IN ENGLAND. By HENRY OFFLEY WAKEMAN, M.A. *Small 8vo.* 1s. 6d.

Welldon. — THE FUTURE AND THE PAST. Sermons preached to Harrow Boys. (*First Series*, 1885 *and* 1886.) By the Rev. J. E. C. WELLDON, M.A., Head Master of Harrow School. *Crown 8vo.* 7s. 6d.

Williams.—Works by the Rev. ISAAC WILLIAMS, B.D., formerly Fellow of Trinity College, Oxford.

A DEVOTIONAL COMMENTARY ON THE GOSPEL NARRATIVE. *Eight Vols. Crown 8vo.* 5s. *each. Sold separately.*

THOUGHTS ON THE STUDY OF THE HOLY GOSPELS.
A HARMONY OF THE FOUR GOSPELS.
OUR LORD'S NATIVITY.
OUR LORD'S MINISTRY (Second Year).
OUR LORD'S MINISTRY (Third Year).
THE HOLY WEEK.
OUR LORD'S PASSION.
OUR LORD'S RESURRECTION.

[continued.

Williams.—Works by the Rev. ISAAC WILLIAMS, B.D., formerly Fellow of Trinity College, Oxford—*continued.*

FEMALE CHARACTERS OF HOLY SCRIPTURE. A Series of Sermons. *Crown 8vo.* 5*s.*

THE CHARACTERS OF THE OLD TESTAMENT. A Series of Sermons. *Crown 8vo.* 5*s.*

THE APOCALYPSE. With Notes and Reflections. *Crown 8vo.* 5*s.*

SERMONS ON THE EPISTLES AND GOSPELS FOR THE SUN- DAYS AND HOLY DAYS THROUGHOUT THE YEAR. *Two Vols. Crown 8vo.* 5*s. each.*

PLAIN SERMONS ON THE CATECHISM. *Two Vols. Crown 8vo.* 5*s. each.*

SELECTIONS FROM THE WRITINGS OF ISAAC WILLIAMS, B.D. *Crown 8vo.* 3*s. 6d.*

Woodford.—Works by JAMES RUSSELL WOODFORD, D.D., sometime Lord Bishop of Ely.

THE GREAT COMMISSION. Twelve Addresses on the Ordinal. Edited, with an Introduction on the Ordinations of his Episcopate, by HERBERT MORTIMER LUCKOCK, D.D. *Crown 8vo.* 5*s.*

SERMONS ON OLD AND NEW TESTAMENT SUBJECTS. Edited by HERBERT MORTIMER LUCKOCK, D.D. *Two Vols. Crown 8vo.* 5*s. each.*

Wordsworth.—Works by ELIZABETH WORDSWORTH, Principal of Lady Margaret Hall, Oxford.

ILLUSTRATIONS OF THE CREED. *Crown 8vo.* 5*s.*

ELIZABETH AND OTHER POEMS. *Crown 8vo.* 6*s.*

Younghusband.—Works by FRANCES YOUNGHUSBAND.

THE STORY OF OUR LORD, told in Simple Language for Children. With 25 Illustrations on Wood from Pictures by the Old Masters, and numerous Ornamental Borders, Initial Letters, etc., from Longmans' New Testament. *Crown 8vo.* 2*s. 6d.*

THE STORY OF GENESIS, told in Simple Language for Children. *Crown 8vo.* 2*s. 6d.*

Printed by T. and A. CONSTABLE, Printers to Her Majesty, *at the Edinburgh University Press.*